THE GREAT JOBS AHEAD

THE GREAT JOBS AHEAD

Your Comprehensive Guide to Surviving and Prospering in the Coming Work Revolution

HARRY S. DENT, JR.

HYPERION
NEW YORK

I would like to thank my agent, Susan Golomb, for her dedication and creativity. Thanks also to my editor at St. Martin's Press, George Witte, for sharing my vision of the book. Special thanks to James V. Smith, Jr., for his valuable contribution to the writing of *The Great Jobs Ahead*.

Library of Congress Cataloging-in-Publication Data

Dent, Harry S., 1950–
[Job shock]
The great jobs ahead : your comprehensive guide to surviving and
prospering in the coming work revolution / Harry S. Dent, Jr.
p.   cm.
Originally published: Job shock, St. Martin's Press, 1995.
ISBN 0-7868-8158-5
1. Organizational change.   2. Career development.   3. Manpower
planning.   4. Labor supply—Effect of automation on.   5. Information
technology—Management.   I. Title.
HD58.8.D46   1996
650.14—dc20   95-49704
CIP

Designed by Richard Oriolo

FIRST HYPERION EDITION

2   4   6   8   10   9   7   5   3   1

This book is dedicated to:

My wife, Cee

Nile, Iomi, and Abel

My parents, Harry and Betty Dent

CONTENTS

CONTENTS

Part Four:
New Skills and Career Paths:
How You Fit In

Part Five:
Leveraging the New
Entrepreneurial Climate

Epilogue:

PART ONE

New Work for a New Era of Prosperity

CHAPTER 1

Explains why more and more people are feeling job shock and gives you the insights necessary for interpreting and capitalizing on the revolutionary forces behind a changing workplace.

CHAPTER 2

Provides simple tools for understanding the forces driving the economy and the great work revolution ahead, which will actually raise our standard of living and the quality of our work environment at a greater rate than at any time in history.

Job Shock—America's Wake-up Call to the Greatest Work Revolution in History

The Industrial Revolution put us to sleep in the name of the efficiencies of functional specialization. It forced us to master very narrow tasks and to blindly follow standard procedures. In many of us, it diminished the capacity to innovate. It's time to reclaim our most creative, most fulfilling, most human functions.

Job Shock

Get ready!

It won't be long before you wake up and find something important missing from your career. Your job may vanish, or maybe your company will go AWOL. This circumstance won't necessarily be due to a terrible recession. No matter where or how you're employed now, in the near future you're going to feel the earth move beneath your feet as the very nature of work is redefined. If you're in middle management, odds are you've already been shifted into a new kind of leadership role—or thrown out of that private office and into the nitty-gritty of things, by investing in a franchise, or starting a small business, or working in small business, or becoming a highly accountable consultant inside or outside your old company. If you're a member of the clerical staff, your job will likely be taken away and you'll be redeployed in a new role you may not be used to or ready for. If you're an in-house professional such as a lawyer or accountant, you'll be competing for work with outside contractors.

We may well stop using the term *jobs* to describe the work we do. You may find yourself running a small business within a company. Or launching a new venture with financial and strategic support from your company. Or you may establish a business of your own, or transfer to a division of your company in a place so remote you only dreamed about living there after you retired from your job in the city where you now work.

Believe me, things are going to change radically, and you can't do anything to stop them. In fact, the worst thing you can do is fight the inevitable—you'll either be steamrollered and thrown out of work altogether, or you'll impede the healthy progress of others who try to embrace the change. These changes will occur without regard to the economy, the President, or Congress. They won't just happen the next time the economy falters. They will progress even as we enter the coming boom period, which I've been predicting.

Am I talking about some miraculous government jobs program? Hardly. I'm talking about what's happening now, what's *been* happening for quite a while, but only in a small minority of our best small and large companies—and even in select school, health care, and government agencies. We are on the brink of a work revolution, a radical and permanent change in the way we work, the way we *think* about work, and the way we live. Imagine Henry Ford quietly tinkering behind the scenes on the Model T and the assembly line in the early 1900s. Then, next thing you know we are in the Roaring '20s and everyone is moving into assembly-line work. Most people can afford cars that were luxury items just years before.

Fact is, if you've been thrown out of a job or if you've moved into a new relationship with your company, you're probably already on the cutting edge of the revolution that's been brewing for the past decade or so.

Just look at all the evidence from one year alone, 1993.

Unless you've buried yourself in the world of game-show television, you've seen symptoms of fundamental change in American corporations—layoffs, plant closings, cost cutting, and benefit slashing. Even if you read only a little news in 1993, you know the headlines were dominated by stories along the lines of "Where Did My Job Go?" in *Fortune* magazine and "Where Did My Career Go? The White-Collar Lament of the 90s" in *U.S. News & World Report.* You've heard the terms *reengineering* and *reinventing* and seen the spate of books and articles as companies downsize, throwing people out of work. You've watched companies shift alliances with more vigor than usual. You've seen the mergers of corporations trying to position themselves to be the first movers and shakers along the so-called information super-highway. Maybe you've noticed that many of these new alliances have a distinctive character—they are not mere consolidations within an industry, but calculated alliances of complementary industries to build corporations of the future.

You've seen all this, but have you figured out what's happening? Are all these things merely isolated items of bad news? Are they the signs of the decline of America? Are they simple spikes on the trend line of business as usual before things return to the way they've always been? Or are they really the signs of an oncoming work revolution and economic boom? What's going on?

There are no simple answers to these questions. But I do offer a few simple principles in this book, principles so fundamental that people at all levels of organizations can make sense out of these times of complex change. ·

The easiest item to address deals with the wrongheaded notion that we're experiencing a brief shudder in the economy and that if we can just wait it out, the country's organizations will blithely return to business as usual. I can tell you with absolute certainty that things will never go back to the way they were! The year 1993 will go down as a watershed in business. It'll be like 1914, when Henry Ford first successfully brought assembly-line production to cars. The assembly line and its organizational principle of narrow functional specialization was the greatest single lever of productivity and progress in the twentieth century. Once it was introduced, that concept defined how we work—until now.

Second-easiest to deal with are the endless items of bad news that have been dominating the picture of the workplace. Naturally, bad news grabs headlines. Such headlines create a condition I call *job shock*. You can define job shock by describing what it does.

- **Job shock creates pain.** Layoffs and restructurings hurt people at the basic survival level. Job shock threatens people's ability to survive, to provide shelter, food, and comfort for themselves and their families—and today, it's white-collar jobs as well as blue-collar jobs that are being lost.
- **Job shock rattles consumer confidence.** Obviously, people without jobs stop spending except for basic needs. But even people who've kept their jobs feel insecure enough to curtail spending as they see their neighbors and coworkers being laid off. This dampens the robustness of the economy and retards the recovery we are in.
- **Job shock terrorizes people you know.** You don't need a news item or even a futurist to tell you individual horror stories about job shock. You probably know somebody who has been thrown out of a job. You may have a recent college graduate still living at home because it's so tough to break into the job market.
- **Job shock points the finger,** creating bad guys in the business community. You may even think that all the ills of job shock are merely the results of corporate downsizing and reengineering, something that big business is doing to the workforce for the sake of making a buck.

As difficult as all this bad news is, it barely begins to tell the story. I've studied the fundamental forces that shape corporations and our economy. My findings lead me to some startling conclusions. Job shock is creating surface news that's barely a ripple compared with what's to come. Job shock is merely a harbinger, a sign of auspicious changes to come. Behind this messenger is a tidal wave of progress. You can't run from it and you can't hide. That's why I say you'd better get ready.

Job shock, the wake-up call

Using a few simple tools I'll introduce in the next chapter, I predict an economic boom, the greatest boom in history. Job shock is only the tip of the iceberg for fundamental changes that will continue to occur even as we see sustained economic growth right into the next century. Jobs are going to be redeployed, automated, eliminated, and regenerated in forms we haven't yet imagined.

Most of our organizations are in for changes more radical than their leadership ever dreamed. These won't be optional, gradual changes, either—they will sweeping, swift, and certain, positively mandated by the economic and technological climate.

What's behind this change in organizations?

Easy. The Information Revolution is finally taking hold, dictating how we will conduct business. Of course, the primary tool of this revolution is the microcomputer. "Well," you say, "we've had microcomputers in offices since the '70s. What's new about that?"

Good question. Two things are new. Let's look at them.

Item 1: Computers are the new office workers

Organizations are finally using computers to revolutionize business practices instead of merely improving the old tried-and-true practices of the industrial age. We are so often tied to the status quo we refuse to risk investing either emotions or capital to make changes. Sure, we've had computers in offices, but we haven't used them to real advantage in most organizations. The workplace has been filled with an older generation used to working in a hierarchical command and control system. This generation is less willing to take risks than the newer generation moving into positions of power now and in the future: baby boomers. The members of this newer generation have already proved they will take necessary, calculated risks to bring in new, creative ways of conducting business when they have come into power. This is exactly what you'd expect to happen. But since the 1970s, computers have been little better than paperweights in many places run by the older generation.

This reluctance to use technology to its true advantage in its initial stages isn't unusual. For instance, in his book *Microcosm*, technologist and futurist George Gilder tells why the invention of the electric motor initially had so little effect on manufacturing. In the age of steam, manufacturers positioned the noisy, hot steam engine outside the factory. The engine drove a long shaft that ran through the center of the building. Individual machines inside the factory drew power from the shaft through a series of belts, gears, and smaller shafts. The adoption of cleaner, quieter, simpler motors changed all that, but not in the way you might think—powering individual machines inside the plant with individual electric motors.

Instead, the first adaptation was to replace the huge steam engine with a huge electric motor to drive the main power shaft. When you integrate an innovation that way, it doesn't seem like a quantum leap, does it? Only later did somebody get the idea of using individual motors to run individual machines.

Keeping the analogy of the electric motor in mind, what did the first computers do? They empowered the paper-shuffling bureaucracy of our giant organizations to shuffle on, moving paper more efficiently than ever. In fact, they added to the paperwork burden, because high-speed printers could churn out even more reports, more analyses, more reasons not to do something—to avoid the very risks necessary in this time of unprecedented change. Computers used in most organizations often merely blocked innovation, rather than advancing it. They permitted bureaucracies to grow without necessarily becoming more effective; workers became only a bit more efficient at secondary work, the furious activity that's often confused with true performance. Computers added complexity to businesses, not to mention adding an entire new order of esoteric specialists: systems people, programmers, and other technicians by the legions. In other words, more bureaucracy.

Nowadays, computers are increasingly being adapted to truly automate the functions of the bureaucracy—repetitive professional, technical, and clerical work requiring people either to perform redundant calculations— or to organize and process data in ways that support front-line salespeople. What does this mean? Simply . . .

New computers are finally being used to *replace* bureaucrats and middle managers instead of to make them more efficient. *That's what's driving job shock!*

Earlier, I said 1993 would go down in history as a watershed year. That was the year when the real benefits of information technologies became headlines, the year corporations first took notice that conducting business in the information age is not about streamlining old hierarchies or improving old methods incrementally. It's about throwing out old methods and starting over. A minority of companies have been doing this since the 1980s, as documented in great detail by Tom Peters in his books, from *In Search of Excellence* to *Thriving on Chaos* to *Liberation Management*. The point is, these new methods are now going mainstream. In 1993, companies began to embrace the message of the latest overnight bestselling book: *Reengineering the Corporation,* by Michael Hammer and Robert Champy. Its theme: start from scratch and "reengineer"—organizing around the customer and around results-oriented processes, not activity-based functions.

Since the recession in 1990 we saw the return of high productivity—more like 3 percent plus—that we had lost after the sixties, when the old mass manufacturing system started to break down. I attribute that to the adoption of computers as the new breed of true office workers—*the automation of white-collar work!*

You can depend on this trend to accelerate because of a second factor.

Item 2: Computers are at the brink of unthinkable power

Computers will continue to exert increasing influence because they will grow in power much faster than we're assuming. We've already seen mainframe power put into desktop computers, moving rapidly into portable computers. Even as Intel introduced its powerful Pentium chip for the world of IBM computers and IBM clones, Apple introduced its line of Power PCs with a chip 60 to 100 percent more powerful than the Pentium chip. In response, Intel announced its P6 chip for late 1994 with a promised increase of 200 percent over its original Pentium chip.

Here's a technological fact that should stop you cold and make you rethink the power that will become accessible to you as an individual and to your company in the next decade. According to George Gilder:

With the predictable progress of information technologies we can project that within a decade we will see the power of sixteen Cray supercomputers on a single microchip that costs less than $100!

Three dimensions of the information superhighway

Imagine what that kind of inexpensive information power will do! It will allow you powerful access to information and expert systems at work, so that you can make many more decisions to satisfy your customers without waiting on bureaucrats to intervene or give you approval. In effect, such information will allow you to run your own business within or outside your present company. It will make available now unthinkable choices both at work and for daily living and entertainment. For example, instead of watching the sporting event the networks decide to transmit to your passive television set, you'll be able to select any game that's being played or has ever been played—and even simulations of games that might be played in the future. You'll be able to bring any movie from any film library in the world right into your home without going through the inconvenience of visiting the video shop—or any training course or educational seminar. Better yet, you'll talk to an expert and get programmed or live answers to your problems and opportunities. But the real information revolution we will experience in the coming decade will occur first at work and then filter into our homes and lifestyles.

I see these three dimensions to this information revolution:

Dimension 1: The smart card

A "smart card" equipped with a microchip memory will replace everything in your wallet, including family photographs, if you want it to. It will ultimately become an entire personal transaction system containing your credit status, your medical history, and instantaneously updated information about your credit cards, bank accounts, insurance policies, medical history, and even your accumulated frequent flier miles. You can choose to record your purchasing preferences on this smart card so you'll be able to enter into any kind of transaction and receive immediate, personalized, and customized service. For instance, express check-in at a hotel would permit you to use your smart card at an ATM-like desk clerk. You simply insert the card and enter your authorization code. The machine reads that you prefer a no-smoking room near the workout room, two room keys, and a 6:00 A.M. wake-up call. The automated clerk offers you several choices of rooms, bills the appropriate credit card, and issues two electronic keys. Since you sometimes purchase hockey tickets through the hotel, it also prints out the team schedule and permits you to order tickets on the spot. Or perhaps you need to go on a vacation or business trip. You would search through a special program for the best rates given your travel parameters and preferences. The computer selects the best itinerary or choices for your approval. You then swipe your smart card into the computer, which downloads all of the information from price and credit card charges to frequent flier miles and preferences into the smart card. You then swipe your card into a machine at the boarding ramp as you enter the plane without any checking in, unless you have baggage, which you drop into a machine that issues you baggage claims. No travel agents, no check-in agents!

The smart card will play similar roles at work: transactions and billing for services in and outside your company; approval of sales and data on credit levels of customers; access to restricted areas, résumés, and authorization codes; and many other applications.

Dimension 2: Mobile computing power—the smart phone

The driving force of the information superhighway in the coming years will be portable computer and communications devices that free up people from desks and offices to interact with customers and to work with other people at remote sites, simultaneously combining expertise from many dimensions to solve customer needs.

The biggest, most powerful trend? Smart cellular phones capable of transmitting voice, data, fax, messages, calendars, Rolodexes, schedules, and more. Beginning in 1996 when Motorola's first low-orbit satellites are in operation, continuing into 2001 when Microsoft and McCaw plan to have a broader network of such satellites in orbit, the smart phone will permit everybody to access a global, wireless network. Phones as we know them will become obsolete, replaced by elegant, powerful hand-held computers. These will become our primary communication devices, capable of accepting data input by handwriting and voice instead of by keyboards. They will be connected to the stationary home office and home databases of information, accessible from anywhere, at any time.

Dimension 3: Stationary computing—the smart television

Powerful digital video telecomputers in the workplace and the home will permit you to access video, complex databases, and networks through fiber optic cables. These stations will become the prime centers of learning, entertainment, and communication in business and the home worldwide. These machines will move into health care and the school system—*and even government!* In fact, one role of government will increasingly be to facilitate and fund the key information collection and monitoring databases in society, and to make such critical information systems widely available to individuals and businesses (through private companies wherever possible) at the lowest cost possible. This will be the competitive edge among countries competing in the world marketplace—not natural resources and landmass.

These stationary computers will become the ultimate information highway pieces allowing the processing of huge increments of complex and visual information. Such machines will serve countless smaller devices from desktop PCs to portable PCs to smart phones to smart cards. These machines will allow more decisions and controls to be implemented on the front lines of companies through access to information at stationary factory and office jobs, but more important, through access to large-scale information databases. Such machines will guarantee the end of middle management and bureaucracy.

Increased personal power

Tomorrow's increased computer power will give you the ability to increase your individual intelligence and give you access to other professional expertise. Using computers, you'll be able to access the services of doctors, managers, consultants, accountants, and lawyers without having to travel to the person's office. Instead of asking a bureaucrat in the home office you'll be able to ask a computer on the spot—your computer will communicate questions to the professional's computer. You'll pay for renting time or pay royalties in accessing these expert systems, but these costs will be less expensive than using professional time for basic or minor questions.

My opinion is that 80 percent of what even highly trained professional and managerial people do is left-brain, repetitive, systematic, computational work. This means expert knowledge can be programmed into computer systems. The 20 percent that we will require from such professionals is composed of more right-brain, creative, complex, intuitive powers and judgments—and we should pay more for that, but only when we need it! We'll be going to doctors and lawyers for their powers of judgment and synthesis, not for complex analysis of systematic logic that is better handled by a machine. Am I saying such professionals will be out of work? Not at all. They'll be freed up to advance their fields of expertise in research. Just imagine how much more effective such professionals will be if we give them 80 percent more time to pay attention to more pressing human and customer concerns than the handling of data and routine analysis.

Powerful computers with proper software will not
merely replace clerks. They will free up every person in
the organization from manager to salesperson to
pursue higher-level tasks.

Already today, we have computer systems that can diagnose patients'
conditions and their chances of survival in an emergency room better than
the best teams of doctors. We also have front-line hospital teams, called
"care pairs," that make and implement as much as 80 percent of the
decisions that an incredibly complex and costly network of hundreds of
expensive specialists used to make. In many areas of business and everyday life, all that's needed is to bring down the cost and increase your
access. The coming generation of powerful computers and the software to
be developed will allow you to process patents, trademark applications,
corporate start-ups, and other complex, expensive procedures with minimal legal participation, thus at far cheaper rates—unless there are complexities that require a professional specialist's intervention.

More important than such conveniences and more valuable than
video-on-demand for entertainment will be the limitless capacity for individualized learning. The interactive computer power we're talking
about will permit acceleration of learning that's unthinkable using the
traditional techniques of today's public school classrooms. The effects
of this new learning curve will occur first in the workplace, then in
the homes and schools. The real payoffs of the information revolution
will be felt in learning and increased productivity for individuals and
organizations. Just think of the personal powers you'll be able to acquire when you can attend classes or participate in live discussions at
any university in the country.

This revolution means much more than movies on
demand for couch potatoes. It means creating a miracle
in how we live by increasing our personal power and
our income. We'll have money to do things we don't
dream of today, and even couch potatoes may find
they don't have as much time to watch today's
popular TV programs.

Power on the job

No matter what your job is, information and user-friendly software will be at your fingertips as a front-line worker. The same information will be at the disposal of the everyday customer. The television set and the VCR will become obsolete, replaced by telecomputers—digital microcomputers that can tap into other computers and data sources to transfer copies of films, TV shows, newspapers, education programs, and business files directly from user to user. The most common form of computer will be in your cellular phone, totally portable and able to communicate globally, using computing power greater than that of supercomputers of today. Everybody will become to some extent an information creator or provider— either you'll be creating information and expertise, or you'll be using it on the front lines to solve customer needs, or else you'll be improving your living circumstances.

The Information Revolution has already extended itself into the workplace of leading-edge companies. Now that profitable, productive results in such companies are becoming clear, the revolution is poised to rush into mainstream companies and transform the corporate landscape as the assembly line did from 1914 on. Networking supercomputers will permit all types of companies to condense enormous numbers of clerical functions into individual workstations. Powerful databases of information and expert systems will be immediately accessible through portable computers to a salesperson or service agent in a customer's office, as well as to mobile executives and even to people working in the home. I'm going to introduce you to salespeople in leading-edge companies that are already using portable computers to respond fast and flexibly to changes in customer's needs—and at lower costs! These salespersons bypass almost entirely the order-processing and accounting functions and send profitable, approved orders directly from one computer to another until the order arrives at the plant. I'll also tell you about flexible factories that can produce very small runs of products, using compact multifunctional teams that require almost no inventories and little supervision and coordination.

The bottom line in the workplace

The arrival of inexpensive supercomputers means with absolute certainty that the majority of us involved as office workers or middle managers are going to be out of work over the coming decades as our left-brain, systematic jobs are automated by powerful computers.

How we work, where we work, how we live, and where we live will change more than at any other time in history. Our standard of living will take an enormous leap. The people who understand these changes first will prosper most.

Compare this increase in power to the way muscle-powered work moved into the industrial age of machines. You might as well compete with a Mack truck at physically hauling boulders across the country as compete against the new breed of powerful digital computers in the systematic work that typifies most jobs today. These computers far surpass us in their ability to perform left-brain functions. Where we surpass computers is in right-brain functions, which are the more intuitive, creative, emotional, and sensory functions and require leaps in information-processing power that digital computers can't make.

Let's face it—digital computers are high-powered, highly efficient left-brain machines that don't get sick, don't get headaches, don't have emotional problems, don't require expensive health care and retirement benefits, and don't sue you for everything from wrongful termination to sexual harassment. No wonder we can say that the very nature of work is about to be revolutionized! This is job shock, and it's real.

So, where do we fit in? Can the elimination of left-brain jobs be an exciting prospect, rather than something to fear? Let's look closer at how the work revolution—the greatest in history—will affect you, and learn how to leverage those right-brain, sensory capacities into new work opportunities.

The Greatest Work
Revolution in History

To advance our standard of living we have always had to automate old jobs. That's what's been happening in the 1980s and '90s. We're in the midst of the greatest revolution in work since the nineteenth-century Industrial Revolution—even *greater* than the Industrial Revolution and the assembly-line revolution that extended it through the twentieth century— a restructuring of work according to a completely different architectural principle.

Here's a quiz to challenge your assumptions about the scope of the revolution I'm predicting. Answer this multiple-choice question: *Where do work revolutions occur?*

a. In the restructuring or "reengineering" of the workplace.
b. In the decades following the introduction of new technology.
c. When people finally begin to accept change after resisting it.
d. In times of crisis and confusion.

What's driving this revolution? Several factors, many of which have been at work for half a century, are coming into play simultaneously. These factors are technological, as I've already discussed, and generational.

The largest generation in history is about to move into its peak spending and productivity years. Baby boomers will be moving into the power structures of business and politics, bringing with them the most powerful technologies ever invented. Result: the greatest work revolution in history—and the beginning of a new era of prosperity. In the coming decades we will change how we work and where we work, and how we live and where we live. For all of its faults and extremes, this is a highly creative, educated, and change-oriented generation.

A brief history of work revolutions

Work revolutions occur every two generations or at about eighty-year intervals. The First Industrial Revolution, powered by steam engines, automated farm and textile work and most other manual labor. This revolution was pioneered by Great Britain in the very late 1700s and then moved to the United States in the early to middle 1800s. At that point we were a country of more than 90 percent farmers, ranchers, trappers, retail proprietors, and other rural people—basically a bunch of entrepreneurial and small family businesses. The rise of the factory system, telegraphs, and railroads allowed us to move into the cities, where, as the Industrial Revolution progressed, a larger percentage of us worked in factories. Today, less than 3 percent of our workforce produces more food than we can eat—and that percentage continues to fall every year. Where did people go when they left the farms?

To the cities and factories, of course. The decline in one sector of the economy during a revolution is always accompanied by an increase in another sector.

We have to realize that the only way we have made progress and dramatically improved our standard of living is by eliminating the majority of jobs in the previous sectors. We ought to embrace such change. Job shock is not a sign of decline, but a sign of progress. It's a necessary component. We didn't become highly paid office workers without leaving the factory. We didn't become highly paid factory workers without leaving the farms. How could such progress be possible without old industries and jobs shrinking? Much of what we hear and see in the media today is a symptom of change, not of decline. We are simply freeing up people to move into new jobs, and seeing the replacement of old products and services that are becoming outmoded and too expensive by higher-quality, often less expensive products and services.

The most recent revolution was the Second Industrial Revolution—the mass-production or assembly-line innovations pioneered by Henry Ford in the early 1900s. That revolution, which catapulted the United States into world leadership, lasted well into the '60s; then mass production techniques were super-refined by Japan throughout the '70s and '80s, and the United States lost some of its dominance. In this revolution we automated the jobs of factory workers, which had been a large percentage of our workforce in the early 1900s, and moved from the cities to the suburbs. Of course, we saw a huge advance in our standard of living, above that of any time in history. Today, less than 14 percent of our workforce is composed of factory workers, yet that segment produces more than we can consume—and that percentage will decline to 10 percent by the year 2000.

Many goods that were once either luxuries or unavailable at the turn of the century have become affordable to everyday consumers. People don't realize that most of our current mass-market, Fortune 500 brand names and products and services that we take for granted were either luxury goods or didn't exist at all around the turn of the century. They were made affordable by the huge efficiencies created by this assembly-line work revolution. Where did the members of the factory workforce go when they were displaced by machines on the assembly line? Into the hierarchical management system that was adopted to make the assembly line efficient. These people became the white-collar workforce.

We are seeing and feeling the mere beginnings of the next revolution— the First Information Revolution. The majority of our workforce today is office workers performing white-collar administrative and clerical functions. These jobs will be the next to go south in the work revolution cycle. We will also see another geographical shift of the population, as the workforce begins moving outside of present-day metropolitan areas to exurbs or outer suburbs and back into smaller towns and communities. This shift will be made possible by the increased power of computers and the ways this power will be employed to decentralize today's businesses and communications.

The downsizing of the white-collar labor force is the first sign that the revolution is underway. The most secure and best-paid jobs of the past era are the ones being eliminated now—and that's the force behind job shock. Middle management jobs were slashed in the '90s recession. They were the highest-paid bureaucratic office functions. Next we are going to see clerical office jobs go—and those are the typical American jobs today.

So we should be terrified by this latest revolution, right?

Wrong!

We have no reason to fear either computers or job shock, or, for that matter, foreign cars, Third World labor, Japanese manufacturing methods, high technologies—*anything* that introduces change. Fear of change is wrongheaded thinking that only makes us reluctant to accept the inevitable.

Change is not your enemy

Computers might take away many systematic left-brain jobs, but they will not replace our highest human capacities—our right-brain, more creative, intuitive capacities—at least not in the coming decades. When is the last time you saw a computer get a flash of genius, have a vision, feel an emotion, enjoy an experience, love a person, think up a new product, read the expression on a customer's face, or even navigate down the street to special-order a Big Mac, your way? The list of what computers can't do can go on forever.

The technological changes I've described are handing us the greatest opportunities in history to advance our standard of living and to humanize our lives, giving us meaningful work instead of mind-numbing bureaucratic functions to perform.

We need to understand change and see it as our ally, not a threat.

Here's a basic but startling fact that might prepare you to embrace change. In *Microcosm*, George Gilder tells us that the most advanced supercomputers are light-years behind performing simple sensory feats like seeing and hearing that are accomplished by people every day:

Two human eyes have more information-processing power than the total of all the super-computers in the world today! The real work revolution is not about reengineering processes per se, but about leveraging the two eyes of every individual in your company and network.

Considering the quality of some prime-time television created by such brains, you might find that hard to believe. But it's true. You can find the world's most powerful computer in the head of any average person. We take that power for granted. We haven't learned how to truly leverage it. We only *feel* that we have been reduced to computers because the Industrial Revolution eliminated most physical tasks and moved us into an era where we mainly perform left-brain systematic decisions in the office or in the factory. Machines put our right brains to sleep in the name of efficiencies of functional specialization. The assembly line forced us to master very narrow tasks and to blindly follow standard procedures. It diminished the capacity to innovate in many of us. It's time to reclaim our most creative, most fulfilling, most human functions.

It's wrong to worship machines to the extent that we foresee a future in which we'll be replaced by mechanical robots in a world dominated by mindless computers. The truth is, our mechanical, computerized world of bureaucracy will be collapsing—sinking out of sight. Bureaucracy and mechanical functions will disappear, all right, but not at our personal expense. The robots we employ will be in factories working when we won't see them. They'll be repairing roads and bridges at night, and cleaning up undesirable waste and sludge when we are asleep.

Technology will free up the right-brain, interactive world, the world where human, relational, intuitive functions count for more than mechanical advantages. Our kids already live in this world—and we wonder why they don't value and respond to our outmoded left-brain educational systems. They can conquer six levels of a highly complex interactive video game without reading the instructions in about the time it takes us poor morons to decide whether to buy Boardwalk or Park Place. Can you imagine how big a joke it is to them that we think they will have a lower standard of living than we do?

The effect of powerful new technologies will not be to expand our mechanical world but to collapse it, leaving room for us to expand the human dimension, the truly human or psychic domain.

To begin integrating yourself into the work revolution, you must first accept that you cannot compete with monster computers in left-brain, computational functions. Big deal! Those are not our greatest strengths as human beings. We still need our natural left-brain capacities, but we can leverage them greatly and free up our higher functions. Our intuitive right-brain sensory capacities are millions of times more complex than left-brain calculations. Computers can presently perform right-brain functions only in the most primitive fashion.

Entrepreneurs, artists, star athletes, gifted political leaders, leading-edge scientists, philosophers, and entertainers are perhaps the epitome of human performance and function. Their trade is leadership, creativity, flexibility, innovation, intuition, perseverance, stress, perspiration, and vision. One entrepreneur like Bill Gates can create more value than hundreds of thousands of everyday officer workers pushing paper through the pipeline. We are moving into an era in which more of us will become entrepreneurs and human problem-solvers and, yes, even entertainers.

Perhaps we can't all be a Spike Lee, a Bill Gates, a Connie Chung, or an Arnold Schwarzenegger, but we *can* multiply our native abilities by using the power of left-brain digital computers, and most critically, by tapping into our own sense of vision and purpose. The most important aspect of this new age is that we must learn to use computers to leverage our perceptive capacities: to envision new products for new needs, to read the feelings and needs of other human beings, to respond in a human way, to test and prove new products and approaches, to question present rules and systems, to design better products and organizations. The truth is, our friend the computer is about to relieve us of the most rote, dehumanizing aspects of our lives and work. More of us will become "designers" of one sort or another in a highly customized, *customerized* world, where Tom Peters claims that every business will be in the "fashion" business.

We are not in competition with computers. They are just the tools to free up and feed our incredible right-brain functions—our superior sensory, creative, intuitive, and even sexual functions—and most powerful of all, our higher processes of the will. The brain, right or left side, is not the entrepreneur, the programmer, the soul or purpose; the mind or will is. We will not be able to practically differentiate between the mind or will and the brain until we begin to significantly automate right-brain, sensory functions as well. This right-brain automation should emerge around 2000–2010 and become practical in the decades to follow.

That is the work revolution, an integration of technology with ourselves.

The answer is . . .

Remember the question I asked at the beginning of this section: *Where do work revolutions occur?* It's time to put together an answer. No single response of the four I offered will do. Instead, it's a combination of all the responses. Here's my conclusion:

Work revolutions begin in times of crisis and emerge
in the decades following the introduction of new
technologies when people finally realize they can no
longer resist the acceptance of inevitable change and
must radically reengineer the workplace.

Sure, that's a mouthful, but it should enlighten you about a process
that is now underway. It might also give you a hint to my next point: the
current popular and productive movement toward reengineering, which
American business is only beginning to practice.

This movement of reengineering actually began in the 1980s with Tom
Peters and crescendoed with his book *Liberation Management*. Peters
showed that radical changes in work, management, and organization were
occurring everywhere—in large and small, service and manufacturing
companies, in both the entrepreneurial and the established sectors. He
chronicled how radical new and futuristic principles could occur in any
business. He documented these changes in incredible detail.

In 1993, attention turned to *Reengineering the Corporation*. More and
more companies accepted the reality that we need to reorganize around
customers and end-result processes rather than functional departments,
jobs, and activities. As I said before, I compare 1993 to 1914—approximately eighty years and two generations ago. In 1914, America was coming
out of a recession. It was also the year the assembly line was successfully
implemented by Henry Ford. The assembly line and later the techniques
of functional, hierarchical management, pioneered by Alfred Sloan of General Motors, allowed America to leverage the existing technology into
global economic dominance.

Reengineering the Corporation is showing us the basis for a restructuring of organizational management. That reordering is mandated by technologies that have been around for decades but are only now ripe for
leveraging into the Information Revolution.

The current approach to reengineering tends to be a blueprint for a
top-down, CEO-mandated restructuring of organizations. No wonder the
book was a hit with executives in large, top-down companies. We must
educate our top leaders to begin extending that picture, moving the process
of reengineering out of the executive suites, downward to the individual

worker—first at the front lines, and then to all levels of companies. Otherwise this revolution cannot be a true work revolution. In other words, to truly profit from the work revolution we have to look . . .

Beyond Reengineering

Let's briefly revisit the automobile production process before Henry Ford's introduction of the assembly line. As the automobile initially gained acceptance and as demand increased, more and more entrepreneurial companies sprang up to meet the demand. Teams of workers produced each automobile almost from a pile of parts to the moment it was driven out to be delivered. This may not have been an efficient way of keeping up with demand, but it did have its advantages, mainly that the team that produced a car could take some pride in it and could be held accountable for its manufacture.

So, do you think people willingly accepted the assembly line? Do you think they liked becoming mere cogs on the wheel of progress, repeatedly performing the same task day after day, week after week, year after year? Do you believe they appreciated having some geek performing time-and-motion studies on them as if they were mere robots? Of course not. These people had pride in their craft and in the products they turned out. They fought the assembly line until they saw how it could increase profits and their own standards of living.

But finally workers surrendered their creative spirits to the promise that they could afford automobiles of their own.

Thus, the standard of living in real wages (adjusted for inflation) for the average worker has grown nine times from the 1870s to today, because of the assembly-line revolution.

The assembly line was able to put even people with very low skills and little education into a large, highly coordinated system that increased their productivity. If you think we have skill problems in our workforce today, just consider the educational levels of workers around 1900. Only

23

2 percent graduated from college and only 14 percent from high school. That was no big deal. Business innovators like Henry Ford did not complain about the inadequacies of the education system and skills of workers. Instead, they leveraged their workers' strengths and minimized their weaknesses with a superior system of management. Companies were able to create enormous economies of scale and tap into the advantages of the functional specialization of labor.

The cost of productivity

The assembly line and the hierarchical, specialized management system it spawned worked for a long time, but it has its own disadvantages. Too many of us have lost the individualistic spirit to mediocrity. Creativity has been sacrificed to the nameless, faceless bureaucracy and the quest for endless entitlements from our enormous institutions, government, and huge corporations. People have come to expect annual raises for seniority—not for merit but just for being alive and hanging on another year. Everything from jobs to health care to retirement benefits has become a right of birth. The problem in business, government, and society at large is that almost nobody is accountable to customers—and to creating bottom-line results. Few people create real value. Seldom are people measured or rewarded on the value they do create.

> **The whole American ideal of independent spirit and individualism has mutated into a perverse notion: "Just tell me what to do and don't blame me if things go wrong, I just did what I was told to do. And, oh, did I mention I'm suing you, and, by the way, where's my 10 percent raise this year?"**

In the hierarchies of management, functions have grown more and more specialized so that work has become an assembly line of staff actions with little connection to the end result or customer. Work is passed from one office to another—thrown over the wall, as they say in the auto design business. Far too many people in the great bureaucracies have removed themselves from accountability. Arguably, that's a trend that has permeated society in a thousand ways. People tend either to avoid responsibility for their own behavior or to blame somebody else for it. This overspecialization of functions is the target of the process called reengineering.

Assembly-line methods and management worked, and continually improved our productivity for most of the last century. Then the progress inevitably started to slow in the 1970s. We all started taking advantage of the system, using it to insulate ourselves from the world of customers and change. As long as the system continued to reward everybody in it, we shifted our focus to locking in the entitlements we earned. No doubt about it, as long as the economy continued to grow, it was a great system that raised our standard of living and production.

However, productivity trends began to slip in the 1970s and 1980s. That's when we saw the most desperate efforts to lock in the status quo, as people attempted to make a secure system out of an insecure world, trying to create heaven on earth. We ended up using the strengths of the system to insulate ourselves from customers and change rather than being responsive to both. Finally it took the recession of the '90s to sound the alarm—the status quo could not be guaranteed. Not our jobs. Not our benefits. Not even the value of our homes!

The changing nature of specialization

That was then. Specialization in tomorrow's economy is the opposite of what it was yesterday. In the old economy the idea was to break down a process into its simplest parts and have an individual or teams of individuals accomplish only one part. These people would likely never see the whole. A person might only put on a bolt or attach the left legs of a chair. That was the assembly-line approach. It naturally required the growth of an ever enlarging hierarchy of bureaucrats to coordinate and control all of these fragmented and overspecialized functions.

The new approach is just the opposite: Individuals or small self-managing, cross-functional teams of people focus on a particular need or solution or problem of a customer and know that customer's need better than anybody else. Call it customer or end-result specialization. Teams, by definition, must become more multifunctional. Small, highly focused teams simply can't afford overspecialization and bureaucracy. They must focus on customers' needs. They must be flexible to do whatever it takes to solve a customer problem. Working in small teams is more efficient than an assembly-line approach in the new economy, precisely because customization and fast response is essential. We'll find that teams require less overhead and have more flexibility to meet customer needs.

Functional specialization is out for the corporation of the future, except in the experts and information providers that support multifunctional front-line teams and businesses—and these people will have to specialize even more in their functions and expertise. For most people, specialization will have less to do with function than with customers. More and more our complex business world and society demand multifunctional people with an emphasis on achieving customized results. This will force specialization toward knowing products, businesses, and customers.

The grassroots nature of the revolution

The real revolution lends itself more to a "bottoms-up" process that makes every individual and small team a real business, as motivated and accountable and as much in control of its operation as the corner dry cleaner. Your local family dry cleaner doesn't have excessive overhead, doesn't lose touch with its customers, and most certainly doesn't return clothing that's still wrinkled and dirty. Why? Because in small business, the proprietor has intimacy with customers. Owners feel accountability. Yes, they are driven by pride, but to succeed they can never lose sight of the financial reality of the bottom line. The most elementary law of business survival mandates that if a business doesn't perform, the customer punishes the owner by going elsewhere.

For the real point of this work revolution to be realized, organizations must leverage the power of the two eyes of every person in that organization. The secret of success will be in getting people at all levels of companies large and small to make more decisions, identify more opportunities, act, make mistakes, learn, get closer to their customers, and become capable of responding in human ways that computers and bureaucrats cannot. That will require more than simply paying lip service to the empowerment of workers. It will take an entire new organization, a new architecture, new values, new measurements, new controls, and new skills, all built from the bottom up around the needs of customers and the frontline units that serve them—not from the top down, catering to the needs and insecurities of hierarchical management.

This new age of organizations will be driven by restoring human initiative and accountability. Does that mean returning to the good old days of isolated cottage industries? Yes and no! It means the creation of a powerfully networked world that allows much faster learning and the ability to tap economies of scale that our nation of independent farmers and small proprietorships before the Industrial Revolution did not have; at the same time, it means we will be working in highly responsive and accountable small business environments.

The motif of the new workplace is: No more jobs, only businesses. People get a life, a mission, a business—not a job. They have customers. They must deliver results. Their monetary rewards are based on real, measured results in their own work domains; their psychic rewards come from solving problems, creating value, and making customers happy. The key trend is restoring decision-making and accountability to the individual, not in merely reengineering overly engineered large-scale business processes.

The inevitability of teams and networks

If we look around our society and think of all the areas where we see high performance, there is a common denominator. Peak performance tends to occur mostly in individuals or small teams. Think of a picture of a marching band compared to a rock band or a jazz trio. Or think of an inefficient bureaucracy you've been frustrated with, and then compare that to a tennis star, golf pro, basketball team, Olympic skater, stand-up comic, juggler, theater group, surgical team, entrepreneurial start-up company, SWAT team, business consulting team, star salesperson, and speakers like Ken Blanchard, Tony Robbins, and Tom Peters.

Individuals and small teams of high-performance individuals always tend to stand out. Look at a sports analogy. A football team is rigidly organized. Enough so that a coach can call every play from the sideline. Coaches can't do that as well in many other sports. Football, then, is organized more like a traditional business, with a CEO, a board of directors, and specialized departments—offense, defense, special teams. In many ways the team is large, specialized, hierarchical, cumbersome, and less flexible than, say, a basketball or hockey team, on which any given player can play the role of almost any other team member—and in no way can a coach call the game from the sidelines. I mean, just look at the speed of the action!

The analogy of a basketball team applies to the way teams will be constituted in the future. Information technologies will facilitate the restructuring of work and organizations to put the emphasis back on fast-moving, high-performance individuals and small teams—in a way that they have real customers and real measures of performance, including bottom-line profitability.

The powerful new microcomputers operate on the law of the microcosm George Gilder describes. Contrary to what your intuition tells you, computer chips increase in power and efficiency by becoming smaller, using low-powered and slower, not larger and faster, transistors to build the network. High-powered transistors create too much heat and resistance, which impedes speed and capacity.

A microchip is a network of transistors that are simply on-off decision switches. The more low-powered, slow-switching-speed transistors that can be crammed into one chip or network, the more power and efficiency will be achieved. What's more, as you add more transistors to a network, the power of the network grows exponentially rather than arithmetically. That simply means that if you add any number n of transistors to a chip, the power increases not by $n + n$, but by n^2.

That unprecedented exponential rate of productivity gains makes networks and microcomputer technologies unique compared to other technologies.

Our mission is to translate these same exponential gains to our people and organizations. It can be done.

We have the blueprint. By designing organizations modeled on the architecture of the microchip, we can get on the same productivity path. The key is to take our everyday, relatively low-powered people, even those who are slow in making decisions, and move them into networks of decision-making in the company. Everybody is an expert at something, and almost everyone knows the task or customer in front of him or her better than people at higher levels. That's a critical departure from the hierarchy, in which all the high-powered decision-makers reside at the very top of organizations, too often isolated by layers of staff and bureaucracy.

Who were the first organizational people to use computers? Too often they were those who already held all the power in the executive suites and the technical experts within the bureaucracy. In the 1970s and 1980s, most of our computer technologies consolidated existing decision-making networks. In the 1990s and early 2000s, the revolution is going to bring all levels of people into computer technologies, linking them into networks closer to the customers and front-line functions. The companies that win their competitive battles will be those tapping into the power of lower-level people and not just the people at the top. The very function of top-level professional, managerial, and technical people will be translating expertise down the lines to the lowest level where decisions are best made—next to customers, the people who matter. The more we can get our lowest-powered people to make decisions and become part of the network, the faster will become the overall speeds, efficiencies, and responsiveness of our organizations.

I've already given you the example of the replacement of steam engines by electric motors—substantial increases in efficiency and flexibility could not be gained simply by replacing the huge steam engine outside the building with a huge electric motor to power a central driveshaft. Let's examine this concept, first from the negative aspects of centralization and then from the benefits of networked decentralization.

The bankruptcy of centralization

Huge bureaucracies and highly centralized organizations eventually destroy themselves as they founder in complexity and inefficiencies that result from self-perpetuation and increasing regulation. You don't have to look very far to see the truth in this. The highly centralized Communist governments of the former Soviet Union and its Eastern Bloc allies, including Cuba, are all in decline, brought down primarily because their economies cannot sustain themselves simply by fiat.

Or look at what happened to the then-fourth-largest army in the world, that of Saddam Hussein, in the Persian Gulf War. The field commanders of Saddam's divisions, who were not permitted any flexibility, became paralyzed when allied forces took out the command and control. The occupation of Kuwait collapsed within a week under the onslaught of allied forces, whose commanders were allowed battlefield discretionary powers.

In the world of computers, the huge mainframes have all but given way to the decentralized power of desktops and portables of all sizes. Yes, it's true that a single microcomputer can't outperform a giant mainframe. But think about the bang you get for the buck today. For only a few thousand dollars, you can accomplish powerful functions at a fraction of the costs involved in mainframes, with efficiencies on the order of sixty to one.

In looking at the business picture, we see the crumbling of giant bureaucratic corporations. You have only to review the headlines of the last year. Sears, GM, and IBM were pictured on the cover of *Fortune* magazine no longer as perennial models of success but as dinosaurs. IBM discovered that it had led the industry in R&D, but corporate bureaucracy so slowed implementation that other companies had taken IBM's scientific papers and beaten it to market with the fruits of its own research.

We should learn our lessons from these examples.

We must all realize that in order to survive, our large corporations must break into networks of smaller and smaller companies and ultimately into more entrepreneurial, flexible networks of small teams and individuals.

Sooner or later, almost all of us will be working in small-company environments. We must all expect to depend more on ourselves and less on Big Brother organizations. Here's a simple analogy to clarify the future of decentralized organizations:

Whales and minnows—a new paradigm for organizing

Imagine two entirely different aggregates in the sea. One is the whale, a single large mass with enormous integrated support systems. The other structure is a huge school of minnows of the same mass. Suppose each must turn quickly—must to avoid an oncoming oil tanker. The whale makes its turn more like a barge, taking many minutes to maneuver. The school of minnows can turn instantly, as if every individual were wired into a central nerve network triggered by its leader or the oncoming threat. The corporation of the future can be represented as enormous schools of minnows larger and more powerful in the aggregate mass than any single creature that ever swam the seas. This analogy is a way of showing how more of us will be working in small, multifunctional teams in smaller business units—networked, flexible, well led, able to turn in an instant. To use an old cliché: Think globally, act locally.

The key difference is not just ultimate size, but speed—a school of minnows can turn on a dime and have the ultimate mass of a whale. In the old economy, size was everything; in this economy, speed counts for far more. In this information-driven age of customized products and services and entrepreneurial spirit, old vertically integrated, hierarchical, bureaucratic structures just don't work. Speed becomes more important—but businesses want the best of both worlds, the speed of small teams and the size and exponential power of large networks.

A real network in action today—the NYSE

Nothing demonstrates the power of information networking, flexibility, and decentralization better than the New York Stock Exchange. Like other financial markets it is almost a pure information system with little hard goods to impede it. It is a working business that works on real-time information systems and has only a few rules, little visible management, minimal hierarchy, and little apparent structure. Some guy rings a bell at 9:30 Eastern time on a workday morning and runs like hell as chaos erupts. Anything can happen in the free play that is the NYSE. All types of political events affect it. Russia makes a decision, oil drops, Federal Reserve Chairman Alan Greenspan announces something, bonds go one way, and stocks go the other. This is a system capable of instantaneously changing in response to any stimulus at any level in the world. And it does it so efficiently that unless you're an absolute expert and devoted to studying it every hour of the day, you are going to lose money in the extreme volatility of short-term trading.

Amazingly enough, it's a highly responsive system operating in a complex world, but driven by simple principles. A board of people you never see establishes ground rules governing what the players can do and what information they can use and what hours they can trade—only as much as necessary for the good and efficiency of the market. Then the operation is left up to the players, who all share access to the same real-time information about the markets. The network expands on its own spontaneously, with no top-down management after the rules are established. Other players jump in to develop software and techniques for participating as they see fit. It is a totally unmanaged system that grows on its own and remains incredibly responsive to change.

The basis of the stock exchange's success is that it functions as a real-time database of price and trading activity. Participating brokerage businesses make information available about trades and profits and losses. Others make daily or minute-to-minute pitches about individual stocks. This information is available to other players. Then the network builds. Individual newsletter writers and investment firms build their own software to give people better measures. Brokerage firms develop their own systems of analysis, and their experts evaluate every stock. Individual investors make decisions every day. They vote yes or no by buying and selling. Governments intervene in the markets with money. It is a highly complex, always changing network, a vast, ever-changing capitalistic free-market system in which every minnow large or small can make decisions that will have an effect on the rest of the network.

Best of all, there is no bureaucracy to say you have to follow a set of arcane procedures. Everybody in the network is free to use information as he or she sees fit to make a profit or become productive within his or her individual milieu. The system responds incredibly well to complexity and customization and chaos; it works every day, and very efficiently at that.

The New York Stock Exchange today is where our most sophisticated corporations will be in the next two or three decades.

In the near future, networks of microcomputers, each with its own memory, will attack either the same or different parts of complex problems simultaneously with sixty times the efficiency of any single mainframe computer.

Internet—where every computer is a minnow

Another increasingly popular and even more dramatic example of a network system is Internet, which allows computer owners to link up with other computers worldwide to work or play. It's the most efficient information system for people communicating around the world, and it's growing at light speed with no formal management. It too is a collection of minnows, a network of end users, with sets and subsets of individuals who connect to each other to share information, to acquire data, and to entertain themselves. Internet has a life of its own, and the way it functions is almost organic.

The Internet has grown from a Department of Defense project of real-time communications and information transfer into a network of over twenty million individuals. These people converse around the world about everything from the newest scientific breakthroughs to sex. It is a learning network.

Who manages the Internet? Nobody. The users manage it for their own needs, and many people will profit from expanding its communications capacities. It's growing faster than Microsoft.

How Do Companies Get There from Here?

The key to the success of reengineering lies not just in the entrepreneurial spirit of individuals and the businesslike performance of small teams, but in how we link both individuals and teams into networks for more power and faster learning. Only a small minority of our large and small companies are really doing this. Too many of us are just reading the various business books and talking about reengineering. And far too many are either ignoring or fearing the change these books describe. In the '90s and beyond we are all going to have to enter the revolution or lose our businesses and jobs.

You can look to the history of computers and learn volumes about how management structures can change to embrace a similar architecture. First came mainframes, the top-down, hierarchical systems. The mainframes were an adaptation of the radical new transistor technologies to the old hierarchical management and engineering processes. The first breakthrough supercomputers were parallel networks of multiple microcomputers able to achieve sixty-to-one increases in performance over mainframes because the networked microcomputers all simultaneously attacked one problem at the same time. Look at a franchise, where many small efficient units are doing the same thing around the world at once—at McDonald's, for example, where you can find a consistent product at a reasonable price everywhere you go. The decentralized management formula has produced enough data from experience to practically guarantee the success of such an operation. But the franchise is not where we're going in the management revolution. It simply doesn't fit the model of the customized economy we're moving toward, a model that places a premium on high quality, customization, localized, fast response and delivery, and personalized service.

A recent breakthrough has come from N-Cube, a leading-edge small company. N-Cube has developed a new architecture using a network of microcomputers that can all attack many parts of a problem or solution at the same time in parallel. This is the ultimate picture of our new corporate world. Not McDonald's, which provides fast response but is hardly customized beyond the point of holding the onions.

What we need in even our largest companies is small, networked teams with different skills that can work on every facet of a problem for the customer simultaneously, teams that grow and change organically, moving like a school of minnows all in synch.

I know of such a network of highly focused and unique small businesses. It's a bed-and-breakfast network with members linked through common world-scale advertising, quality standards, and an 800 number for reservations and information. As far into the future as I can see, that's the vision for corporations. Hierarchical architecture will be increasingly out of business in coming years, both in computers and in organizations.

Don't get the idea that such change is a lifetime beyond the horizon, although it will take many years and decades in most companies to come to fruition fully. I could list any number of highly innovative, entrepreneurial minnow-like companies that have already successfully prototyped the corporation of the future. Most companies are hoping that their gradual and superficial changes will be sufficient. They won't! So . . .

Get a Life!

The recession and job shock of the early '90s were tough for many corporations and individuals, but it was necessary to help us shed old practices and principles faster. The increased power of new technologies will expedite trends that have already begun. Sadly, most people in this country hope that either big corporations or the government will take care of them, or that change will slow down. I have a message to address those harboring these false hopes:

Stop clinging to the whales of old. If you think big bureaucratic companies or the government will take care of you, you will be crushed when they go down and you find your security has been ripped away.

Once change comes, we're never going back to the good old times when you went to work for a giant paternal organization for life. Stop looking to the government or IBM to provide heaven on earth in no-risk jobs that require no innovation or no productivity, yet offer endless raises in wages and entitlements. In the larger scheme of things, when the very survival of huge organizations is at stake, you will be of small concern to the behemoths thrashing about as they try to catch up to the future that's being written by smaller, more flexible organizations.

What's more, the Band-Aid corporate fixes that have always gotten a company through lean times aren't going to work anymore. Simple layoffs, cost-cutting, and reshuffling won't be enough. Why not? Because times have changed. Things won't be returning to the way they were.

Lost jobs and lost markets won't be back!

Stand by to watch companies change fundamentally and forever. That means we'll see a totally revamped job environment. It means the very nature of work will be redefined.

Prepare for every job in America to change

We're seeing a permanent reengineering of corporate structures and processes. Leading-edge companies have recognized this for a while. As the rest catch on to this fundamental change in the way we use technology, we'll be dealing with its implications for the rest of our careers.

Work in the future is going to be conducted by individuals, most often in team settings. And where will team members come from? Back-line clerical people and experts will either be pulled into front-line teams or become specialized consultants available either inside or outside the company. They will be paid by front-line teams only if they can create value for them.

35

As I mentioned earlier, jobs in America will change so much that we'll have to stop calling them jobs. People will be getting their own micromissions rather than a job description, and will be allowed greater latitude than ever to be creative in fulfilling these missions. The work people do will vary from situation to situation, even from day to day in some cases. Rather than complying with some checklist from a job description, workers will exploit that underused organ the brain to help companies and customers solve problems. Individuals will be performing a variety of exciting functions and exercising independent thinking. In many ways, each individual will become a business or a valued member of a team. These teams will work exactly like a business, with a profit-and-loss motive and customer accountability. In return, business will give people worthwhile work and not just a job. We'll all see higher earnings potential based on value created or added by such teams.

In this book we will focus on the simplest principles that everyone can understand, at all levels from management to the front-line workers, to learn the secrets of how we can construct organizations and the workplace so that we can be as efficient and flexible as schools of minnows. Two other excellent books have formed the current thinking on how organizations will perform in the future. These are *Reengineering the Corporation* and *Liberation Management*. Like the authors of *Reengineering* I see a total restructuring of work, but not a restructuring that can be mandated from the executive suites across America. I see it more as a grassroots revolution incapable of succeeding without the understanding and support of people at all levels of companies. That is precisely why leadership is more critical than management in the new economy. That's why we've focused so much of this book on individual preparation for the revolution.

Liberation Management also brings its focus to individuals. However, unlike that book, with its excellent detail of reporting, I focus on the big picture. That's why I've brought forward only a few sets of very simple, overriding principles that keep people from getting lost in the complexities of change. Complexities are inevitable, but can confuse everybody and force us to revert to obsolete, old management techniques and destroy the reengineering efforts that are so critical. These principles can be understood at all levels from corporate executives down to individual workers. The themes and principles I'll be sharing will help you leverage the power of your two eyes, bringing every single person into the equation for solving problems for customers. Meanwhile . . .

Take heart—job shock is giving back your soul

The coming work revolution will force us to rediscover our greatest strength, individual initiative—thus nurturing a spirit of real entrepreneurialism. This is precisely why the advantage is going to return to America. We have an entire history and culture of entrepreneurial peoples fostering new technologies. Europe and even the vaunted Pacific Rim nations are slower to embrace these principles. Only individual initiative creates tangible results. People will work effectively only in an environment where they can make worthwhile distinctions and issue responsible decisions. Out of that comes job satisfaction and genuine self-esteem—the real thing, not the Pollyanna "virtual reality" self-esteem generated by "visualizing your way to success" techniques in motivational seminars.

We have the strongest entrepreneurial sector in the world. Baby boomers are more creative than any generation in the world, as are the baby busters who are to follow. Because of that, America is going to lead the greatest boom in history. We are defining this work revolution. We dominate the information technologies and emerging customized products and services that will rule the world economy in the future.

Don't resist the work revolution because you're trying to rekindle the apparent security and familiarity of a tired, failed workplace and the good old values of the past. It's clear that in companies that have taken the lead in the work revolution, the overwhelming majority of people are both happier and higher paid. But some people, especially the ones that branch out on their own, are simply happier! Maybe a Yale graduate lives on a remote island and runs a dive shop and wouldn't trade places for all the money in the world.

Workers, professionals, and managers at all levels of companies need to hear that the reasons and rewards for the work revolution are a booming economy, rapidly rising personal standards of living, and a greater quality and choice in life. What they're hearing instead is that they need to work twice as hard just to compete and survive. People will be motivated by fear, but not for long. Psychologists have proved that fear only motivates simple repetitive tasks and retards more creative, complex tasks. Creative and complex tasks are the focus of the new, customized economy.

Most of us are tired of being told to run twice as fast just to keep what we've got. That's one reason this book was fun to write—my message is that you will enjoy more fruits of your labors. You will be rewarded materially and experientially if you take the risk of participating in this work revolution.

When the dust settles, more people will have been forced to move into new jobs and more entrepreneurial opportunities. People will be saying, "What was I afraid of? I'm having more fun than ever at my new job. I have more influence on my job and with the people I serve, and the rewards, both tangible and intangible, are far better than the bureaucratic entitlements I used to have."

"I even feel like a human being again instead of an automaton."

In Chapter 2 we will look at how growth and competition in our economy are going to be much stronger than most of us expect. We will read the signs that tell us we are about to enter the greatest boom in history, learn how to identify the right companies to work for, and discover how to benefit from the new information-driven, customized economy.

2

Get Ready for the Greatest Boom in History

Once you accept that the economy is predictable
and that you can see where the growth industries
are, choosing to work for or create the right
company becomes the most important decision
you'll make. The fundamental factors that drive
our economy suggest that we are about to
enter the greatest boom in history. You should make
sure you are a part of it.

The Economy Is Predictable!

Economists analyze all types of complex statistics that don't really matter—focusing on symptoms, not causes. As a group, they have proved no more accurate in predicting the future of the economy than the average guy on the street. The truth is, the factors driving the economy are simple and readily accessible to everybody. How can you plot your career and job prospects without some understanding of our economy and what types of businesses will grow in the future?

The economy is far more predictable than economists have led us to believe. It is driven by very simple fundamentals like family life cycles of spending that we can easily understand, chart, and project. It's time to bring economics back to the people!

That means we can identify trends driving the economy and see the basic directions in which we're moving.

Contrary to popular opinion and all the best-selling depression books, we are on the verge of an exciting era of growth and another huge advance in our standard of living that will last into the next century. Three trends will create the greatest boom in history:

- **Disinflation.** We will continue to see lower inflation and interest rates after 1997 as workforce growth and restructuring of the economy fades and productivity returns. A new generation entering the workforce drives inflation up by bringing on an innovation cycle that results in high investment in technological retooling. Imagine the effect of the huge baby boom generation. The turmoil is then followed by a period of high productivity when the effect of those investments is felt, driving inflation back down. Inflation has little to do with government deficits, growth rates, and debt, which are the commonly perceived causes. The continuing disappearance of inflation will restore huge purchasing power gains to consumers, eventually including 6 percent, thirty-year fixed mortgages, and reduce the cost of borrowing for families, businesses, and the government.

- **The Baby Boom Spending Wave.** We're about to witness the movement of baby boomers, the largest generation in history, into their peak spending, earning, and productivity years. Family spending follows a very predictable life cycle that rises until around age forty-six and then tapers off into retirement. It is generations or greater numbers of consumers moving into and out of their peak spending years that cause corresponding booms and busts in the economy. The baby boom Spending Wave began in the roaring '80s. Baby boomers will move into their peak years of spending around 2007, creating the biggest spending boom in history.

- **Mainstreaming of the Information Revolution.** As we saw in Chapter 1, new technologies are moving into our organizations and

40

homes, changing how we work and live. This will result in the emergence of a new, customized economy and an unprecedented surge in productivity. This trend will be driven by the movement of baby boomers into their power years when they have the capacity to change organizations to accommodate the new technologies and their very different skills and lifestyles. The combination of the microcomputer revolution with the individualistic tastes of baby boomers will mean that growth in the economy in all segments—high-tech, low-tech, manufacturing, and service—will accrue to companies that offer customization to individual needs; high-quality and value-added products and services; fast response and delivery; and personalized service. In the coming decades, we'll also see information technologies leading to a major population shift back to small towns and cities, reducing the cost and increasing the quality of living.

Let's look at how these fundamental trends will be driven by three successive waves of the baby boom generation cycle.

The Generation Wave

The driving force behind economic growth and change is the movement of a new generation into society. I call this pattern the Generation Wave, which is composed of three stages following the initial Birth Wave: the Innovation Wave, the Spending Wave, and the Power Wave. I describe the Generation Wave in great detail in my first book, *The Great Boom Ahead.*

New generations coming into the economy and aging and doing predictable things have more to do with everything from inflation to deflation and growth to recession than any other single factor, including all our politicians put together.

The Birth Wave

The Birth Wave is nothing more than the pattern of birthrates of a given generation. Birth surges peak about every forty years and create new generations of consumers and workers. The baby boom generation is by far the largest in our country's history, eighty million strong. Just look at

Figure 2-1 to see the birth pattern of baby boomers in comparison to the previous generation, which I call the Bob Hope generation, and the generation following it, called the millennial generation.

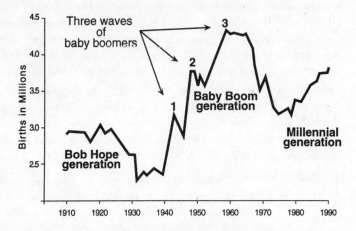

**Figure 2–1. Cycles in U.S. birth rates in this century.
(Source: U.S. Census Bureau)**

Figure 2-2 illustrates how eighty million baby boomers have been rolling through our economy in three successive waves, as has occurred for previous generations. You'll see that all I have done to arrive at the Generation Wave is project this birth pattern forward to the three important stages in the lives of adults: the age at which the generation enters the workforce (Innovation Wave); the age at which the generation reaches its peak spending years (Spending Wave); and the age at which the generation moves into power positions (Power Wave).

These waves will cause economic and management changes that we can predict on a very reliable timetable in direct proportion to the size of the generation. Therefore, the baby boom generation's unprecedented size will distort and magnify all of these waves of change. Let's look at each of these waves separately.

The Innovation Wave

As any new generation enters the workforce it brings new social and technological ideas and spawns an entrepreneurial revolution. Young people are the innovators in society. This forces older, mature industries and companies either to decline or restructure and entrepreneurs to launch many new ventures. Of course, such turbulence requires large investments at all levels, consumer, business, and government—but at a time when the new generation is young and not very productive, with low earnings and savings rates.

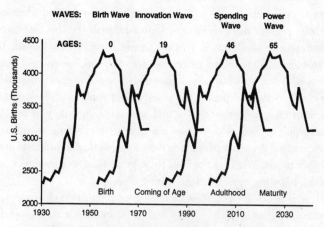

Figure 2-2. The baby boom Generation Wave and its various phases.

Refer to the Innovation Wave in Figure 2-2. You can see that from the '60s into the late '70s the huge baby boom generation entered the workforce in larger numbers. Eighty million baby boomers, including more working women than ever before, demanded a huge expansion in our fixed capital stock. Just think of the requirements in office space, desks, chairs, computer terminals, parking garages, shopping malls, and cafeterias alone!

But these young people were also experimenting, testing, overthrowing old rules, and causing a social and technological revolution that their conformist, civic-minded parents may never forget. For opportunistic individuals and entrepreneurs among them—Bill Gates and Steve Jobs are examples—it has been a heyday. The most important aspect of the Innovation Wave is that we see new products, services, and technologies emerge into niche markets in all industries. These don't remain as niche markets, but become the seed of a two-generation growth cycle of powerful new industries that will come to dominate the marketplace in the boom to follow.

The growth markets, industries, and technologies
for decades to come were largely established
in the '60s and '70s!

These growth markets have emerged in every industry. Examples range from Ben & Jerry's superpremium rain forest macadamia nut crunch ice cream to customized semiconductor chips to luxury cars to white-collar pool halls to home maid services to adult education services like Anthony Robbins tapes and seminars. The key trends are not technological. Technologies are only the means to the end, and that end, the greatest trend of our times, is the social change from outer-directed to inner-directed behavior. Outer-directed people are reactive and conformist, looking to the system for cues as to how to live and where and how they fit in. Inner-directed people look to their own inner needs and strengths and weaknesses, and are proactive, designing their lives, work, and products to meet their own needs. Whereas the Bob Hope generation was generally outer-directed, baby boomers are clearly inner-directed.

Here is a key insight. New technologies, products and services, and social trends all move into society and the marketplace on a projectable life cycle called the S-curve. Figure 2-3 shows the simple S-curve formula that can give us remarkable insights into where things are going. We tend to think and project in straight lines, but reality follows the S-curve. A new product takes a long time to form and undergo the difficult trial of being accepted in niche markets. Customers may be afraid of it and not understand it. Often it is high-priced and not very user-friendly at first. Growth consistently underperforms the grand visions of the entrepreneurs and pioneers promoting the new products.

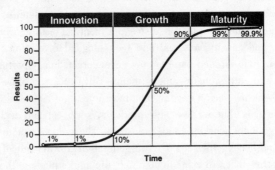

Figure 2–3. The S-curve.

Then when it reaches a critical mass, it mushrooms into the mainstream far faster than anyone expects. It took cars fourteen years after invention in 1886 to reach the first stages of commercial production in 1900, when only 0.1 percent of urban families could afford a car. In the next fourteen years, cars slowly penetrated the upper-income markets to the point that by 1914, 10 percent of urban families owned a car. Then the assembly line in 1914 exploded cars into the mainstream, and fourteen years later, in 1928, 90 percent of urban families owned a car. That is how new products and technologies have always moved into society. It's time we recognized this simple fact.

A **new technology or product will move from 10 percent to 90 percent of its market potential in the same time it took to move from 0.1 percent to 10 percent. The Information Revolution is about to enter its powerful 10 percent to 90 percent move in the coming decades much as automobiles did in the Roaring '20s.**

Change and progress will be faster and greater than most people and forecasters expect. Today's niche products and services will move into mainstream affordability more rapidly than in past decades; the niches of today will become the dominant, mainstream industries in the coming decades. This is where the productivity and new jobs will come from, even as our older technologies and industries continue to downsize and lay off workers.

Here's another important insight into why we experienced inflation in the 1970s and why it will continue to fade, making our lives easier and more affordable. It took a huge investment to launch these new technologies and industries, and consumers paid an "inflation tax" to finance them. But their movement into the mainstream will bring high productivity that will beat back inflation. Most economists are not aware of the historical correlation between inflation and technological revolutions. Entrepreneurial revolutions require a lot of investment to retool old companies and even more investment to launch new ones. So it was no accident that we saw the highest inflation rates in history in the late '70s as the largest generation in history went through its Innovation Wave. We also saw inflation as the Second Industrial Revolution was emerging in the early

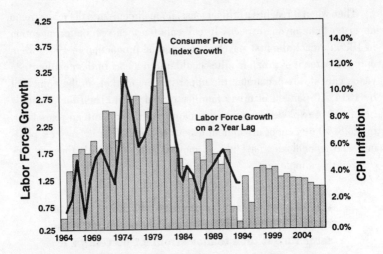

Figure 2–4. Baby boomers entering the labor force. A tool that indicates inflation predicts prices will continue to stay low throughout the coming boom.

1900s in this country and in many prior technology revolutions. It was also no accident that the most powerful innovations and technologies in history emerged: The digital revolution—from the personal computer to cellular phones to fax machines—arrived at the same time that the peak of this huge enterprising new generation moved into the workforce.

Trend 1: Disinflation

This is a trend we are able to project from the Innovation Wave. Remember I said inflation was caused by the entry of baby boomers into the workforce and the technological revolution they brought with them? In this view, inflation can be understood as the means by which our economy finances the transition from old to new technologies, old to new industries, and old to new generations.

You tell that to economists and they fall off their chairs. But I have a tool, illustrated in Figure 2-4, that proves my assertion is no joke. Just look at the correlation!

I haven't been able to get anything close to correlating with inflation as well as this factor, the rate of labor force growth moved forward two years. I found this indicator by accident and eventually rationalized it through understanding the Generation Wave.

This chart would have told you that inflation would have peaked in 1980 regardless of government policies. From 1980 to 1986 the economy was growing like crazy, and the conventional wisdom would have predicted a bounce in inflation. It never happened. Inflation fell from 1980 to 1986 in line with this indicator despite very high growth from 1982 to 1986, high debt accumulation, and an exploding government deficit! Likewise, inflation is going to continue to fall again after 1997, with mild inflation rises into 1997 after falling inflation into 1995 or 1996. The Federal Reserve does not think that way. Neither do the bond markets, nor most businesspeople.

I strongly warned subscribers to my newsletter that we were going to see a great investment opportunity in bonds and stocks in late 1994, because bonds and stocks were falling based on rising inflation expectations that would not fully materialize with the economic recovery, just as occurred in 1984.

This indicator would have told us to expect a strong disinflation period from 1980 to 1986 and then a mild bounce-back of inflation into 1990. Now it's telling us to look for continued disinflation after 1997, and mild deflation after 2010.

Baby boomers are going to soon realize that they are the *richest*, not the poorest, generation in history as disinflation continues to expand their purchasing power, especially reducing the cost of their mortgages.

There will be high economic growth ahead because of the baby boom Spending Wave, which I'll cover next, especially from around late 1998 to 2007. At the same time, labor force growth will be very low. This means companies will have to redeploy the workforce and make everybody nearly twice as productive just to keep up with the high growth rates. This will be entirely feasible, both because we are learning how to leverage information technologies and because the baby boomers will be aging into their most productive years.

The Spending Wave

This part is going to make you wonder where economists have had their heads for most of history. The boom and bust periods in our economy are caused by new generations moving into very predictable family cycles of earning and spending.

The secret to forecasting the direction of the economy for decades in advance is right out of the consumer expenditure surveys the U.S. Bureau of Labor conducts and publishes every year.

No matter how much we declare our free will and spontaneity, we are largely predictable animals. The economy is far more predictable than most of us assume, because we consumers are highly predictable.

Life insurance companies make money by predicting human mortality with a high degree of dependability. There's no big secret to it—these companies know, on average, when you're going to die. They know exactly how much they will have to pay out in benefits over time, and thus how much to charge in premiums to cover payouts and overhead and to leave something for profit and investments. No matter how complicated life insurance gets, it can be distilled down to a simple thing: average life expectancy.

Whether our economy booms or busts is determined by something just as reliable: the earning and spending cycles of people as they age and raise families—what I call the Spending Wave.

Figure 2-5 shows how the average family earns and spends more from their late teens or early twenties into their mid to late forties, peaking between the ages of forty-five to forty-nine, or at around age forty-six for the baby boom generation. After age forty-six, the kids have left the nest and the parents have already purchased most of the family's durable assets, from the house to the appliances to the cars. Therefore, people can work and earn less and have very high discretionary income and save for retirement to boot. Understanding family spending and the durable goods cycle that peaks around age forty-six is the most important factor in predicting our economy.

There is a subcycle within this family cycle that I also adjust into my

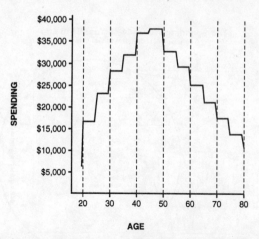

Figure 2–5. Average annual family spending by age (5-year age groups). Spending for the average family peaks between ages forty-five and forty-nine.

projections. There is a steep surge in durable goods buying into age twenty-five around the initial formation of households after kids leave their parents. You know, the used car, a bed, a sofa, and so on. The average family slows down spending for a few years as children are born, then moves forcefully into peak durable goods purchases into age forty-six, as parents advance in their careers and raise their kids. We can forecast most of the booms and busts in our economy decades in advance by projecting this forty-six-year dominant cycle of durable goods buying, and by adjusting it for the secondary twenty-five-year family formation cycle of durable goods buying.

Trend 2: The Greatest Spending Boom in History

The forty-six-year leading indicator of the economy

Figure 2-6 shows what we can project from the Spending Wave. You can see a remarkable correlation with the economy that results from taking the birth index in the United States, moving it ahead forty-six years to project the peak spending of that generation, and laying it down on top of the S&P

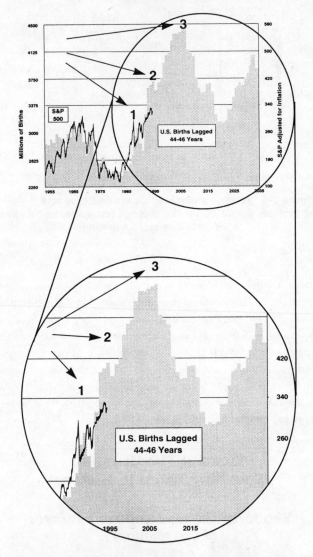

Figure 2–6. Projecting the Spending Wave forty-six years ahead to predict the direction of the economy into the next century!

500 index adjusted for inflation. The logic is too simple for economists! The peak impact of a generation on the economy is when its members are peaking in their spending.

We can see the direction of our economy and the stock market nearly five decades in advance. Isn't that enough time for you or your business to plan and react?

The economy will expand as a new generation progresses in higher numbers into the peak of this spending cycle, and then the economy will contract as the generation rides down the other side of the spending peak after age forty-six, until the next generation comes along.

Look what happens when you use the Spending Wave as a predictor by projecting the birth index forty-six years ahead.

I wish I could make it more complicated, but it is this simple—as most fundamental trends are. The baby boom generation will predictably cause a booming economy lasting until around 2007—the greatest boom in history, with a Dow peak around 8500 at the top. The economy will first slow into 1996 and then surge strongly after 1998, when 46- and 25-year-olds are up and inflation is declining again.

During a Spending Wave, the niche products and services of the Innovation Wave period move into the mainstream markets as the spending power of the new generation is felt. An example is the personal computer, which was at first discounted as a serious product by IBM and other mainframe manufacturers. But baby boomers saw they could afford the first PCs and immediately invested in the increased productivity they could put in their offices and homes, leading IBM's CEO, Lou Gerstner, to say in a 1994 *USA Today* interview: "To be blunt, the failure to capitalize on this sea change . . . is the single most important mistake IBM has made." This mainstreaming of niche markets drives the growth markets and results in many new businesses overtaking old ones for industry leadership.

The Power Wave

The third and final wave is the Power Wave. As you can see in Figure 2-2, this wave exerts an influence when the generation cycle matures, as baby boomers move into the power structures of organizations and politics in their forties, fifties, and sixties. This is when the new generation finally inherits the power to change organizations, management, and work to suit its lifestyles and talents. This is the time for a generation to accommodate new technologies it either invented or embraced during its period of the Innovation Wave. As you know, baby boomers are a lot different from their parents. They don't work the same way. They are more entrepreneurial and more individualistic, and a lot more experimental.

We have yet to see the real impact of the Information Revolution. This will last from the early '90s and into the 2020s as the Tom Peters and reengineering management revolution goes mainstream. We will see companies entirely reverse the old principles of hierarchical and assembly-line processes as they switch to front-line, customized, and customer-focused processes that can deliver customization and personalized service at increasingly lower costs.

When this Power Wave is felt, we'll see a substantial productivity leap. Products and services once thought to be confined to premium and niche markets will move rapidly into the mainstream, with an unprecedented rise in our standard of living. The Power Wave *is* the work revolution.

I've already introduced my vision of the work revolution ahead wherein every one of our jobs from the top down to the front lines will change as we witness the automation of white-collar and managerial work.

Remember what I told you in Chapter 1 about the projected increases in computer power. The power of sixteen Cray supercomputers on a single chip is simply unprecedented. This stride forward in technology is greater than Gutenberg's invention of the printing press. Mass printing allowed universal educational opportunities and created an enormous leap in the power to communicate. The next leap will be even bigger, because it will do more than educate and inform. It will allow people to leverage their intelligence and creativity into fantastic leaps in productivity.

Most people, including many managers, are scared to death of computers because they are improving so quickly and are so powerful. We've already seen mainframe power move into desktop computers. No technology—not automobiles, not railroads, not anything you can think of from our history—ever came down in cost or increased in power at anywhere near the rate of information technologies, especially computers.

The typical manager from the Bob Hope generation looked at the new information technologies and said, "Wow, what a wonderful way to streamline our command and control hierarchies." So they used computers to fortify bureaucracies. What a blunder!

Information technologies are about smashing bureaucracies, not fortifying them.

Even today, where is the typical desktop microcomputer, the most powerful business tool in history? Is it sitting out in field with the sales force? No. Do executives have them? Some, but not many, because computers are seen by the older generation as secretarial tools along the lines of the typewriter. Microcomputers are mostly in the possession of people who sit at their desks in offices all day long. These are not the innovative sectors of most companies. But now the baton is clearly passing from the Bob Hope generation to baby boomers, and we are going to see rapid changes in how computers create productivity.

The Power Wave gives us the ability to project the coming of a new, customized economy and a massive new population migration, both features of the last of our three trends.

Trend 3: Mainstreaming the Information Revolution

The emergence of a new economy: the customized economy

The confluence of the spending, technological, social, and organizational trends extending from the huge baby boom generation wave is resulting in one overriding megatrend: A new economy is emerging. I call it the customized economy. This is the biggest trend emerging out of information technologies. It is an economic leap even greater than the assembly line of the past century that allowed an unprecedented array of standardized products to move into mass affordability and a ninefold increase in the average wage adjusted for inflation. What we are going to see in the coming decades is that customized products and services are going to move increasingly into mass affordability. Our standard of living will increase even more dramatically. The critical driving force is ultimately the very work revolution I'm talking about, just as it was the assembly line that standardized cars and all types of products and services and made them affordable to the mainstream in the standardized economy.

New economies emerge every two generations. Where one generation is individualistic, the next is conformist in nature. It is the individualistic generations like the Henry Ford generation and the baby boomers that bring radical innovations in their Innovation Wave and launch work revolutions in their Power Wave. They give birth to new industries, technologies, and work methods that grow into the mainstream over two generation cycles. The role of the conformist generations like the Bob Hope generation is to foster incremental innovations that greatly extend the new technologies and industries into mass-market affordability.

Let me give you an example. The Henry Ford generation innovated the airplane through the experiments of that crazy Orville Wright, who just couldn't understand why man couldn't fly! The Bob Hope generation innovated the jet engine, which greatly extended the affordability and distance of air travel. The Henry Ford generation brought us the automobile. The Bob Hope generation added power steering, power brakes, automatic transmission, and superhighways, which greatly extended the affordability, drivability, and range of cars. New economies begin with the individualistic generations' Innovation Wave and emerge into the mainstream with its Spending and Power Wave. New economies then move into mass markets and mature progressively with the Innovation, Spending, and Power Waves of the conformist generation.

The microcomputer revolution and the extremely individualistic tastes of baby boomers will mean that the growth for decades to come in all industries will revolve around these four principles:

- Customization to individual needs
- High quality and added value
- Fast response and delivery
- Personalized service

To compete in this new economy, companies will have to change top-down, hierarchical management structures into bottom-up, front-line-oriented organizations that can tailor products and services to customer needs at lower costs and make decisions instantly with little or no bureaucracy. That is the primary topic of this book—how companies will do this and how your career and opportunities will be affected.

Figure 2-7 depicts this summary trend of our times. The growth in the coming decades is going to be generated by this new economy, and the old economy is going to decline even faster. Therefore, the most important decision any business can make is to identify and move into the growth markets in every industry that are being generated by this new economy.

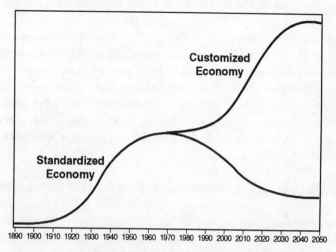

Figure 2–7. The customized economy that has been forming over the declining standardized economy.

The most important decision any individual can make is to work for or start the right business. People should choose companies that will benefit from the largest megatrend of our times: customization. Information technologies and companies are the means or infrastructures. Such companies are only in their infancy, comparable to automobiles and oil in 1914 when the assembly line first emerged. But the end is customization. Products and services in all industries will grow with companies that can employ this new work revolution and bring customization into mainstream affordability in the coming decades. This will be the prime source of job growth and security and profits in business.

A study of growth companies and job creation by David Birch of Cognetics showed that a very small percentage of high-growth companies, which he calls "gazelles," create most of the jobs in our country. His startling finding: Only a very small percent of these companies were what you would typically describe as high-tech. Most were everyday manufacturing, service, and retail companies that were bringing higher levels of service and customization. These are the companies to look to for job growth and career opportunities.

Here are the highlights of this customized economy:

A new logic in a new economy

The logic of the old economy was simple. You standardized the products or services and produced them on an assembly line where every process was broken down into its simplest functional parts and arranged in a linear sequence. Greater and greater capital investments were made in larger and larger machines that were fueled with more and more oil and energy that made them run faster and faster. Longer, faster production runs meant lower and lower prices, until the economy was saturated with low-cost goods by the 1970s.

A shift from the assembly line to the front line

The customized economy has the opposite logic. This is why managers and companies and workers are having such a difficult time adapting. Now you custom-design the products or services around the individual needs of customers. You produce them on the front lines as close to the customer as possible, and you perform all of the functions simultaneously in multifunctional self-managing teams.

Software is the key driving factor

The leverage comes from greater and greater capital investments in software: from the marketing database that allows you to measure the needs of your customers individually and know exactly what they want and when and how to pitch them; to the software that runs your production or service machinery that allows you to make short runs for individual needs and quick-changing markets without the setup costs and delays of the old assembly-line system; to the management software that allows you, among other things, to pinpoint the bottom-line profitability of every order, every customer, every self-managing team, and every employee! And of course, the fuel is knowledge and information, not energy.

Premium niches move into the mainstream

But to move into the mainstream such customized products and services will have to become more affordable. The greatest business trend of the coming decades will be that the premium niche products and services of the past decades will move rapidly into mainstream affordability. To accomplish that, companies will have to adapt the new organizational methods: again, moving power, information, and decision-making to the front-line people.

A brief summary of how you can fit in

This will be a time of incredible growth and prosperity—and incredible change. This book is written to help you see the simple principles of change and profit in your career as a professional, worker, or entrepreneur.

The first priority for your career will be to make sure you work for the right companies, the companies positioned to grow much faster than average in this great boom. Look around. These are the companies that are not now experiencing job shock and layoffs, because they are already tending to lead the workforce revolution I describe in this book.

But there is another megatrend emerging from the information revolution. Many of us are going to changing where we live and work in the coming decades.

Trend 4: The Next Great Population Migration

Whereas generation cycles of births and spending come about every forty years, cycles in basic innovation and population migration come about every sixty years. Look at Figure 2-8. Interest rates, inflation rates, and commodity prices have peaked approximately every sixty years: first between 1861 and 1864, then in 1920, and then again between 1980 and 1981. This graph is of long-term government bond interest rates, which

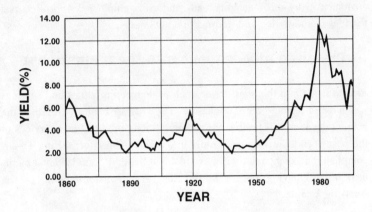

Figure 2–8. Long-term government bond yields (annual average) show the sixty-year cycles in interest rates.

peaked in 1861, 1920, and 1981. This sixty-year cycle is most fundamentally a real estate and credit cycle, but it is caused by cycles of breakthrough innovations that alter our communications, transportation, and energy infrastructures. It is the second most important cycle driving our economy and it is almost as predictable as the Generation Wave.

New basic technologies and infrastructures open up new low-cost land areas that increasingly attract consumers and businesses. This is similar to the move to the suburbs from the cities after the Great Depression. The door to this move was opened by cars, telephones, and electrical energy. All of a sudden, you could buy a lot of land and a big house for not much money in places that used to be wasteland. But as larger and larger numbers move into suburbs, prices and the costs of living and doing business ultimately rise. Eventually the area becomes the maturing high-cost place to live. This happened to suburbs progressively into the late 1980s. Then prices collapse as families and businesses move to the next area to escape high costs, taxes, congestion, and crime. This is what primarily drives this sixty-year cycle of falling prices and interest rates (as such new areas open up) and rising prices and interest rates (when they get saturated).

Think about it. Do we create land and natural resources? No, they exist, deriving their value from how we use and consume them. When large numbers of new businesses and consumers move into a new area, the value

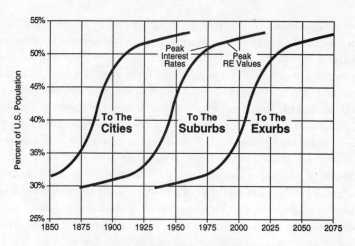

Figure 2–9. Three migration waves: A sixty-year cycle from cities to suburbs to exurbs.

The long and short of it is this: New communications, transportation, and energy infrastructures allow consumers and businesses to move to new, lower-cost areas of real estate, thereby increasing our standard of living.

of the land beneath the structures grows in value and ultimately raises the cost of living and doing business.

The introduction of basic innovations has always initiated or expedited major business revolutions and population shifts. Just look at the effect of the steam engine that emerged in the 1760s and ultimately ignited the Industrial Revolution in Great Britain and the move into the cities there. Then sixty years later, around the 1820s, the railroads, the telegraph, power plants, and steel-making advances emerged. As railroads moved into the mainstream economy, they allowed a substantial portion of America's population to migrate from the eastern region of the country to the West and from the farms to the cities. As we can see in Figure 2-9, the greatest migration came between about 1875 and 1905.

The cities then became increasingly saturated and costly as places to live and do business until real estate values peaked in the late 1920s, then collapsed in the 1930s, exacerbating the decline of the Spending Wave of the Henry Ford generation. In the 1880s, automobiles first emerged, sixty years after the railroads. From about 1935 to 1965, the growth into the mainstream of automobiles, telephones, and electrical energy allowed the shift from cities to the suburbs—again, sixty years after the migration to the cities led by the railroads. The transistor, the basis of the information highway that will be emerging powerfully in the coming decades, will allow a massive shift of our population—something on the order of 20 percent, or sixty to seventy million people—from the suburbs to "exurbs," which are suburbs farther out, typically fifty to one hundred miles from a major metropolitan area. These exurbs will also include small resort, recreational-oriented, and low-cost small towns and cities, especially those with universities and business infrastructures.

Note that about a decade after the peak in interest rates in Figure 2-8 a real estate and banking crisis occurs. Falling interest rates ignite a final blow-off boom in the saturated areas of real estate. Then real estate values collapse, taking down the banks and creditors that financed them. We saw debt- and real-estate-related depressions from 1873 to 1875, from 1930 to 1933, and just recently from 1990 to 1992. The Great Depression in part represented the death of the cities, and the early 1990s saw the death of the suburbs.

The Great Depression was a rare confluence of the downturn of a sixty-year real estate and credit cycle and the downturn of the forty-year spending wave of the Henry Ford generation. That's why it was the worst depression in history. Even the downturn of the huge baby boom spending wave between 2007 and 2022 is not likely to be as severe, because it won't coincide with a sixty-year down cycle. The sixty-year real estate and credit cycle actually turned down in the early '90s with the collapse of real estate values in the suburbs. This was the mildest sixty-year real estate and credit cycle collapse in history, because it occurred in the midst of the most powerful baby boom Spending Wave in history.

Most of the sixty-year-cycle proponents still expect a great depression in the '90s. They will be dead wrong!

Any business that can relocate to the exurbs or small towns and cities will be able to reduce its costs and therefore be more competitive. Any business that can market its products or services to these growth towns will experience much higher than average growth and less competition. That's because it takes most businesses a long time to recognize that this migration is one of the greatest megatrends of our times. Only customization is a greater trend.

It therefore follows that the greatest opportunities in the coming decades for entrepreneurial, job, and career opportunities and just a plain old greater lifestyle at a lower cost will come in these smaller suburban-like communities, or exurbs, the growing small towns and cities that retirees and baby boom families and small companies are flocking to.

Summary

Understand that we are about to enter the greatest boom in history. It will be a time of unprecedented opportunity for businesses and individuals who understand the megatrends in customization and population shifts. For people who resist these changes and slug it out in the suburbs and in the declining standardized industrial-related industries, life will continue to be job shock, even during this great boom.

To escape this trap, first look for companies that are well positioned to exploit the high-growth information technologies and customized products and services at competitive costs. Second, look for companies and entrepreneurial opportunities that take advantage of the growth of small towns and cities and the lower-cost, easier lifestyle they offer.

In Part Two we will look at a composite of leading-edge companies that are successfully implementing this great work revolution. You can get a feel for the types of companies that are leading this revolution. I'll show you the dynamics of this new work environment and how it will change our skills and interactions. And I'll tell you how such companies will also reward you with much greater personal and career growth opportunities.

Get ready to take a ride in the corporation of the future . . . *today!*

3

The New Look of
Sales and the Front Lines

The salesperson or "customer consultant" carries
the full capacities of the entire company in a
notebook computer—perhaps even a palmtop
computer. The salesperson reconfigures products
and services to the customer's inventory and needs,
reveals past trends in sales and profits for optimum
stocking decisions, product performance, and
pricing information, checks credit limits, and inputs
orders with automatic checks and controls—all
functions that once depended on bureaucratic
clerical and back-office staff.

A New Vocabulary
for the Customized Economy

Chapter 1 identified job shock as simply the surface phenomenon of a
much broader revolution in work. Chapter 2 emphasized how important it
is for you to use available forecasting tools to spot the leading-edge companies and the industries that will matter in the coming customized economy. You can begin your journey of embracing change by adopting a new
vocabulary. As long as we're in the middle of a work revolution, we might
as well stop using the obsolete terms. For starters . . .

Forget "jobs"

In the work revolution ahead there won't be jobs. People will be running businesses and getting results. This is not the narrowly defined functional job of performing a single task over and over as you're used to seeing in the standardized, assembly-line economy of old.

Working in the corporation of the future will require you to be proactive, creative, and flexible.

If the environment changes, you have to shift—to form new alliances, develop new markets, devise new strategies, and incorporate new technologies. To define a job with a standard checklist of a job description is counterproductive. You must see yourself in the role of a businessperson, however small.

If you're looking for a job in the new economy, you'll be disappointed. You ought to be learning to contribute to solving problems and creating value for a business in which you have a substantial personal and professional stake. That most emphatically is not a job.

Forget traditional "rewards"

Companies keep trying to use "carrots"—bonuses and other rewards. Sorry, those things just don't orient people toward results. And they don't create a sustained motivation. The only real motivation for baby boomers at times like this is to give them their own businesses. Today's people are increasingly invested in internal motivations. They look good if something succeeds. The only motivating reward is to run your own business doing something that really motivates you. Managers should spend time making sure people are doing something they're already excited about.

Traditional reward systems work well only for rats and fearful people.

It's been proved in psychological tests that rats work faster if fear is introduced to the equation. This is fine for simple repetitive tasks. But in complex situations, fear retards creativity—yes, even in rats.

Rewards set up with fear and greed in mind may have once worked to get low-skill people to perform low-skill jobs faster. Baby boomers are not motivated by such factors. They would prefer to be creative while allowing computers to eliminate the more rote, clerical, left-brain functions.

Forget blame

In the future, the word *responsibility* will not be a synonym for *blame*. In the environment of small business and the atmosphere of teamwork, a key accountability measure—besides profit, which is by definition a business motive—will be human intimacy, relationships in which people feel responsible for meeting the needs and exceeding the expectations of their customers.

Once intimacy is restored to the business equation by moving people forward from a faceless bureaucracy into front-line teams with face-to-face contact, members of the workforce will feel responsible for helping customers solve problems.

In the corporation of the future, you won't need a manager to kick butts and take names. People will feel the urgency of satisfying their own customers.

Peers will also bring pressure on teams, because one member's failure hurts everybody on the team.

Customers "R" Us

Face the inevitable—the nature of work and the structure of organizations is going to change whether we like it or not. Our only choice is to change our work environments and organizations to accommodate the future. The alternative is to accept failure.

You and I have to take the steps to make the right changes in our companies. We can't sit back and wait for the federal government or even company presidents to show us the way—this work revolution has a bottom-up dimension to it that won't be subverted to a top-down approach. But no matter how it's implemented, what will the successful corporation of the future look like?

Despite great reengineering strides made by our most innovative large companies, like General Electric, the real future can be seen by looking at the visionary organizational innovations of smaller emerging companies.

I'm not just talking high-tech companies like Cypress Semiconductor, Microsoft, or Apple, either. Many of the examples for this chapter come from Leegin Creative Leather Products, once an ordinary $10 million belt company in City of Industry, California, led by Jerry Kohl. Leegin pioneered a bottom-up revolution that employs most of the lessons of successful reengineering and has grown from a $10 million to a $70 million company, with no ceiling in sight.

However, before we discuss Leegin and the principles salient to organizing for the work revolution, let's look at an ideal situation, Customers "R" Us. CRU is a company I concocted by combining real examples from large and small companies and very minor adaptations from what I've been able to project from expected advances in information technologies.

CRU, part of a network of the future

Customers "R" Us represents a typical corporation of the future, a small-focused business unit. CRU specializes in fashionable medium-to-upper-priced women's wear. Owing to the need to fit into an alliance or network, it is a small division of a large company that maintains part ownership and provides a highly efficient production, distribution, and information network for hundreds of specialty mail-order firms and brand-name clothing producers.

The larger entity has very little to do with the mail-order and brand-name clothing firms and their daily operations. It simply provides the latest in information systems and software and highly efficient warehousing and production facilities these firms can share when it makes sense. It also can provide financing at lower costs than the company could achieve on its own—as long as CRU remains profitable. Individual firms have their own brand names, customer policies, and clothing designs. They each manage their own advertising, although the parent company has negotiated discounts on media buys.

CRU is intended to show you the workplace and lifestyle you'll be looking for when your company reorganizes—as it must to enjoy the benefits of the coming, customized economy.

A typical telephone sales transaction

A mail-order catalog customer is calling. While the phone is ringing, a microcomputer is at work behind the scenes analyzing the number to decide if the caller is a past customer. If he or she is, the computer will access the customer's summarized file of age, income, past buying history, credit approval levels, ages and birth dates for the entire family, comments about past preferences, experiences with this caller, credit card numbers, and so on. The file will pop up to the sales representative as he or she answers the phone. And if it's not a past customer, the computer will determine the exact address or at least the calling area code from the phone number and access an on-line marketing database to pull up an approximate demographic and lifestyle file on the caller—age and income, lifestyle preferences, propensity to buy, and so on.

All this will be done within milliseconds, before the sales representative can even pick up the telephone to say:

"Hello, this is Customers 'R' Us. How can I help you?"

"Well, I'm interested in ordering a jacket out of your catalog."

"Oh, is this Mr. Kearny? Hi, this is Linda. I helped you last year when you called in. Is this for your wife's birthday coming up on June 24th? I remember that you ordered the leather pants and vest outfit last year. How did she like it?"

"Oh, great. How did you remember?"

"We like to keep track of our customers—kind of like one big family!"

"I was looking at the red coat on page 25—you know, with the rhinestone buttons."

"Oh, Mr. Kearny, you have such good taste. These gorgeous coats have been running out of the store, and I won't have more in stock until June 25th, too late for your wife's birthday."

She refers to the family's past purchases and notices that the wife tends to buy higher-quality brands than Mr. Kearny and again notices the leather ensemble bought last year for her birthday. She also quickly accesses a file listing the new items on sale and locates a red leather jacket on sale.

"Guess what," she says, "you may be in luck. We have a beautiful red leather jacket on sale that would go with the leather pants and vest you purchased last year, and it's only $200 more than the rhinestone coat—I know I would like it more!"

"Do you really think it will work? It's just two weeks away, and I want to get something really nice this year. Maybe she wouldn't like the rhinestone coat anyway. She always says I have incurably tacky tastes."

"Let's do this. I can ship this to you overnight, no charge." Linda is allowed to authorize such a shipment if she thinks it will help close a deal or if the dollar sales are high enough—she is measured on the net profit of her sales after all expenses, not just volume, and she gets a percentage of those profits as the main component of her salary and benefits. "You can look at it, or even consult with one of your wife's friends. If you decide you don't like the coat, just call me back tomorrow and I'll have it picked up, no charge, and we can try another option."

Mr. Kearny is deeply impressed. "That sounds great."

Linda completes the transaction. She suggests a credit card he might use. She thanks Mr. Kearny, and she assures him she is his contact inside the company by saying something like "Next time you need anything, or have any questions, ask for me, Linda, and I'll be glad to help you."

After the customer disconnects, Linda posts an instruction to the computer so it will automatically route the next call from Mr. Kearny's home or business phone to her.

Personally speaking

Linda is one of several phone salespeople highly trained and motivated to know each line of clothing. She is backed up by powerful technologies that can help her to sell and to know and precisely meet the needs of her clients with the kind of personalized service she gave Mr. Kearny. Linda loves to interact with people, but just gets a little too nervous in face-to-face sales. So she's at her best on the phone.

CRU uses personality tests as well as intensive interviews to identify people like Linda. Actually, Linda used to be an accounts payable clerk and now says, "I can't believe I was a such a bureaucrat!" She was laid off in a restructuring of the apparel giant Clothes, Inc., a year ago. She applied to work in the CRU accounting department because she heard that CRU was involved in a smaller, more personalized work environment and that was growing rapidly and not laying off workers. She wanted to be more closely connected to the action, with more contact with salespeople. Linda admits she was bored in her old job. She stayed there for the security, but that's gone now.

Her personality test, instantly analyzed on the computer that administered the test, told the hiring manager that Linda's personality profile closely matched that of the company's most successful phone sales representatives. How would she like to interview for that job instead of work as a clerk?

CRU has found that courteous people with backgrounds in clerical work make better information-providers and problem-solvers with today's "smarter" customers than the stereotypical aggressive, outgoing sales types of the past.

Former clerks readily adapt to the newer sales technologies that rely on information systems. They are willing to answer questions and patiently let the customer come to their own decisions. With the help of some subtle closing techniques they learn in a sales seminar, they close more sales than the blowhard types.

Like most CRU employees, Linda loves her work.

Contrast Linda's scenario with the typical large mail-order company of the past, or even the present. You talk to a harried, overworked $7-per-hour person only after being placed on hold to listen to elevator music. The phone rep knows nothing about you and would have very little flexibility to deal with your special needs. If one coat was out of stock, you would probably just get a peremptory apology. The operator would be eager to go on to the next call, since performance is measured by the number of calls handled in a day. Or in the event the product was in stock, you'd likely be told: "Our policy is to allow four to six weeks for delivery."

That wouldn't be of much help to Mr. Kearny, whose wife's birthday is next week.

The qualities that distinguish Linda's new career

Linda pays for the expenses of her operation, including the phone and software that makes her so effective. She can give discounts, ship overnight, expedite orders—anything she determines will make more profits and create long-term loyalty on the part of the customer. The CRU software helps her do all those things. It also measures her on the profits she generates. She also has the flexibility to allot her share of profits among salary, medical, pension, and vacation benefits she desires—this lets her decide how she will be rewarded. She gets to deal on a repeat basis with many customers and can converse with them as if she knows them; ultimately she will know them individually in many cases. And her clients like her, as is measured in her growing volume of repeat business and high sales-per-transaction statistics.

Linda is literally her own, independent business within Customers "R" Us.

The company hired her because of her desire to make her own decisions and to interact with people. They want some of their best people on the front lines dealing with customers, not their worst. Besides training her in product knowledge, CRU educated her on the philosophy of the company and taught her how to work the information systems and how to make trade-offs in costs and customer loyalty. Two of the most critical day-long courses were given by the marketing and sales VP of the multibillion-dollar parent company. Another was given by an outside seminar leader on simple business principles such as how to use demographics to analyze customers and optimize sales, and how to understand variable and fixed costs to optimize your profits. The president of CRU and the marketing VP also gave critical seminars.

Linda says, "I learned simple things about accounting—things that I thought only managers and professionals could understand and that I never learned in the accounting department of my past job."

Linda finds the CRU system as comfortable as one of the suede suits she sells. She has been given the tools not only to increase her profits and pay, but to create personal relationships and satisfy customers so that they trust her enough to call her whenever they need something—even if they aren't sure what they need. But most of all, Linda has fun interacting with her clients. She likes the idea of helping them solve their problems. She enjoys making people happy.

Linda is not what would be traditionally considered high-skilled or technical, but she does know how to operate computers and she now makes $35,000 to $45,000 a year. If she'd taken a similar job in the telephone room of a traditional mail-order company, she'd be lucky to make $25,000, including bonuses for performance.

Of course, Linda particularly enjoys working out of her home.

Home, sweet workplace of the future

A CRU computer automatically routes incoming calls to Linda's work telephone number in her home. This gives her fewer distractions from the commotion and gossip of the office and more time for her family and hobbies. The company started this program when a valued salesperson threatened to quit because she needed to be at home more after her daughter suffered an accident requiring her to convalesce. CRU, a bit reluctantly at first, went along with what was deemed a special situation. But they found that not only were costs and overheads reduced, but this salesperson was able to handle 28 percent more calls and sales a day at home because of greater focus and fewer distractions. Now all CRU phone salespeople work out of their homes. Same with the field sales force.

Unthinkable? Hardly. What does it matter that some junior assistant middle manager is not around to look over Linda's shoulder every hour or so to make sure she's not goofing off on company time?

Like all employees, Linda gets paid on performance, which is tracked by computer. Employees can't cheat anybody but themselves. The result is less supervision, less stress, and, most important, higher levels of performance.

Diffusing responsibility

All employees at Customers "R" Us work as individual profit centers or in small teams that are profit centers, really businesses. Every such business unit has clearly identified its customers. Every employee or small team is their own business. Let's look at the field sales functions of CRU.

Outside sales

Jeff is a mobile sales rep who visits specialty retail stores two to four times a year to sell the company's seasonal new lines. Jeff, of course, is armed with a very powerful notebook computer and miniature printer that he carries with him in his car and briefcase. He uses the computer to help him analyze his clients and new prospects so that he can plan his time correctly. All of his appointments and notes for follow-up and to-do lists are in it.

Jeff can contact the central office either through his cellular phone or computer and get information or updates—he hardly ever has to waste time on pilgrimages through traffic to report in person.

He handles calls and what little clerical work he has to do from his home or hotel room or his car. Jeff closes twice the business he used to in less time, leaving more time with his family and for his hobby, golf. This is partly because he uses his time better and doesn't have to commute back and forth to the office. But it's more because he can use the computer to meet his clients' needs more effectively.

He pulls up to the next store and has a brief chat with the buyer. He then moves quickly to analyze the store's inventory of his clothing lines. Jeff fires up his computer, and it's ready to take inventory with no commands or computer jargon. He merely refers to a menu-driven program that asks for the first item number and quantity and so on until the inventory is completely entered. His computer can then spit out all types of reports on sales by line, color, size—and he can compare such statistics (anonymously, of course) with other stores in the area or in other areas.

Jeff can come back to the buyer with important information that helps him or her buy better or turn inventory faster.

"Did you know that you are selling three times as many black belts than red this season? We'd better keep you better stocked here. Our analysis tells us that if you could increase your sales of belt line X by 20 percent or more if you expanded the size range to include 36 and 38. We show that the best competitors in your area are focusing on the new narrower belt lines. Would you like to try more of these this season? We also show that despite slowing sales in popular white belts, you still get your highest dollars per square foot on these lines, so let's maybe not cut back on these unless trends slow down a good bit more."

"Jeff," asks the buyer, "our home office has been leaning on us to carry more low-end belt styles. What's your opinion on that?"

"I can print out a report from our broader customer database that shows that although revenues per square foot rise, profits per square foot drop as much as 20 percent to 30 percent. Therefore, I would recommend that you lean more toward the medium-to-higher-end lines unless your customers start demanding the lower-end lines more. I'll give you a copy of the report to send back to your management so that they don't just think you're blowing a smoke screen here."

The computer as a true sales tool

Jeff not only can provide all of this information with his sophisticated inventory and sales analysis program provided by the parent company's experts, but also he can process an order quickly with no paperwork and no delays or hassles from the home office. He can check credit, inventory availability, shipping schedules, and so on, through his wireless, cellular modem.

He, like Linda, has access in his computer to costs and margins and has a certain level of pricing flexibility depending on the volume and past history with the client, without begging somebody in the home office for approvals. He is likewise measured by the net profits he generates for the company and rewarded accordingly, regardless of whether the rest of the company is doing well this year or not. Jeff is his own business.

The inventory analysis automatically generates the optimum recommended order for the customer, and Jeff only has to adjust that order for any changes that the client makes after their discussions. Then the computer performs order processing checks and prompts Jeff to make simple corrections and adjustments when necessary—for instance, if he misspelled a word or entered a figure in the wrong column.

Jeff is a salesperson, not a numbers guy or administrative type, so the computer handles those things for him and allows Jeff to take credit for the success.

Once the order is approved through the computer on the spot, it is then transmitted directly to CRU computers over wireless networks. The order will be scheduled and shipped the same day—next day at the latest.

Jeff is on to the next profitable client after booking a $3,000 order. He now completes most orders in one visit instead of multiple visits and has doubled his daily sales from what he was making in the days before notebook computers. Jeff is making close to $100,000 a year, and he doesn't have an M.B.A. in marketing—just a B.A., in psychology. Thanks to the company's training program, he has gained a working knowledge of portable computers—which is easy enough to acquire nowadays.

Late in the afternoon as he is finishing a $2,000 order for his last customer of the day, he gets an E-mail message on his computer confirming the shipment times for all orders from today. That allows him to call his clients and let them know exactly when to expect their orders—it gives him that personal, caring, quick-response dimension that the customized economy demands. Store buyers like doing business with Jeff, and he likes doing business with them. He makes twice the salary he did before, in 80 percent of the time.

Before he heads home, Jeff stops for coffee and pulls up the day's news summary on his computer. He sees more sales layoffs at his old company, Acme Clothes. "Boy, I'm glad I got out of there," he says.

Once a month, the company throws a dinner party where the phone salespeople and field salespeople can meet and exchange customer trends and sales tips. That's how the company keeps these people in serious communication. But on a day-to-day basis, any salesperson can communicate, accessing others through an electronic bulletin board that also updates recent trends in sales and sales tips from other salespeople anywhere in the company. Jeff posts a note to the bulletin board about how the report on the better profitability of high-end versus low-end belt lines was the critical factor in booking a $3,000 order versus $2,500. Maybe other salespeople should use this as a selling tool.

The Missing Piece

Notice anything missing from the sales picture I just painted? In case you missed it, I'll tell you:

What has disappeared is the bureaucracy and middle management. Neither Jeff nor Linda had to run the obstacle course of people and procedures who get in the way of high performers delivering the goods to customers.

The salesperson or "customer consultant" carries the full capacities of the entire company in a notebook computer—increasingly, a palmtop computer. The salesperson reconfigures the product or service to the customer's inventory and customized needs and reveals past trends in sales and profits for optimum stocking decisions, product performance, and pricing information. He or she checks credit limits and inputs orders with automatic checks and controls—all functions that once depended on bureaucratic clerical and back-office staff.

When the sales rep transmits the order, it goes directly via modem over the phone lines to a flexible production facility, so that the order goes out immediately for overnight or even same-day delivery of a customized product. Ideally, the salesperson produces a report or a customized service right in front of the customer, if it is an information service.

You think this is too futuristic to be believed. Hardly. I interviewed a Washington client of USAA, the San Antonio insurance company, concerning this kind of service. USAA doesn't require its customers to deliver a damaged auto to receive a damage assessment. The agent drives out to inspect the vehicle, writes an assessment into the company's main computer, accesses the driving and insurance history, prepares a claim, and authorizes a payment—all through cellular technology—and prints out a report for the customer within twenty minutes. The agent can write a check on the spot. The entire transaction takes less time than you'd require to drive to a fast-food restaurant, order, and eat a meal.

In a logical step further, the corporation of the future will provide customers with software that allows them to directly analyze their needs and place orders into your system without sales staff assistance. In that instance, the salespeople educate customers on how to use the system for maximum results.

So what's going on with the in-house staff of the corporation of the future? That's where most of our jobs are! Let's look in on them in the next chapter.

4

Out of the Office

No matter where you look, the corporation of the future is no longer staffed with overspecialized, unaccountable, non-valued-added workers.

Customers "R" Us Revisited:
A History of the Nonbureaucracy

Jeff and Linda perform their services at the front lines of the company. That's what matters most to customers. But do they have the full skills and resources to deliver the total product to customers? Where's the support behind them? There must be at least a little, scaled-down bureaucracy tucked away on an unlit floor of the company headquarters, right?

Wrong on bureaucracy. *Right* on support!

Let's look at the accounting department where Linda initially applied for a job. You don't see accounts payable clerks and stacks of paper and computer printouts here. The people in this department are now called sales facilitators. Most of the accounting and order processing has been built into the computers and software that the salespeople use to serve customers better and close sales.

Mass firings, mass hirings

Over a year ago, once the first team of field salespeople started booking orders direct with manufacturing through the new computer system, CRU's president entered the accounting department and declared: "All of you are fired—your jobs no longer exist. I've authorized our computers to take them over. However, we have a new position you can apply for immediately called *sales facilitator*. The skills will be higher, as will the earning potential, but you're going to have to learn some new things and talk with customers."

About half of the crew were scared out of their wits and left the company. The others entered an exciting period of learning and growth. And note that there were no wrongful-termination lawsuits as the employees chose to leave rather than learn new skills.

Team functions

These new sales facilitators, and Mark is one of them, were formed into teams of two that each cover a sales territory. These people spend a lot of time on the phone interacting with shipping, finance, and manufacturing. Their job is to make sure that salespeople get the information that the computer system can't deliver to their fingertips, and that the orders they promise get out on time so that they can close more sales and keep customers as raving fans.

Mark says, "We provide the most crucial link to sales and customer service, while the outside salespeople get the most credit. That's all right—we're not into the glory, just the action. Besides, we don't care for all the traveling and schmoozing." The company's personality profiles have helped facilitators identify these traits so that people don't get misplaced in jobs they're destined to fail at.

Facilitators are also salespeople in that they handle calls from specialty retail stores that Jeff serves only on a seasonal basis. They process small orders and reorders, or just answer questions about the product line or delivery schedules for the customer. They lend the same personalized touch over the phone and provide the same quick response to these customers as they provide for Jeff.

Each team of two individuals covers a territory, including one team to serve the phone sales reps. Why? Because one person can't be there twelve hours a day to handle customer calls, and they have to jockey to cover vacations, illnesses, and normal interruptions. Only when Mark's partner, Jean, is on vacation, will he have to work twelve hours a day. Otherwise, in normal times they overlap during the most busy hours from 10:00 A.M. to 2:00 P.M. Neither Mark nor Jean gets to eat at a "normal" lunch hour. They don't care. What they're doing beats being an accounting clerk. They have much more flexibility as a team to trade off hours or to take vacations to fit their personal life circumstances—the fact is, in the corporation of the future, they actually have personal lives.

What do Mark and Jean do? Almost anything. They provide the latest inventory information to salespeople not on the computer system yet. They fill in when a salesperson's computer is down or the company's computer system goes on the blink. They keep in contact with the shipping team to make sure an order gets out on time—even if it means they have to go down to post orders and pick the items personally. They make last-minute changes to the order for the salesperson or the customer. They can resolve credit problems on the company's accounting systems, or track down errors in accounting. They can help the salesperson resolve cost or price questions that may go beyond the simple rules in the computer system.

The support staff of the future does whatever is required to help the salesperson close the sale and deliver the order. These aren't pinheaded bureaucrats, but action-oriented generalists with a bent for numbers.

The company spent much time retraining the former accounting, accounts payable, accounts receivable, and general ledger clerks to learn broader accounting and financial skills, and to learn to make more decisions and to communicate with different areas of the company—especially shipping. In essence these teams are back-line support people that have been incorporated directly into the front-line sales function. It's just that they are more useful back at the home office to resolve the very problems that a salesperson cannot deal with in the field or on the phone with the customer. These people, like the front-line salespeople, have had to become generalists to provide the prompt and informative service it takes to constantly adapt to their customers' changing needs.

The missing in action—Vernon, for example

Of course, many of the old accounting employees, almost 50 percent, left, saying things like "I can't handle the new demands," or "Who can deal with those sales prima donnas?" or "I don't care what anyone says . . . those people need to be controlled, not supported—they will sell or spend the company down the river every time," or "The thought of helping those people make more money makes me sick to my stomach."

That last was from Vernon, the accounting manager, and a perfect example of the vanishing breed of bureaucrats. He left CRU rather than adapt. He was recently laid off by Amalgamated Apparel. This time he is throwing in the towel, applying for early retirement rather than continue to reenter the rat race as a tired, irrelevant rat, as in bureauc-rat. The new manager of the corporation of the future is a facilitator, not a bureauc-rat.

The new system of rewards and emphasis on training the right people for the right job

Mark used to be a general ledger clerk and went through the transition successfully to sales facilitator. "It was chaotic for the first six months, but now I love it. Our new manager, Barbara, really spent the time helping us vent our frustrations and learn how to communicate with people in other departments with different perspectives."

Jean just recently hired on and was put with Mark because his experience and performance made him one of the best trainers for new recruits. Mark gets bonuses for training Jean. These come partly out of the company and are partly charged to Jean's costs in the first six months. These charges count against her profits. She was told when hired: "You can make double the money of most clerks or facilitators, but you have to make an investment in learning and stick with it for at least six months to have it pay off. We aren't looking for temporary workers."

What we're talking about here is an employee becoming vested in his or her own success and developing a long-term intimacy with the sales force and customers in the territory. Any parent who requires children to contribute financially to their own college expenses knows the outcome:

How can Jean fail to take her education seriously when she's paying for it?

Mark and Jean are rewarded on a percentage of retail store sales less their direct and indirect expenses. Salespeople are required to pay a percentage of revenues to support the facilitation team. Most are more than happy to pay for this service, just as they would have to pay for services hired externally.

If sales facilitators don't perform, the front-line sales staff lets them know about it and ultimately can refuse to pay for their costs. Management hears from the front line if facilitators don't respond.

One field salesperson refused to be charged the facilitation percentage one month when she felt that the team had lost sales for her by not responding on time.

Team members get their main satisfaction from serving people—both the salespeople and the customers who call in month after month for special reorders. Mark says, "We know the customers and feel obligated to help them even when we get in spats with the salespeople. But the salespeople are our real customers. If they look good, we look good—and they tell us when we're cooking. And when they're cooking and closing sales, we get our share of the pie."

So the revolution turns bureaucratic accounting departments into a responsive team that's dedicated to supporting front-line functions!

The Final Frontier for All Bureaucracies—MIS

There's one place you might expect still to find good, old-fashioned bureaucrats—the management information systems department. Why? It's obvious. They control the computers that make this company run. In most companies, you can't get anything done without kissing the cheeks of and bowing before the MIS guru!

Not at Customers "R" Us. In the old days its MIS department was fairly typical. It developed and ran the inventory model that helped make recommendations for optimum stocking quantities for retail customers.

Salespeople had to send in handwritten tallies of the inventory and wait for MIS to get back to them—of course, when it was convenient for MIS. Which meant the salesperson almost always had to make at least two trips to a customer to close a sale and had little flexibility to perform analysis or answer technical questions for the client without calling MIS.

That was until the president of CRU spent a few months working with a small group of the field sales force to develop a laptop computer system for sales automation in the field. MIS people just laughed when they heard about this. The president didn't even know how to program, much less understand the complexities of computer systems. They thought he'd soon come begging to MIS for help.

Not at all. The president invested himself in learning how to program— that's how important he thought this project was—and worked with customers and front-line salespeople to determine what really was needed to solve customer needs and how computers could facilitate the process. He was only able to get three of his thirty-five retail sales reps to buy into his vision, but that was enough. One of these "guinea pigs" was Jeff.

Success speaks for itself

Within a year, Jeff and the two other guinea pigs were operational in the field, closing sales in one trip and dazzling the customers with information and strategic advice on how to turn their inventory faster and stock the best-selling items. Within another year, almost all of the old sales force that had once rejected the mere idea of carrying one of those "sissy" computers into the field volunteered to be trained by one of the original trio of guinea pigs so they could change over to the new system. They finally saw that the computer was their ally, not their enemy! Besides, it's not so hard learning from a fellow salesperson—certainly it's better than trying to communicate with the tekkie bureaucrats in MIS!

MIS was humbled to discover that noncomputer people had come up with a sleek, workable sales system. The president had a quiet meeting one afternoon with Jack, the MIS director, and let him know that he could either get on board or find a new job! The president was committed to change and had a lot more leverage now with Jack at MIS than he had had over salespeople when he originally suggested the laptop idea to them.

Jack saw the light. In fact, excited by the new system, he signed on to reengineer his department. He worked closely with field sales and phone sales representatives and, of course, the president.

First, he corralled his best software engineers to help fully install and debug the rudimentary system designed by the president and the salespeople, making it very fast and user-friendly. For example, the salespeople were concerned that any old computer could become a bigger bureaucrat than the "order prevention department," which was their term for the old accounting and order processing operation. Computers can be the ultimate bureaucrats—they do what they are programmed to do, with no exceptions. At least with human bureaucrats—pinheaded as they were—you could scream at them or threaten to kidnap them and ultimately get some action if you were creative. Computers managed by MIS might be even more tyrannical and less responsive than human pinheads.

Making computers responsive

To address concerns, Jack hired a small outside software firm that specializes in sales force automation to turn out an improved version of the old system, which required the computer to follow preprogrammed rules and controls. The new system would allow the salespeople to have more decision-making authority and information access in the field.

It turned out that there was an easy way to create exceptions. The programmer from the outside firm, after a creative brainstorming meeting with the president and sales staff, drew upon his experience with other firms to come up with an override program for the computer. Here's how it works:

Let's say a salesperson is in the field with a customer and CRU screwed up the last shipment by being late and costing the customer sales. Normally the allowable discount level for the order today would be 10 percent, and that is what the computer would allow without approval from the home office.

The sales rep can now enter a one-paragraph message that comes in with the order that overrides the 10 percent discount rule by the computer. It might read: "Hey, you guys in manufacturing (who are receiving this order) screwed up last month and were three days late in shipping the order. I am buying the customer a steak dinner on your expense account, and giving him an extra 10 percent discount. If you don't like it, tell the president and have him fire me." At least nine out of ten times, such exceptions will be approved routinely. But note—not only does it keep the home office more accountable, the salesperson is kept accountable by having to enter a formal written explanation for his or her action.

The biggest problem the field sales reps had was that they were on the road at odd hours and were mostly not computer-literate. Now that they depended on the computer system as the very basis of their sales operation, they needed a security blanket. So, Jack took three of his most people-oriented MIS employees and had them restructured into a twenty-four-hour technical hot-line team to handle whatever technical questions or software problems arose and to feed back potential improvements to the software to the development team in MIS. The salespeople had to agree to put their money where their mouth was and pay for the costs of the system. This they were glad to do after seeing how the portable computer systems could as much as double their profits. Notice, it's not commissions and not salaries, but profits—they get a share of the profits they generate for the company. That's how real businesses work, even if they're one-person operations.

The MIS department? Half the original tekkies are gone and the remaining people are organized into teams. Only two real front-line-oriented functions remain. First, a small MIS team maintains the home office information and hardware systems that keep the front-line phone and retail field operators efficient. Second, there are people who man the twenty-four-hour technical hot line. Two outside accounting and software firms work closely with the sales force to design and upgrade the software to stay on the cutting edge of the technology.

For these services the sales people are charged, albeit for in-house services, at about a 20 percent discount from what it would cost to go to an outside computer consulting firm. They pay for the service because, once again, that's how business works. They get a discount because you don't have to pay for heavy marketing efforts to an in-house customer. The twenty-four-hour hot line is charged largely to the field salespeople, as they use it more than the phone salespeople.

As long as in-house functions are efficient and cost-effective, CRU salespeople are only too happy to pay for them. But if there's a cheaper, better way to get something done, they'll find the service outside the company—that's business.

As I've said, the primary software functions in CRU have been sub-contracted to two outside firms that specialize in sales force automation.

These were the only real *specialty* areas of expertise that could not be easily adapted into the company. A Big Eight accounting firm helped program and continues to maintain the accounting system in the software for allocating fixed and variable costs to the various salespeople and departmental teams. Management has to arbitrate any disputes over the fairness of such allocations. Indeed, such an arbitration process provides new insights for controlling costs. CRU uses the accounting firm as an objective sounding board to help. In many cases a dispute over high costs being charged to salespeople has led the company to subcontract to outside firms, saving money and reducing internal management complexity.

A local software firm works directly with the salespeople and sales departments to add new features and to help maintain the portable field hardware. The firm has one programmer who is like part of the company now and spends half of his time on this ongoing project. So, he knows the company's people, systems, and needs.

The Role of Top Management

Top management sets strategy for the firm, putting together alliances with customers, vendors, competitors, allied companies, and support companies, forming long-term relationships. They remain focused on getting the best information and support for their front-line teams. They spend time with customers and at the front lines, determining needs and training. Their primary job is providing resources for communication, education, strategic vision, and training. Except for strategic matters, top managers are no longer decision-makers but coordinators and facilitators for front-line teams, whose members make most of the decisions for their customers.

Middle management and the bureaucracy?

You already know where they are. They are *gone*, missing from action—and *that* is the revolution!

The great majority of accounting, MIS, human resources, R&D, and marketing people have either been eliminated or moved to the front lines to become part of customer-oriented teams. Or else they have been assembled into lean, efficient, multifunctional back-line support teams that provide services to the front line and are held accountable to treating those front-line teams as their customers. Or the function has been subcontracted to an outside firm that specializes in providing such services efficiently to many companies. Many supervisors have moved forward to run teams on the front line. Some have moved onto entrepreneurial development teams to form a separate business within the company or to spin off a new business. Some have left the company to buy a franchise, work in a smaller growing company, or start their own company.

The back-line people at Customers "R" Us are highly accountable and in synch with the customer and front-line needs of the company. No unaccountable pinheaded bureaucrats here!

Ah, but what about manufacturing? How on earth will the corporation of the future incorporate the factory and production systems for goods and services into the rest of the program?

In the next chapter we'll address how exactly that was accomplished at CRU.

5

A Factory of Factories

Managers have to learn to let people make
mistakes, force them to learn to think for
themselves and to analyze problems,
to look for solutions and opportunities that aren't
apparent on the surface—and people must stop
expecting to be spoon-fed!

A Miracle in Manufacturing

At first it was good news that the sales and office functions of CRU had
reduced response time for orders placed from weeks to a maximum of one
day. Then it became painfully obvious that the manufacturing plant's
highly complex assembly-line process was unable to fill those orders in a
timely manner. Most products typically spent weeks being processed as
they were passed through as many as forty different operations and workstations. Scheduling was a nightmare of complexity, with hundreds of
styles, dozens of lines, and numerous sizes. The plant would carry large

amounts of inventory to compensate. Still it required an average of ten days to produce and coordinate all of the inventory to get an order out, and sometimes the process was as slow as three weeks.

Everybody knew something had to give. The people out front would not bother continuing to improve their efficiency if manufacturing couldn't allow them to fulfill the first tenet of customer service— deliver the goods you promised.

The process of orchestrating change

Manufacturing was the last bastion of the company to restructure. CRU's president also knew it was the most complex and critical. So, no gun-to-the-head strategies here. The process he and the plant manager used took years to orchestrate.

The first step: introducing change

The president had come up in the field sales force and hence was comfortable working with field salespeople directly to make the transition to portable computers. Even then, he had to begin only with a handful of guinea pigs because of strong resistance to using computers. In the plant, the operation was even more complex and the skill levels more varied. So the president knew that the plant manager would have to proceed slowly to enlist the support of other plant management before reengineering manufacturing.

The first step was to allow the plant management group to become acquainted with concepts in manufacturing like "total quality management," "quality circles," "self-directed work teams," "electronic data interchange," and so on. The president took the plant managers to seminars and brought in outside experts. The plant managers slowly bought into the concept until people began on their own to show an initiative toward a reengineering process.

The first idea came up from the VP for plant administration. He thought that people needed to feel more pride in their workplace and that the management team needed to walk the talk to get this going. So . . .

One day at lunch the entire top management crew walked into the cafeteria with buckets, mops, and sponges and started cleaning the floors and walls on their hands and knees. Did this send a message? Indeed. The message: *Something's changed around here! We are leaders, not merely managers, and workplace pride is important.*

What followed was an even better idea. One of the plant supervisors for the belt lines walked into his top-performing shop late on a Friday afternoon and called all of the employees together. He told them: "Every one of you is staying overtime this weekend with *double pay!* I am shutting down all of the computer systems and giving you boxes of crayons just to get us back to our most elemental human state. It takes us weeks to process an order from beginning to end following many complex steps. There has to be a simpler way. Your assignment is to figure out, regardless of cost, how to reorganize yourselves and your machinery to process an order from beginning to end in three days! And your deadline is Monday. No excuses. Don't worry about failure, just come up with a way. I have a simple theory that I will establish as a standard for you to shoot for: It can't cost more to produce an order in three days than it does to produce it in three weeks."

Teamwork

On Monday morning the group had a solution. One of the employees had sneaked out and brought in a copy of *Reengineering the Corporation* and studied it until he could summarize the key points to everybody. This led to some obvious insights about how they could reorganize their assembly-line process into small cross-functional teams, each team producing a narrow line of product. By Monday afternoon they had proved, albeit in an awkward manner, that a small group of people could combine skills and functions and turn out a complete order in three days.

This was the breakthrough. Over the coming months, all the plant supervisors experimented with differing team sizes and product line ranges per team. Finally they found that teams of six to ten performed optimally. Eventually the plant was divided into over twenty small teams that focused on narrow product lines they would produce from beginning to end.

The secret was getting people invested in making worthwhile changes. Not just any people—the very people who know the ins and outs of their operation and have to live with the changes.

Growing pains

Getting the process established was not without its inconveniences. At first, teams had to address shipments by hand until automatic devices could be brought on line. They were forced to order materials using manual methods until management could get the outside consultants to come in and reengineer the information systems around the new management system.

Training

The plant managers knew that many new skills would have to be introduced to allow workers to broaden the individual skills required by the multifunctional approach of small teams. He knew people couldn't be excessively specialized, especially in small teams. People needed to train in a number of functions and steps in the production process of each line of clothing rather than only perform one step. But most of the functions were similar, so it was easy for most teams to spot the functions that most logically should fall with each person on the team and to have that person learn those skills from others.

But people also needed to learn basic math and statistics to monitor quality control. And since teams would be running their own operations and making cost-versus-quality trade-offs, everyone had to learn the basics of fixed and variable costs. Since many of the workers were Hispanic, the managers brought in teachers who could train in Spanish. Later English language training was introduced as well so workers could communicate better in the intimate team settings.

Salary and benefits

The pay and incentive systems had to change to reflect payment for performance and cross-functionalization. Workers on each team now get a base wage that rises as the number of skills they have mastered increases.

Multifunctionalism is the key to productivity in the new environment, so rewards are structured around the ability and willingness to take on a broader position on a team.

Teams are measured on the revenues that top management charges the sales departments for their products produced less their costs—fixed and variable—for producing them. A lot of work and analysis was required in cooperation with the outside accounting experts to come up with a system of cost allocations that was considered fair. That system is being further refined today—and will continue to be refined, because in the new economy, anybody who rests on the old laurels will be left behind by fast-changing markets and technological innovations.

Each team at CRU gets a monthly bonus to be split according to base wage level by every member. So these little factory teams are their own businesses. They get measured on customer satisfaction, quality defects, and so on—by team. If there is a problem, the team knows about it and rework or waste is charged to it.

Everybody's job on the factory floor changed, but none more than the plant management and supervisory jobs. Leaders not only had to master a whole new body of management principles and tools, but also had to learn that their primary job is teaching and facilitation of the team process with a very difficult new discipline. The fundamental message of change is this:

***M**anagers* have to learn to let people make mistakes
and force them to think for themselves, to analyze
problems, and to look for solutions and opportunities
that aren't apparent on the surface. *People* have to
learn to stop expecting to be spoon-fed!

That insight can only lead to . . .

Breakthrough!

Customers "R" Us no longer has one factory, but many small minifactories. Each team makes most of its own decisions about the layout of machines, quality control, hiring and firing for the team, who learns what skills, who takes charge in what circumstances, who is responsible for keeping track of costs and productivity and quality, and what volume of materials and parts inventory to keep on hand.

It's not enough that a CRU manager discovers that small, cross-functional teams producing narrow lines of products are the best solution to the plant's need to shorten its production cycles and cut its costs. Workers must arrive at the same conclusion. The CRU manager created a crisis to achieve this, forcing his people to think differently on what is now widely referred to in CRU as "The Weekend."

Today when you walk into the plant manager's office you find the walls covered with charts. He spends most of his time educating the factory workers and team leaders and "hawks"—the people on each team primarily responsible for tracking efficiency and knowing the numbers. Hawks not only report how costs are faring for their teams and the overall plant. They also cross-pollinate success and failure stories between teams and product lines so everybody is aware of what's going on.

Fred, the plant manager, shares all the numbers and data with all of the workers. One example Fred gives from a previous week: "We had a meeting with all of the plant employees, and after running over the normal weekly statistics, we showed an analysis of how the latex gloves that most people throw away every day actually add up to 15 percent of the profits of the entire plant operation. I had to say no more. In the next week people started keeping their gloves and reusing them, and costs dropped substantially. People aren't irresponsible, they just need to know!"

When people are given information continually, they begin to develop a feeling for the pulse of the organization. They adapt, willingly, quickly, and concertedly. This is exactly the phenomenon you'd expect to see when a business networks as a school of minnows does.

Fred says, "The new system allows us to produce shorter runs faster and to greatly reduce waste, inventories, and obsolete stock—we are in the fashion business." It's easy because everyone at CRU knows what's selling day to day to day. Why? Manufacturing is linked directly to the front-line sales efforts through the portable sales computers that send in orders direct every day. Plant management hears immediately about customer quality problems or late shipments. But most of all, the plant management can track what is selling and anticipate most of the order flow so that they can have on hand almost exactly what customers will want, while maintaining minimum inventories.

Continual innovation

Fred just instituted a new express shipment policy. Any order that comes in from sales by 1:00 P.M. and that is on the plant's growing list of high-volume products will be shipped the same day. So Fred has gone beyond the original goal of next-day shipment for most products. It is Fred's goal to have virtually every item capable of shipping same day within the next few years. This will require even closer integration of the sales and manufacturing scheduling systems. Each team will have to be immediately notified of orders for a particular line and work on getting them to shipping by the end of the day.

Other plant managers have also come up with innovative alliances with small, entrepreneurial clothing designers to expand the company's "just less than leading-edge" product line. In similar styles and fashions, the firm represents the lines of innovative designers chosen by a two-person team in the design department. The company hasn't yet shown a great track record in picking the more trendy lines, anticipating what will be hot, and deciding how much to produce. But it has become even better at delivering high-quality, steady, basic lines at low costs.

These outside designer firms must go along with CRU's demanding internal standards to earn the right to play along. They are required to have enough inventory and flexibility to get orders to shipping at the plant or shipped directly to customers within two days. The next step, of course, will be to integrate these firms into the order system electronically so that they are immediately informed of requirements and can ship on the same day, next day at the latest.

Once a hot new line from one of the outside firms catches on in the mainstream, Customers "R" Us takes the product into its own product line and plant and pays the outside firm a nice royalty.

"They focus on innovation for more upscale customers, we focus on low-cost delivery of broader product lines," says the CRU president. "That way we guarantee we won't go out of style and lose growth in the future.

"In fact," he says, "we had one of our designers come up with a very innovative line that didn't fit into our main lines. He ended up convincing us to spin him off like one of these outside firms. Now we have part ownership of his venture and he is supplying us as an alliance and markets his products to other specialty stores direct."

Such a system of external entrepreneurialism and variable alliances will become a defining characteristic of corporations of the future.

In Summary

Customers "R" Us is now a network of small teams and individuals at every level that run like a school of minnows. It's hard to find a bureaucrat anywhere. Most important of all, customers are happy. The firm has seen its sales quadruple in the past three years since it first converted over to notebook sales computers across the sales force. Now competitors are coming to Customers "R" Us and asking if they will sell and/or produce their lines, as they just can't seem to compete.

The example of Customers "R" Us is taken from a number of examples of real-life large and small companies today that are leading the greatest work revolution in history. Therefore, we can all see the future by studying the simple principles that drive these companies regardless of their size or industry or technological sophistication.

If you think Customers "R" Us is impressive, just wait. Imagine how much more we will be able to streamline companies and break down into networks of highly responsive small businesses and teams as we approach the next decade which will bring us the power of sixteen Cray supercomputers on a $100 microchip!

Sound like the type of company you would like to work for? That's entirely possible. In fact, you might be responsible for helping restructure one of today's companies into a corporation of the future.

In Part Three we will look at the four simple principles that you as a manager, professional, or front-line worker need to know to understand the changes that will continue to shape your work environment in the coming boom—to create your corporation of the future.

Four Principles Driving the Work Revolution

CHAPTER 9

**Tells how you can use real-time information systems
to link everyone in your business network and have
the network truly move like a school of minnows.**

Four Simple Principles
for Introducing Change

Most meaningful human change is complex and unpredictable, especially in its early stages, when we can't detect behavior patterns and logic. When we encounter a flaw early in a new process, there's no way to be certain when it will recur—often and regularly, or rarely and randomly. As I've pointed out, the work revolution ahead will bring on much more meaningful change than the job shock of the early '90s. It will bring radical changes in how we conduct business, and each change is likely to be answered by even newer technologies that we futurists haven't fully anticipated.

Furthermore, although we can predict a rough timetable for when that change will come and the general forms it will take, nobody can tell you exactly how it will strike your business or when it might wipe out your job. So, what are you supposed to do—sit tight, trembling in paralysis, and waiting for the ax to fall?

Absolutely not. The best strategy I can suggest is for you to introduce change yourself as an owner, manager, or professional in your company or as an employee in your department or small company, and manage the inevitable chaos rationally.

And do you think that a change management strategy is necessarily complicated and abstract? Not at all. Change can be difficult and challenging, but it's usually not that complex in principle. The most successful people I have seen in implementing revolutionary organizational change have been the more naive types who didn't know that much about management or didn't know how complicated it would be. They just set out to do it. The only way I know to plow through radical change and the accompanying human resistance and turmoil is to have a clear vision of what you want to accomplish and to operate on simple principles. I have learned this and relearned it from my background in turnaround management in large and small companies.

In a crisis, change comes so fast and so radically that you don't have the luxury of a step-by-step plan. You simply have to have a clear understanding (through thorough and realistic analysis) of what went wrong with the company and a strong vision of where the company must go. Then you simply have to operate and communicate on very simple principles and keep hacking away!

By simple I don't mean magic or instantaneous. Sure, you can read those Tom Peters illustrations where he describes how an entrepreneurial type goes into his company and completely reorganizes it in a weekend. That's what I call a random genius occurrence—a truly visionary entrepreneur found specifically the right time to introduce exactly the right changes using precisely the right people, and somehow it worked out. Unless you're a genius yourself, don't expect your own program to turn out that way in your company. Or just as likely, some crazy or creative person happens by chance to do the right thing at the right time. That's a pure accident of nature, like the appearance of an orange mutant butterfly that just happens to be a better survival color so that generations later all specimens have become orange. What these rare occurrences show is how direct and simple change can be. Chances are it won't work that easily in your company.

On the other hand, you are much more likely to learn from observing geniuses and crazy people who have failed their way to success than from the everyday garden-variety business school professor. You're not quite as likely to get it from watching most of our large companies that try to introduce change in a top-down, orchestrated way, although a few of these have proved to be solid leading-edge innovators.

In the next four chapters I'll introduce you to four simple principles I use when I go into a company to manage organizational change in turnaround situations. These are principles I have also summarized from studying the successful and not so successful reengineering efforts of large and small companies. I assure you, very few change situations are more radical than a turnaround. Yet, I find nothing works better than a simple approach. It allows you to keep sight of the forest without getting overwhelmed by the trees of day-to-day reality.

Here's how I work: I first identify a few key things wrong with a company, identify the measures that will bring about change, and then just dive into the change process. After the process is underway, the most important thing to do is to stick to your commitment to change. Of course, you'll make mistakes and encounter new problems along the way—some of which you will have introduced yourself. You make adjustments and go on. If you can resist the natural tendency to complicate things and resort back to old principles of management, you'll be all right by following these four principles:

- Hone and maintain your strategic focus.
- Organize around your customers and your front lines.
- Establish every individual, team, and unit as a business.
- Link everyone in real-time information systems.

Obstacles to implementing change

My four principles summarize the essence of what you are trying to create so that you can use them as a vision to simplify change for your employees and coworkers and get them to cooperate instead of resisting change.

Two of the biggest liabilities I have seen with people trying to implement organizational change are that they don't have a strong understanding or vision themselves of what they are trying to create but are only acting out of fad or competitive pressures; and that they don't communicate their intentions clearly to the very people they want to change, so they don't involve them effectively in the process of change.

Workers need a compelling vision of change: not just why it is good for the company, but why it is good for them—what benefits they are going to get out of this change. Unlike many work revolutions in the past, this is very much a bottom-up revolution that demands heavy involvement from below.

These principles have one goal in common, and hence all of these principles have to be applied to achieve it. Piecemeal doesn't work here.

The goal is to convert your business from a
hierarchical assembly-line operation to a network or
school of minnows that exploits the speed and
flexibility of change in small self-managed units and
at the same time exploits economies of scale,
organizational learning, and world markets
where appropriate.

But the key challenge is to bring a fragmented school of many small units
to move and change together. That is the secret to the new organization.
That's what these four simple principles are about. It easy to break things
into small units. It's very hard to then get them to move and work together.
That's where we try to go beyond the popular concepts of reengineering.

What these principles can do for you

- **Principle 1** helps you develop the minnow theme at the highest level
  of your company's strategy. Using it as a guiding principle, you can
  become a highly focused minnow as a company and then join the
  best school of minnows in your industry for competing and best serving the end customer.
- **Principle 2** instructs you in moving your critical value-added functions to the front lines where company meets customer, and aligning
  the rest of your company's units internally to the customer and your
  front lines. This creates a fundamental orientation to what ultimately
  counts, so that everything changes naturally with the customer and
  customization to the customer's needs becomes the natural path of
  least resistance in your company.
- **Principle 3** guides you in breaking your company's operations into the
  smallest possible business process teams and becoming a network of
  minnows within. It is about insuring that every unit is self-managing and
  naturally as responsive and accountable as a small family business.
- **Principle 4** sets in place the idea of linking the whole network within
  your company together so that everyone sees critical information and
  changes simultaneously and can adapt without cumbersome bureaucracy through human communications. It is about linking internal units and strategic partners and suppliers into a seamless
  network that serves and responds to the customer.

Many companies are already implementing these principles piecemeal or to different degrees. I think it's necessary to implement them all in concert to achieve a new organization that actually works in a coherent manner at all levels.

Most important, the four principles have been designed to work in a logical sequence. Put them into play in the implementation priority indicated— that is, in the order I've listed them.

Although many aspects of these principles will occur simultaneously in what is unavoidably a messy process of human change, there is a logic to successful implementation. There's no need to spend a lot of time figuring out how to reorganize into front-line teams around the customer's needs (Principle 2) unless you first understand what your strategic focus should be— what you're best at and what customers will value and pay the most for (Principle 1). Without first considering Principle 1, you don't even know who your customers are, or, more to the point, who they should be. Why waste efforts reorganizing around the wrong customers or customer needs?

Similarly, it doesn't make sense to make huge investments in real-time information systems (Principle Number 4) until you have made every front- and back-line unit a real business with self-managing teams accustomed to making decisions and trade-offs like seasoned businesspeople. Otherwise, they won't know what to do with all the great information you make available to them. In fact, they are likely to not use it at all—to stay in the bureaucratic mode of avoiding risk and waiting to be told what to do. Or worse, they will abuse it by making unprofitable decisions with the best of intentions, because they don't know how to make basic business trade-offs.

Two final, crucial reminders

First, always make sure something works manually and at the most basic human level before you try to automate it with computer and information systems.

Second, remember the overriding principle of KISS: Keep It Simple, Stupid!

Maintain Your Strategic Focus: Do Only What You Do Best

Traditional companies try to do everything and suffer because they are mediocre at everything instead of excellent at some things.

Sharpening Strategic Focus

In the waning standardized economy, gargantuan corporations continue to perform every imaginable function—doing few of them well. These will give way to companies focusing only on what they do best and what adds the highest value for their customers. Some of those processes will only get larger in scale and be suitable to large companies, but more will continue to get smaller.

In the new, customized economy the leverage comes from being focused, intimately aware of the needs of your customers, and quick to change while maintaining low overheads—again, the flexible, instantaneously reacting minnow concept. It means tapping the incredible innovative and motivation power of small cross-functional, highly empowered teams and individuals. This obviously means even stiffer competition ahead for giant corporations from smaller, more specialized companies.

But it doesn't mean that larger companies can't adapt and survive or that the future advantage will continue to accrue to small companies. Minnows may be able to beat whales by carving off small niches in their markets, but as customization goes mainstream, the spoils will go to schools of minnows. These schools can evolve in two very different ways: as networks of smaller, independent companies that band together to combine economies of scale from national and world market scope with their inherently fast, focused, flexible innovation at the local and specialized level of business; and conversely, as large-scale, global corporations that can break themselves effectively into smaller units to achieve the flexibility of small businesses and creatively use information technologies to share the world-scale economies they already possess.

So this chapter is about the concept of developing minnows and schools of minnows at the largest scale and strategy of your business. When you're done reading, you should have the basis for choosing where to focus as a company or a department to become a highly focused minnow that fits into a strong broader network or team of players for meeting the end customers' needs in your industry.

Here are some practices and principles for sharpening strategic focus in your company at the highest level. I've arranged them into two steps that should help you get started in a rational way.

Step 1: Decide What the Focus of Your Company Should Be

Above all, the leadership in a company has to decide at which qualities and parts of its process the company truly excels, and which have the biggest impact on customer satisfaction. Some businesses get along just fine only until some eagle-eyed competitor notices a vulnerability that could become a specialty niche or expansion opportunity, allowing the competitor to come in and stomp on the vulnerable party.

Ask yourself this question: *Why make major human and financial investments only to have some other company walk in and take that function or market away?* Invest human and financial resources only in areas in which you can sustain a competitive advantage.

How long did it take Lexus to take the lead in luxury cars from BMW? One year. How long did it take IBM, with an inferior product, to take the lead from Apple in personal computers? Two years. Apple uses a superior operating system and is a better designer of personal computers. But Apple was not the most efficient producer, distributor, and marketer of computers. IBM had that cold and beat Apple, despite an inferior product, a bureaucratic organization, and an arrogant sales force.

To look at strategic focus, you always have to consider the entire value-added chain you are part of—all of the activities that combine to create an end product or service that is of value to the end customer. This is an important concept that we will refer back to again and again, so make sure you get a clear picture of this simple concept. It is basically the same principle emphasized in *Reengineering the Corporation.* You could also call this a business process at the highest level of an industry.

You may be a small company targeting only a certain mail-order market, a specialty retail store, a specialty distributor, or a specialty manufacturer—or you may be a broad-based competitor across many product, distribution, and retailing channels attempting to get synergies from those combinations. But large or small, you are a part of an entire value-added chain from raw materials to retail sales that reaches a set of end customers with final products or services that they value and pay for. You need to be constantly evaluating what matters most to customers in this chain and where each competitor in the chain is best at what they do. And of course . . .

You must never lose sight of where you are best in providing what matters most to your direct customer, and also of how you add value for the final or end customer in the chain.

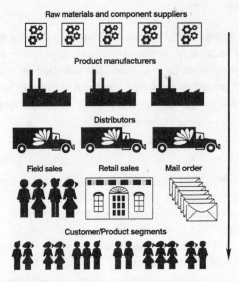

Raw materials and component suppliers

Product manufacturers

Distributors

Field sales   Retail sales   Mail order

Customer/Product segments

Figure 6–1. The typical value-added chain.

Determining your place in the value-added chain

What you must do is identify all of the critical processes by which key products or services are created—by which value is added for the end customer. Once that is done, you must choose which of those arenas you have a real competence to compete in, which key business processes in your industry you are going to specialize in, and where you can sustain a competitive advantage.

The first decision a company must make is where to be a minnow in its school or broader value-added chain—simply where to focus. The second decision is to identify a network of other minnows—the best strategic partners in their respective areas of competence—you must join so that you as an entire school of minnows have a sustainable competitive advantage. In the course of self-evaluation, ask yourself these questions:

- **What have we historically and consistently proved to do well?** Which specific functions and roles for our customers? Do we just think this, or would customers and outside parties verify it?
- **What do our direct customers value strategically** the most of all the things that we do? What creates the most value for them?

Where will they pay the most and be the least price-sensitive if we can really serve their needs? What do they value highly that other direct or indirect competitors do well?

- **Where is there the greatest match** between what we do best and what the customer values most and is willing to pay most for? This should become our strategic focus as a company.

- **Is there somebody else today or in the future** that could be better than us in these areas we have chosen to focus and compete— if they decide to enter our market—because of their greater economies of scale or shared learning and knowledge or customer intimacy? This might or might not be someone who competes with us now, and it might even be some company outside our traditional industry boundaries.

- **Are there related functions or other customers** that could benefit from our proven skills and strengths and allow us to further dominate our arena of focus and sustain a competitive advantage through extended knowledge and learning, economies of scale, or customer intimacy that we build from expanding into these areas?

The main point here is simple. You have to find an arena where you can satisfy real customer needs and sustain a competitive advantage so as to remain profitable. Otherwise your investments in time, money, and learning will be wasted. Worse yet, the investments your employees have made, including intangibles like moral support and enthusiasm, will be lost. If your company does not have a clear strategic focus and cannot communicate it well, then you should be concerned, because your job may be at stake sooner or later.

Using outsiders and your front lines

To address these issues of strategic focus it is often useful to tap the objectivity and expertise of outside consultants. You may even move your executives off-site for a weekend retreat to isolate your critical issues.

Such measures are all useful, but I can tell you this:

If you don't involve your front-line people and your customers in the process of answering your key questions, you won't have all the answers you'll need.

What's more, you'll be neglecting an important opportunity. Only in making changes at the grassroots level, using the very people most familiar with problems in the trenches, will you truly make a difference for your customers and your company's organizational evolution.

On the front lines you've got people intimate with customers, and they know their customers by name. There is no substitute for that in top management. On the front line you're face to face with the people who count and the machinery that makes your company go. Forget about some centralized computer or staff department for a moment. Remember that supercomputer in the heads of people who can process customer responses. People on the front lines are your little geniuses. Sure, they're often very low-powered in comparison to all the people on bonus plans in the ivory tower. But when you put bunches of them together, they have the collective power to interpret everyday signals in their machinery, their customers, and their coworkers. You can't read that up in an ivory tower. When making changes to the corporation of the future, ignore your front-line people only at the risk of failure.

Strategic focus at Dolby

Traditional companies are getting picked off every day in increments by smaller, focused companies who outdo them because of a lack of strategic focus in the giant. But in the best cases the giants don't mind.

Just ask makers of sound equipment. Most leading manufacturers advertise that they are the best at making cassette decks, or speakers, or turntables. Dolby Systems cut those distinctions even finer—and that's the trick in this new age, to focus more sharply than anybody else thinks possible.

Dolby entered the market with the sole intention of producing noise-reduction systems for cassette decks. It makes so much sense for one company to make an enormous investment in R&D to master the art of noise reduction rather than having dozens of major manufacturers duplicating the process with a variety of components and methods. For the consumer, it is an important element, but not *that* important. It doesn't affect the tonal quality, it just cuts out some noise. But does the end consumer want to go to the store and evaluate twelve different qualities of cassette decks and twelve different noise reduction systems? No. Dolby simplifies it for everybody, setting one standard—in fact, *becoming* the standard, like Microsoft for personal computers.

Dolby has, in effect, negotiated strategic alliances with all the major cassette deck manufacturers that agree to incorporate Dolby noise reduction systems exclusively or near exclusively into their cassette decks. The manufacturers then handle all of the distribution and most of the marketing and service for Dolby. Dolby can focus on designing and producing the next generation of noise reduction systems, educating the end consumer on the benefits of noise reduction and building a solid, trustworthy brand image for Dolby. Dolby is a company that focuses on R&D and design and creating a quality image for that design—very simple, very profitable!

Dolby's unique niche gives it a near monopoly in its field. The company has carved out the kind of recognition for specialization that we'll be seeing in the new economy resulting from the great boom ahead. What's best about Dolby's position is that no one dares or cares to challenge them. (However, Dolby's expertise lies in a mature market; CDs are replacing cassettes as the consumer market choice. In order to grow, Dolby will have to innovate again.) Dolby's credible brand name and low-cost specialization is an advantage to all the cassette manufacturers and to the end customer. It is a critical player in a broader network or value-added chain, and it is valued for its role.

The very term *Dolby* has become the generic name for noise reduction in much the same way *Xerox* is used to mean photocopy and *Scotch* represents transparent tape.

In the new economy, things will become so hyperspecialized that no single company will be able to be the best at everything. You have to focus on something you can absolutely dominate in.

Step 2: Form or Join a Network of Strategic Alliances

You may already recognize that Dolby's arrangement with sound component manufacturers is just such a strategic alliance. Obviously, you should form such alliances with companies that are the best in the areas you choose not to focus and compete in.

Completing Step 1 will tell you where you are best at meeting the critical strategic needs of your direct customers, and, most important, of the end customers in the value-added chain. These are the consumers who pay the final bill for everybody's services in the chain. In going through this process, you will have identified the competition for your products and services, as well as potential allies. Next you will ally your company with them in a strategic fashion—through long-term agreements, through joint ownership or investment, or through merger and acquisition, with the best available companies.

The most important point is this:

The team of strategic partners you choose to join at the highest level of your company's strategy may be more important to your overall success than your strength and competitiveness in your own arena of strategic focus.

To turn to sports for an analogy, it doesn't matter how good a field goal shooter you are on a basketball team if your point guard and rebounders never get you the ball to shoot!

As the idea of alliances continues to mushroom in the great boom ahead, you will see an earnest race among competitors to lock into networks with members that contribute the highest performance possible to fend off the competition. Many of these agreements may be long-term and exclusive. Your clarity and competitiveness in defining your own strategic focus is critical. You must become as attractive as possible to a strong network. Your degree of excellence at what you do will determine your leverage in negotiating favorable long-term agreements with potential alliances.

A strategic alliance by the book

Here's a quick example of one company's strategic focus and its ability to form strategic alliances to complement its own strengths.

We're used to hearing about complex mergers and alliances among large companies. This is a case of a small company orchestrating a highly productive network. A client of mine, a small specialty publisher, was perplexed by the enormous sales costs of getting its books through the complexities of the distribution chain into the bookstores. It was costing about 50 percent of sales revenues just for sales and distribution, whereas the typical cost in the industry was 25 to 30 percent. Obviously the company wasn't the best at sales and distribution and was too small to take advantage of the economies of scale in distribution that many larger publishers enjoy.

The publisher touched base with a number of other specialty publishers and found they were singing the same sad song. So they formed a new, separate sales and distribution company. It now sells and distributes books for more than forty specialty publishers, appealing to the same segment of book chain and bookstore buyers.

All these companies share a single sales force. With their combined sales and distribution scale, they have the ability to develop an individual focus and to cut their sales costs to 25 percent of sales—half the original percentage—by exploiting economies of scale through the cooperative distribution arm. Together they now have a broad enough line of books to interest most book chain buyers. Yet all forty publishers maintain independent editorial control. Each still controls its own marketing and promotion programs to cater to its individual niche customers, who are similar lifestyle types with varying interests within that lifestyle.

The trouble with big

An alliance of small companies, in this case built around a large distributor, can muster clout where it counts. Yet each company can remain small and responsive to its own niche. You only want to be big where it counts and where customers don't feel intimidated by size.

Big alienates customers by generating hierarchies and bureaucracies. Big removes the personalized touch that will become so important in the new economy of the individualistic baby boom generation. But note in the book publisher example that individual readers never see the sales and distribution process that gets the books into the stores at the lowest cost. They only see the promotion efforts and the book itself, which the small publishers still control and are efficient at producing because they know their readers so well. Of course, the next step for the distribution company is to negotiate advertising discounts with magazines for its forty publishers.

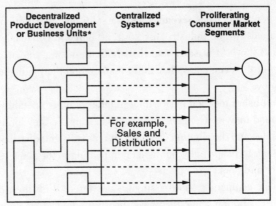

* See Figure 6-3 for a chart of these units and systems

Figure 6–2. The corporation of the future.

Yet big can play the strategic alliance game, too

With Dolby you saw how a smaller, very specialized company could ally itself with many global companies. In the example of allied book publishers you saw how small companies can choose to focus and ally themselves to establish a larger, yet limited entity to obtain cost economies of scale.

But big doesn't have to get shut out of the benefits of forming alliances. Larger, more mature, world-scale companies have increasingly realized that they are best at more standardized, world-scale functions like brand maintenance, sales and distribution, large-scale production, and broad-based, basic R&D. They will focus on building economies of scale around these functions. Increasingly they will either develop strategic alliances with smaller companies or break off small, focused niche units within their corporate structures. These niche units can share economies of scale while focusing on customizing products and services to specific markets through concentrating on applications R&D (product design and development), local promotion and PR, direct sales, and customer service. In other words, the large companies within the alliances focus on large-scale information and logistics systems to lower costs. The small companies focus on dealing with the customer and delivering the customized, personalized service— the best of both worlds.

Decentralized Functions	Centralized Functions
Product development	Sales and Distribution
Product R&D	Basic R&D
Marketing	Large-scale production
Advertising and PR	Information systems (MIS)
Market research	Strategic vision
Production	Strategic direction
Quality control	Funding and evaluation
Shipping	Advertising placement
Technical service	Shipping coordination
Acquisitions	Service coordination

Figure 6–3. Centralized and decentralized functions in the corporation of the future.

The forces driving alliances

Two great megatrends are driving this paradox of maintaining the advantages of large companies while striving for small, independent business and independent units within business: the customization of products and markets, and the movement toward a world marketplace. Even though we hear a lot about information technologies taking away the advantages of economies of scale in many areas (small-scale production machinery, front-line sales, and order-processing information systems), there are certain functions like sales, distribution, and the others I mentioned that still benefit from large-scale economies. The movement to world markets is only amplifying those scale economies.

Schools of minnows that can attack many customized segments of a broader market and share critical economy of scale functions will be the winners in most industries and marketplaces, as the race for leadership in the emerging customized and information markets intensifies toward the top of the great boom ahead, around 2007.

Summary of Principle 1

The first thing your business, large or small, must do to join the coming customized economy as a corporation of the future is to establish your strategic focus.

You begin that process by determining where you are best at serving critical customer needs. Then you decide where you must ally with other companies that can complete the process by doing what they do best in a way that offers the best end product for the best price.

Ultimately, in Principle 3 we will apply this concept of strategic focus down into every unit in your company. But before you can do that, you must adopt a new organizing principle at the most fundamental level of your company. Once your macro strategy is clear, you must design a macro organization or structure to support it.

Structure always follows strategy, so no real reengineering effort can start without a full consideration of strategic focus. Strategic focus is the end—the satisfaction of customer needs. Organizational structure is the means to accomplish that end.

In short, you must start with your customer and restructure your company from the bottom up. The guide for this restructuring is your customer's unique needs and the front-line aspects of the value-added processes you have chosen to focus on in using Principle 1.

In the next chapter we will look at this macro-organizational principle that must permeate your company.

Organize Around
Your Customers and
Your Front Lines

The shape of the new economy is to provide goods
and services that answer the four key needs of every
customer: customization, superior quality, fast
response and delivery, and personalized front-line
service. As a general rule, this can only be
accomplished in small, front-line teams that can
have a natural human intimacy with customers.

Organizing Forward

In the preceding chapter we looked at Principle 1—becoming a minnow
in the most efficient school in your industry to best serve the end customer.
Principle 2 is to align your company at all levels to the customer and the
all-important new principle of customization. This is the first step in building an effective school of minnows within your company to serve your
strategic focus.

In this chapter we'll look at the leading trend of the '80s—focused
customer service. I'll tell you how I see that trend developing to its natural

end in the '90s: the total reorganization of companies to focus on the front line where company meets customer—at all points of interaction—and most important at the point of transaction or sale.

As the importance of customization grows, companies will be forced to add as much value as possible to their products and services and to make decisions at the front lines. Most job growth will come from moving skills and processes from back-line functions into front-line teams.

To me, it's self-evident that by the year 2000 the organizing principle of most companies and hence the driving force of your company's operations will be the front-line operations—that's where the decisions will be made.

As I've said, in the new, customized economy, companies won't produce goods and services in assembly-line fashion one step at a time. Instead they will produce many steps simultaneously using multifunctional teams at all points along the production cycle—with the weight of the effort pushed far forward.

The ideal of the corporation of the future will be systems that allow customers to tailor their own product or service to their needs, using your software and systems. Your mission will simply be to manage the delivery and follow-up service—and, of course, to educate customers as to why they need your products and services and how to use your software systems. That will become the focus of your front lines. So, even sales as we know it will change as we move our organizations toward the customer.

You've already seen examples of this trend. For example, what is an ATM if not a customer-operated station for conducting banking business? No doubt you've visited the computerized printing kiosks that allow you to design and print a personalized greeting card on the spot. What about the newer generation of gasoline pumps that allow you to fill up and pay at the pump with a credit card, avoiding a trip inside to stand in line while some dope ahead of you buys fourteen different lottery tickets, a diet beer, and frosted cupcakes?

Many companies, like printing operations, have already set up software and computer links with their customers so that customers can design the layouts of their brochures or fliers in-house and have those designs translated directly into lower-cost, fast-response printing. It's not a great leap

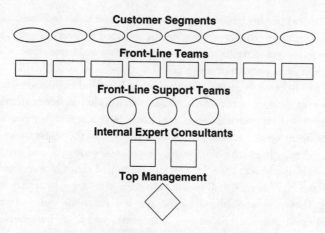

Figure 7–1. Upside-down organization chart.

from there to the moment when the placing of orders, checking credit, starting production, order processing, restocking, collecting marketing data, and reordering of raw materials will take place instantaneously—in many cases under the control of the customer, using your software, which controls the transaction and protects both your interests.

Let's look at some of the principles for organizing around customers and front-line teams.

Principles for Organizing Forward

We'll start with the customer and borrow a page from the customer service gurus who have been preaching since the '80s that you should turn the company organization chart upside down as a starting point in reorganizing.

Organize from the customer up, not the top down

This may sound like a simplistic cliché, but it's not simple at all. It's a total revolution in management principles. Turn your organization chart upside down, putting your customers on top. What this really means is that the entire organizational and decision-making process in your

117

company has just been reversed. Every decision you make organizationally stems from those customers, their needs, and their differences—not from the preferences and needs of your top management and home office, which is the way most companies organize.

Why? Because in the era of scarce information and cumbersome manual storage techniques before the Information Revolution, information was so scarce and expensive that you could only have a few highly educated or intelligent people access it, make decisions, and then pass those decisions down a hierarchy of captains, lieutenants, sergeants, and privates who would implement them in a tightly controlled chain of command in which the implementors had no idea why they were doing what they were doing. They were specialized by the simplest functions and performed according to policies, procedures, and orders, which, as bureaucracies became more complex, began to contradict each other and hasten the breakdown of traditional organizations.

Computers didn't help very much, because they were so costly. In 1972 it cost $7.89 to store and access one bit of information in a computer. Today it costs less than a penny to store and access one bit, and even that is falling at the speed of light into fractions of pennies. With that type of lower-cost information, you can afford to reverse your information flow and make more decisions on the front lines, where decision-makers can be far more intimate and responsive to customers' needs.

In fact, you can't afford *not* to put your information flow at the front lines.

Let's look at two steps I've developed to help you restructure to achieve a customer focus:

Step 1: Differentiate customers into their narrowest segments

If you've done your homework on strategic focus, you already know what your customers have in common. Next, reverse-engineer your working data and determine as finely as possible how your customers' needs are different.

Here's what you're looking for:

- **What levels of customization** in your products or services are necessary to meet your customers unique needs?
- **What different quality levels** or tolerances do they require?
- **How do their needs for response** and delivery times differ?
- **What degrees of personalized service** are expected?
- **What different information needs** and decision processes are involved for them to make a decision?

This is simply a matter of grouping your customers into the smallest groups of similar needs. Don't be afraid to take it to an extreme. Segment customers into the widest groups of differences and then back up and start questioning if many of the differences are really that consequential to your business or decision-making processes or even to the customers themselves. Finally, back up into fewer groupings for business practicality.

The ultimate goal is to have every _individual_ customer become a market.

Companies that gain the largest market share and earn the deepest loyalty in the new customized economy will be those that meet the _individual_ needs of ever finer customer segments. The natural extension of this logic leads to the point that every customer becomes a point of strategic and organizational focus—a market. Always remember that the ever expanding trend toward customization will force you to constantly refine your segmentation of customers. And that the dramatic progress of computer technologies will give you the power to achieve this goal.

Step 2: Satisfy these needs on the front lines if at all possible

Once you identify the finest, most significant segments of your customers, you can make your first organizational decision: to form front-line cross-functional teams, even if a team is as small as a multiskilled individual, that can focus on meeting those particular needs with as little back-line intervention as possible.

Teams will focus on meeting each customer
segment's needs like a small entrepreneurial business
attacking a very narrow niche market.

Some guiding principles to forming front-line teams

- **Identify the skills,** information, training, software, and hardware
  you'll need on the front lines to satisfy the special needs of each
  small segment of customers.
- **Eliminate every interference** and intervention you can from the
  back lines and upper management.
- **Assume no limitations** in costs at first and back into those realities later.

Why no limitations on cost? Simple. This is a radical shift. It often
takes extreme thinking to break the molds of old management practices.
Sometimes only by going to extremes do some of the apparent limitations
to front-line operations become less formidable. Your mission here is to
bring together direct value-added business processes that have been fragmented into many back-line functional departments along the logic of the
assembly-line-driven functional organization of the past. You must strive
to do more than to reunite them into natural business processes that can
oversee entire end products or services. Strive to reorganize these processes first and foremost around the needs of the front lines, which in turn
revolve around the customer. You must strive to make customization the
natural path of *least* resistance for your company.

You simply *must* see customization
as an opportunity, not a threat.

Business processes versus functions

Face it, you're going to have to learn a new vocabulary in the new economy.
One of the most powerful points in *Reengineering the Corporation* is that
companies have to reengineer around business processes, or value-added
chains as we referred to them earlier, not around functional departments

or mere activities. Most of the controls and bureaucracy burdening our corporations result from the excessive need to coordinate all of the functional parts that have been split out of natural "whole" business processes into narrow functions in the name of the efficiencies of functional specialization. Remember, this was the workforce revolution that drove the industrial age—functional specialization is not intrinsically wrong. It's just that we're in a new age, one that makes it obsolete.

Hammer and Champy's definition of a business process in *Reengineering* is: "A collection of activities that takes one or more kinds of input and creates an output that is of value to the customer." That customer can be an internal one or an external one, and the process can be large or small. Creating an end result or product that has *value to the customer* is the key point here.

What I am emphasizing is that the starting point for such a reengineering back into basic coherent business processes can only originate from this point of view of front-line focus on individualized customer needs. You can reengineer around natural business processes and still fail to provide the customization and personalized service that are ultimately the critical trend of this age. Therefore, we can't just take a large-scale view of our businesses and reconstruct them into logical business processes. Such a point of view only tends to end up reconfiguring businesses around large-scale factors. Yes, that point of view results in a more effective and efficient process, but it doesn't achieve its full potential.

I have the greatest respect for *Reengineering the Corporation*. I see it as a landmark book highlighting 1993 as a watershed year for the workforce revolution, much as 1914 was for the assembly-line revolution of Henry Ford. But I remain suspicious of how fast it caught on in corporate America. It's too easy for executives in large companies to think that they can now apply the usual heavy, top-down methods of management and control by creating "reengineering czars." That approach won't succeed without addressing the most fundamental change in our times, one that ultimately defeats the very notion of top-down: the empowerment of individuals.

The driving force in the new economy is the empowerment of the individual—customers and employees—a concept that was nearly obliterated in the assembly-line economy.

Individualism among consumers is requiring us to place a premium on entrepreneurial workers and company leaders at all levels—but especially on the front lines where company meets customer. Only people with a front-line orientation who share a vision of change and customer needs can drive that vision through to reality. *That's what's driving business processes in the corporation of the future.*

So we return to the central point of this chapter: The most critical organizational principle is not reengineering, but organizing totally, at all levels, around the customer and the front-line operations that interact and transact with the customer. Don't try to define larger business processes and value-added chains in your company until you have clearly established the optimum front-line entrepreneurial processes for interacting with the customer—and that should revolve around the smallest cross-functional teams that can meet the customer's needs with a minimum of back-line intervention. Necessary back-line functions only flow from and exist in response to the needs of those front-line operations and what is not economical to put on the front lines. That is what makes this such a radical approach from the past. This is what I meant in the first chapter when I talked about going *beyond reengineering*. In a sense, that's how we'll define the very term *customer service.*

Redefining customer service

Let's get back to the customer, the basis of business process. You can now see the implications of fine segmentation, can't you? Segmentation allows you to refine your strategic focus down to even smaller groups of customers and to cultivate a high level of intimacy between your front-line people and your customers.

> **T**his is the secret to customer service: creating a natural, simple structure that promotes, maintains, and rewards intimacy between small groups of customers and small teams of front-line workers responsible for and empowered to meet their needs

It's like a relationship between family or close friends. You don't need a complex structure or controls or checks and balances to recognize or respond to the needs of people you are intimate with—like your kids or spouse or best friends! The motivation, the accountability, and the responsiveness are inherent in and directly proportional to the closeness of the relationship.

And, of course, small, intimate teams can adapt and make decisions much faster than larger organizations or bureaucratic structures of any size.

Caring enough to restructure to the very best

An example I read about Hallmark Cards is an excellent demonstration of this principle of segmentation to arrive at a new level of customer focus.

The story goes something like this. When Hallmark reexamined its customers, the company found that the key differentiation for card shoppers is the holiday or occasion they are experiencing. That really boils down to differing emotional and psychological events in the lives of people. This was more important a differentiation than traditional customer segmentation schemes like lifestyles and demographics and regional cultures. So Hallmark decided to reorganize around holidays and experiences.

Hallmark formed small teams of people dedicated to a holiday or occasion (customer specialization), pulling people from formerly back-line functions like art design, editorial, and production coordination (functional specialization—and note these are direct value-added activities that affect the quality of the product to customers, not bureaucratic administrative and control functions) into front-line teams that live and breathe, say, birthdays for kids. That's all they do year-round! You get to know kids—you talk with kids, crawl around the floor with them, color with them, go to kids' birthdays, have them slobber on you—so you can develop an intimate and unique understanding of what a birthday means to a kid. You learn to understand kids' birthdays better than anyone else in the world!

Your successes, failures, and feedback are clearly traceable to the results with this customer—whether this customer is happy or not. Obviously, kids' birthdays are different events from adults turning sixty or Mother's Day or Christmas.

Hallmark's extra degree of customer focus and efficiency was obtained by moving many value-added functions from back-line, larger-scale departments into smaller, more intimate front-line teams that focused on one special occasion in the lives of customers.

Exceptions to restructuring at Hallmark

Sales was an example of a function that could not be practically moved into front-line teams. Why? First, the stores that sold the cards to customers didn't want to have hordes of focused sales teams visiting them and wasting their time hawking only one narrow card line at a time. Likewise, it would have wasted the economies of scale the company enjoyed to pay the high cost of flying around an army of salespeople.

But just wait five or ten years until direct video sales become feasible with advances in computer technologies. Then it will likely be feasible to have stores receive visual representations and promotions of the narrowest of card lines. They could then interact and even make customized modifications to those cards directly with the teams responsible for them through video conferencing, without the need for human sales representatives physically interacting with store buyers. Then the sales function will be incorporated into the front-line teams.

The point: Many people who used to be in large, specialized, direct value-added functional departments on the back lines, from art to editorial to production, have been moved into front-line teams where they have to broaden their functional skills and shift their specialization more to understanding the specific needs of a small group of customers.

Hallmark is a case where a prominent feature of the corporation of the future is already in effect in the here and now. It's going to happen on a much wider scale. You'd be a fool to ignore the inevitable.

Let's continue examining. . . .

The back-line impacts of the Hallmark restructuring

Of course, a small group of front-line people would not be able to master all the specialized skills required to compete in the greeting card business. They must be able to call upon an array of specialists on demand. So, Hallmark still uses back-line experts, outside consultants, and specialty services to support front-line teams.

For example, the design artist on the team is multifunctional enough to draft the overall design of the card and do most of the artwork, but might have to call in an airbrush artist for special effects. The design artist has two choices: either contact an in-house airbrush specialist and pay a fair rate; or go outside the company to hire airbrush skills by the hour or on a project quote.

The important principle here is that front-line teams can focus on customer needs. They are empowered to meet those needs and can change with the demands of the marketplace. Teams remain responsible for delivering an end product to a customer without a complicated bureaucracy, controls, or systems that block their ability to respond to obvious needs. Front-line teams are responsible for highly focused, largely self-contained, self-managed processes.

As a rule, the greater the focus on individualized customer needs and the smaller the teams, the better the performance.

The efficiencies of such a structure can be astounding. We'll look at this more in the next chapter.

There simply is not room for overspecialization inside front-line teams. And there simply cannot be a gargantuan bureaucracy to impede their performance. Think of a small business like your local dry cleaner. Does it have excessive overheads? Does it to go through five or ten approval levels to make a simple decision? Does it lose touch with customers? Does it fail to measure the returns on advertising dollars spent in the yellow pages? No, a small business can't afford to do those things because it would soon be out of business. Teams and small businesses rely on strong human connections with their customers. Both need natural accountability and flexibility. Both, in effect, are small entrepreneurial businesses. We need to restore that quality to our larger corporations, and by that, I mean corporations larger than fifty employees.

The new specialization

Embrace front-line customer specialization as the secret to survival for a corporation of the future. You must know your customer and be able to solve a particular need or problem better than anyone else in the industry—or else you won't stay in business. Functional specialization, by skills, is still required, but it becomes increasingly secondary to customer specialization or the ability to deliver solutions and solve problems for particular customers.

That is the new specialization trend: *from functional specialization to customer specialization*—restoring the best of the old family or proprietorship business, combined with the economies of learning and scale of world markets through the power of information technologies that can instantaneously link many small-scale units vertically and horizontally around the world.

To do this you must first reorganize around your customer's specialized needs and the front-line processes that can best serve them and change with them. You'll have to put every process and function in your company to the Front-Line Test, starting with the processes most pertinent to your customer's needs. Question every process in your company and ask:

Why can't this be done on the front lines?

That is the key question for this chapter. The function of the CEO and everyone involved in restructuring at all levels is to ask that question again and again. Often you will get good answers for why it can't be done. But someday, if you keep asking, you'll find out that new software or technology or approaches or techniques or creative people will find ways to perform the function on the front lines. In many cases you can do it on the front lines right away if you are willing to start from scratch and rethink your business. Most managers are instead trying to change slowly and streamline present bureaucracies.

The first areas to question are the direct value-added processes that the customer is aware of, not all of the bureaucratic supervisory, control, measurement, and accounting functions—although those are absolutely critical to deal with, and we will get to them later. Why does the production require large machines back in Chicago or in Korea—aren't mini-mills producing steel in smaller mills closer to customers? Is there a technology that would allow us to do that? What will allow us to customize the production of our (or our suppliers') larger factories to produce smaller runs to demand closer to the order date? Why can't we produce the sweaters in large volume and then delay the coloring until orders are placed and then do it in the warehouse? Why do we have to go back to R&D or engineering to make minor changes in product specifications and costs or prices? Why can't such changes be built into a software system that allows the salesperson or customer to alter the specs and have modified costs and pricing flashed out by the portable computer?

The difference between value-added and not

An important principle to be understood at all levels in companies is the difference between direct value-added and indirect non-value-added work and processes.

The way to define value-added work and distinguish it from non-value-added or bureaucratic functions is simple. Ask what the customer actually feels about your product or service. Here are some examples of what matters to customers.

Value-Added: What Customers Care About

- R&D and the design that went into it
- Quality of production and assembly
- Quality of the components that went into the product
- The sales process and the people customers have to deal with directly from your company
- The quality of customers' relationship with those salespeople
- The quality, the tone, and the information content of the advertising or promotion that educates customers
- The speed and accuracy with which you process customers' orders
- Your credit policies and billing process
- The speed and accuracy of your shipping or delivery process
- The follow-up service customers get
- The quality of customers' relationships and interactions with service personnel.

These are the processes that you need to first reorganize and move to the front lines or as close to the front lines as possible, as Hallmark did with card design, art, editorial, and production coordination.

Always reengineer the value-added functions

Focus first on reengineering the value-added processes and let non-value-added, more bureaucratic processes fall into line on their own—or fall out of the company. In *Reengineering the Corporation*, the authors flatly state:

You can't reengineer a non-value-added function, because it's not a business process!

When you reengineer specialized functions into more natural processes and front-line units, much of the complex bureaucracy of controls and measurements will disappear naturally. This is why you should concentrate on moving direct value-added functions to the front lines first.

A front-line hospital (the secret to health care reform?)

Another great example of how an organization took real value-added processes from the back lines and moved them to the front lines is in Tom Peters's book *Liberation Management*. He describes a large hospital that effectively moved about 80 percent of the activities of many medical and technical specialists, which drive most of the complexity and bureaucracy in hospitals, to front-line care units. Note that these specialists are very much direct value-added workers who diagnose and deliver specialized care to the patient, not accountants or administrators.

The hospital trained "care pairs," a nurse and a technician, to handle most of the more straightforward tasks of the specialists on the front lines. Each care pair was to focus on the front-line care and needs of patients with similar types of illness. These two people became the direct interface with small numbers of patients—six or so beds each in twenty-bed mini-hospitals within an eight-hundred-bed hospital.

The results? Care pairs were able to give the kind of specialized and personalized service you rarely see in the highly sterile and bureaucratic atmosphere of most hospitals. Their care came at lower cost and with many fewer delays because they were able to avoid bureaucratic mistakes and the expensive and timely intervention of specialists. You can see how much of the bureaucratic checks and procedures would naturally fall away with such a direct, front-line process. What's more, there were fewer malpractice lawsuits! People aren't likely to sue someone who shows them close personal care, but they will sue faceless bureaucrats who mistreat them casually.

That brings us to non-value-added functions:

Non-Value-Added: What Customers Don't Care About

- How you manage, coordinate, and supervise
- Your bookkeeping, control, and tracking systems
- Your annual report and stockholder meetings
- What computer and software systems you use internally
- Your training and hiring programs
- Your legal policies
- Your goal-setting and planning systems
- Your evaluation and pay systems
- Your retirement and health care benefit plans

That is, customers don't care about any indirect, non-value-added bureaucratic functions unless they fail and impede the value-added functions they do care about!

And customers don't care about your management, bookkeeping, personnel practices, and employee health plan—unless it costs them money. The truth is, *they always do cost the customer!*

It's not that bureaucratic functions aren't necessary. It's that they are internal to your company's operation and that they should be minimized, not maximized. They entail real costs and delays that the customer pays for. Customers don't want to pay for something that they don't feel as a direct benefit. Of course, most people, being reasonable, realize that those functions are a necessary cost of doing business. They understand that somebody has to pay for them and that it's usually a cost built into the product. But the last thing they want is to be reminded of it. So tell your people that next time they feel the urge to say, "Sorry for the delay; our new, multimillion-dollar computer is on the blink," they should keep quiet. The customer doesn't want to hear it.

In most companies, the bulk of the payroll is consumed by people who supervise, keep paper, advise, screw up, and give reasons not to do things—indirect work. Yes, most such people actually end up subtracting more value than they add. But it's not their fault. The old system of functional specialization and command and control management required these bureaucratic layers. Our old structures rewarded bureauc-rats for following policies and orders and not seeing the bigger picture or innovating. That's what they were supposed to do. In a fast-moving, customized economy, that doesn't work anymore; but our structures still value and reward such people for stifling rather than promoting customer focus, innovation, and flexibility.

These areas offer a huge cost savings potential. To keep a company's products from being priced out of the market or to bring premium-priced, customized products and services into mainstream affordability, you have to pare down the back-line functions. More important, if you try to bolster and empower your front lines but keep your bureaucracy in place because you don't want to fire people, what is the bureaucracy going to do? Right— it will spend time justifying jobs. It will find reasons to interfere with the front lines and prevent innovation because innovation will only put bureaucrats out of a job. So managers are going to have to put these people out of their predicament and force them to move into new, more productive, more enjoyable, and ultimately more secure positions, something that most bureaucrats will resist mightily at first.

I've heard some consultants say that most companies run a ratio of something like 70 to 30. That is, 70 percent of people are non-value-added and only 30 percent add value. This is *at best*. Some real laggards run ratios of up to 90 to 10. The trick of this revolution is to increase the percentage of our direct value-added employees—dramatically!

It's your job to handle that "stuff" and not to allow your internal workers' desire for security and avoidance of change to result in an organization that uses bureaucracy and systematic rules and policies to protect employees from the customer. That's a detriment to customers. Unfortunately, it has also become the path of least resistance in most hierarchical and functionally specialized organizations.

If you expect to succeed as a corporation of the future, you'll have to make a religion of smashing the back-line bureaucracy in your company.

The second most important question

To help organize around your front-line processes it helps also to put every process and function to the Back-Line Test. Question every back-line, non-value-added, bureaucratic function in your company that remains after you reengineer your value-added processes into and around the front lines and ask:

How can we obliterate or minimize back-line functions?

No matter how thorough you've been with the Front-Line Test, always focus endlessly on eliminating, automating, outsourcing, moving forward, or redeploying all back-line, indirect, bureaucratic functions to simplify them and make them more accountable. Ask why your sales staff always must go back to accounting to get credit approval. Is there anything that says that the information or the formula for evaluating credit can't be right there in a salesperson's portable computer, which is linked by a wireless modem to the customer database in the home office? Why does order processing have to be done back in the accounting department? Couldn't a portable computer perform the same checks and controls at the point of sale? Why does *any* function have to be performed on the back lines or by some more bureaucratic fiefdom or functional department?

Options for Minimizing Non-Value-Added Functions

You want to add as much value and information as possible as close to the customer as you can. You want to make as many decisions as possible on the front lines. The companies moving to the front lines are eventually going to win even if they stumble on the way, even if they make some mistakes, even if they make some trade-offs in economies of scale and controls. The greater customer satisfaction and the savings from reducing bureaucracy ultimately will offset disadvantages in companies that keep pushing to do it right.

Do you want to work for a company that is not making these critical changes? Do you think you can maintain your present job security and benefits in a more bureaucratic, back-line job that is about to be obliterated? Foreseeable changes will cause the elimination of more jobs in the coming decades than at any time in history.

Back-line administrative and clerical jobs will continue to be eliminated even faster than we saw in the early '90s. That was just the tip of the iceberg, when the highest-paid middle management jobs started to be permanently eliminated by reengineering and computerized expert systems. This restructuring will spread further through the remaining middle management jobs and then extend deeply into the greatest single category: clerical jobs. People in these areas are more vulnerable to pink slips than factory workers or any other class of worker.

I have identified five ways companies can create higher responsiveness and efficiency by demolishing middle-level jobs and bureaucratic functions. Your options in order of priority and logic: Eliminate, Automate, Move Forward, Outsource, or Redeploy.

Option 1: Eliminate

The first question you should ask of any bureaucratic, non-value-added function is:

Do we need to do this in the first place?

Remember a lot of the restructuring of front-line and back-line value-added processes will eliminate the need for many controls, checks, and balances. If front-line teams have the proper information and broad enough skills, they can monitor their own performance and control their own processes.

Much of what companies have been doing for ages is simply no longer necessary, may never have been necessary. One example: checking credit. If you do your homework you may find that 95 percent of the time it doesn't pay to check credit, that the costs outweigh the benefits and the extra time delays hurt your sales closing ratios to boot.

Think about it. If you make a gross margin of 50 percent over your fixed overhead costs on every item you sell, your operation will stay in the black unless every other customer fails to pay you! I'll show later why the real margin may be even higher than that. Have you ever wondered why many jewelry stores that have very high gross margins offer easy credit to anyone, even people who have been through bankruptcy?

Accounting or finance specialists in charge of credit are typically measured by and focused on the lost revenues from the minor percentage of defaults versus the cost of running their department. So they may be rather tight about credit policies and look like heroes while actually preventing many high-margin sales. Maybe you find by taking a bigger picture that checking credit only on customers with a high-risk profile can save 95 percent of the credit checking. And of course, customers are going to be happier if you aren't constantly holding up their orders and querying them for credit information as if they are questionable people to do business with.

If you can't eliminate a function because it has value or you have to retain a portion of that function, then your next option is to automate it.

Option 2: Automate

As I've pointed out, most clerical and control functions are systematic and can be done by computers. Thus computers and software provide the greatest opportunity for eliminating bureaucracy, costs, and time delays in companies. If your people do not require right-brain creative input to make a decision, then look to a computer.

Portable computers make information available on your front lines, to your most mobile customers, and to your sales and service people. We often hear this capability called sales force automation. That's a misnomer. You're not automating the sales force but the back lines, placing their information capacity in the hands of the salespeople and freeing them up to do what they do best—serve customers in the most human ways, but with much better, faster information capacities.

When automating, the most important question you can ask is: Why can't this procedure or check and control or accounting function be put into our software and computer systems? If you decide credit checks are necessary, even after this discussion, then program credit formulas into your front-line computers. Allow sales staff access to databases so customers' records can be instantly checked, the formula applied, and credit approved—*on the spot!*

If you need controls on discounts, just program your limits into the computers. Let the software warn the salesperson on the spot when the limits are being exceeded, and if you want absolute control, have the computer refuse to issue the order—just like a bureaucrat! Or better, allow salespeople enough discretion to override the computer's objection with a written explanation that makes them accountable for their decision later, as we saw in the CRU example of Part Two.

Above all, don't let a software program dehumanize a process that belongs in the hands of people who read customers' needs.

Automating can truly be a magical process. You are taking sluggish, costly bureaucratic functions and making them disappear into the software of your computer systems, or into the invisible microcosm that George Gilder describes. Every function that you can put into the software brings you closer to the incredible efficiency of the microcosm.

Automating is sure to be the most important weapon against bureaucracy in the future. Never give up on automation. If you can't automate today, technology to come is likely to allow you to do it tomorrow. If you do postpone for now, then it's on to Option 3.

Option 3: Move bureaucratic functions to the front lines

If you can't eliminate or automate a function, the third option is to ask the same question we asked before of direct value-added processes being performed on the back lines: *Why can't this bureaucratic function be done on the front lines?* But note that with back-line functions, this isn't the first question we ask, because the goal with bureaucratic functions is to eliminate and minimize, not to move closer to the customer and front lines as is the thrust with value-added processes. Here we are asking if a back-line function that can't be eliminated or automated can be moved to the front line so as to simplify and minimize its impact—in other words, make it disappear into the microcosm of small self-managing front-line teams.

Can specialists in the professional, clerical, or technical ranks teach your front-line teams how to perform the simplest aspects of their jobs without adding overheads and delays? And then be available to intervene when their highly specialized skills are truly needed?

Let the sales office secretary or even the salesperson check the credit just as the accounting department does, if it can't be done automatically in the computer yet. The sales office staff will have much more motivation to serve the salesperson and help close the order instead of preventing it. In other words, put this bureaucratic function on the front lines where it can be more directly handled and more accountable to the front-line process.

In short, eliminate your Order Prevention Department. The sad part, again, is that the back-line bureaucrats are just doing what they are structured and told to do: making sure everything is in order and in compliance with company policies. They have no structure that makes them accountable to the customer's needs and urgencies; those on the front lines do.

Accountability to a customer is what ultimately makes a difference as to whether the company succeeds or fails. Companies have no choice but to demolish Order Prevention Departments wherever possible.

If you can't move a bureaucratic function simply and efficiently to the front lines, then try outsourcing it.

Option 4: Outsource to competent, efficient, strategic vendors

Sometimes a bureaucratic function is too complex, requiring specialized expertise that can't easily be programmed into the computer or transferred to front-line generalists. In that case, you should consider subcontracting it to a firm that focuses only on that task, using the best people, equipment, training, and information systems. Why do anything inside the company— unless it can be efficiently automated or simplified by being moved to the front lines—that would distract from your strategic focus?

How can a front-line team focus on keeping in touch with changes in customers needs and designing and delivering the best products if it has to spend a high proportion of its time dealing with accounting, payroll and benefits, and complex coordination processes? Better to subcontract such things to maintain your focus on what is most important to the customer. Let outside specialists in bookkeeping, computer systems, software systems, strategic planning, team building, or whatever do what they do best and handle more indirect or less strategic functions for your teams when and if they need it.

Considerations in outsourcing

▪ Keep control!

Remember, bureaucratic functions are necessary and useful, despite the fact that they've been overdone and are now out of control in most companies, driving up overheads and reducing innovation. You can't afford to lose control of these functions any more than you can afford to dilute your focus with them. You need your outside subcontractors to be few and just as intimate as an in-house department, sharing strategic information and forming close, long-term relationships, so that the fragmentation of these functions does not result in chaos or lack of strategic focus.

▪ Outsource to a firm that fits

I hear many businesspeople claim that they have tried outsourcing and it didn't work because the vendor was not able to be as sensitive to their needs as an in-house department. (In fact, I've heard more people claim that in-house departments are less sensitive!) What this simply means is that they did not take the time and care to select the right vendor and to communicate the requirements and rewards of being a preferred or exclusive vendor. I have also seen many small firms fail by going to a very large vendor that has many much larger clients; the small firms were surprised that they weren't treated like royalty or that they got the junior people to work on their projects. Often you are wise to work with a smaller firm that will treat you as its top client rather than with a bigger, more powerful firm that will see you as its last priority. This is just a matter of strategic focus in reverse. It doesn't mean that a small firm can't get high-priority service from a large vendor. It's just that you have to communicate your strategic value to the larger firm.

If all else fails and you can't outsource a more bureaucratic function, then you must redeploy it to serve your front lines like an internal consulting service, instead of being a bureaucratic fiefdom.

Option 5: Redeploy

Your last resort: If you can't eliminate the function, automate it, move it efficiently to the front lines, or outsource it, then you have to form an internal consulting or service team. As usual, orient such a service toward your front lines as much as outside consulting firms or subcontractors are oriented toward their customers.

This option is a last resort because of our first principle: strategic focus. Companies have to strive to keep doing what they do best, delivering what is critical to the customer and not getting sidetracked into too many tangential functions. But some functions are too expensive to farm out because of communication or transactions costs. In other cases, a function might involve strategic information too sensitive to let outside of your company.

Hewlett-Packard and many other large companies have successfully reengineered their highest, most strategic staff functions into voluntary consulting services that have to bid for and justify their services to internal value-added units. The process was difficult at first, because people weren't used to being accountable or having to justify and market their services. The end result: H-P now has internal businesses demonstrating high returns on investment for the corporation. They are more satisfied as professionals now that the internal units highly value these insider services.

You can redeploy people as well as functions

How do you redeploy your people? It may not be as tough a task as you imagine. For instance, what makes a good salesperson in today's new information age isn't what the mythology says it is. The smart customer wants to make decisions with information and a variety of choices. Nobody wants to have a product crammed down his or her throat. You're going to find that a lot of office people in your back lines are better suited to being sales and service people than the typical gung-ho aggressive sales type of legend. Back-line people are used to dealing with information. They are more courteous. They aren't as pushy. They aren't as likely to be afraid of information technologies and computers.

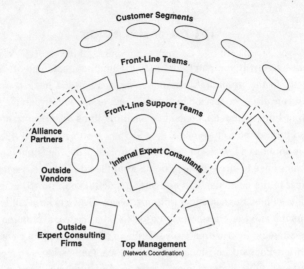

Customer Segments

Front-Line Teams

Front-Line Support Teams

Alliance Partners

Internal Expert Consultants

Outside Vendors

Outside Expert Consulting Firms

Top Management
(Network Coordination)

Figure 7–2. Organizational network.

You can redeploy people to front-line teams or they
may stay on the back lines and directly serve as
front-line support functions, in effect becoming part
of the front-line process.

But you are likely to have to teach people communications skills, such
as subtle closing techniques in the case of new sales staff. Remember the
sales facilitators in Customers "R" Us? These were examples using actual
people in Leegin, the small belt company. They became phone sales reps
for follow-up orders to the field sales trips, learning to interact directly
with customers as well as serving field sales staff.

Bottom Line

Every decision you make about your organization starts with your customer,
then moves to your front lines. Everybody else in the company exists only
if he or she is necessary to serve this front line (see Figure 7-2).

My final word on this subject is good news: The bureaucracy is the area where most jobs will be eliminated in the future. More than anybody else, clerical and middle management employees have to carefully consider their options for the future. Remember this is *not* bad news. The greatest growth in jobs will come in front-line teams in larger corporations and in smaller businesses, and many former bureaucrats will be able to move forward and contribute to companies in eminently more rewarding positions. But there will also be fruitful opportunities in back-line and outside consulting and services. You can still specialize in very specific functional skills and provide information on demand effectively to front-line teams at low costs and overheads. Many such services will be run out of a person's home at very low overheads and an increase in family and leisure time. That is a different focus in skills and career. We will look at that issue more in depth in Chapters 10 and 11.

In the next chapter we will look at how we turn the front- and back-line teams into self-managing businesses with the same accountability and responsiveness as outside entrepreneurial businesses. Meanwhile, remember this:

It isn't enough to put up posters that say you are a front-line company.

Don't make the mistake of paying lip service to the idea of organizing around the front lines or restoring your company to the entrepreneurial principle. Don't simply make your accounting department 10 percent more efficient—or even 100 percent more efficient. Work toward eliminating departments altogether if they don't add value or serve customers directly. Build it into the software entirely and put more people on the front lines.

Never require a salesperson to have to go back and ask a bureaucrat for permission to help the customer.

8

Establish Every Individual, Team, and Unit as a Business

Break every process in your company into the smallest, most focused teams possible. Structure every front- and back-line team to be self-managing, to have a well-defined customer, to monitor its own productivity, and most of all to have a bottom-line P&L. You're not a real business if you don't have a P&L! Teams at all levels have to learn to think like businesspeople.

Get Everybody Involved in the Business of Your Business

In Chapter 6 we discussed Principle 1, the principle of strategic focus at the highest level: making your business a minnow in a strategic network of minnows in your industry. In Chapter 7 we discussed Principle 2: reorganizing every process in the company around the customer so as to link your company's school of minnows to the customer as the key driving force. In this chapter we are going to discuss Principle 3: making your company a network of highly focused individuals and small teams that are as responsive and accountable as small entrepreneurial businesses.

I give this principle the highest emphasis at my business seminars. Why? Because it's the factor I see that is most neglected. Some companies make great efforts to get their employees focused on the customer. They train them in all types of new skills, empowering them to go out and serve customers. Then they leave them in the same departments and bureaucratic business structures and expect them to act differently.

Don't underestimate the importance of structure. Structure determines the flow of energy, decisions, and outcomes because it establishes the path of least resistance. People look to structure for motivation and rewards as they try to fit in. Most managers have overlooked the importance of entrepreneurialism and its relationship to structure.

The point of Principle Number 3 is to ensure that you break your company into an effective structure, a school of minnows within your company, so that every unit is as responsive as an entrepreneurial small business.

Growing entrepreneurs

If you want people to act like entrepreneurs or small businesses, put them in the same proven structures that work for entrepreneurs and small businesses out in the real world. Get them out of the secure, insulated environment of most companies.

Remember the example I gave earlier about the local dry cleaner. It doesn't build up overheads or lose touch with the customer. It can't afford to—it would go out of business overnight.

Why are garage start-ups more effective at launching new products than in-house, R&D, or new product projects? I mean, the corporate in-house units enjoy all of the advantages, right? They have more funding, access to distribution channels, a trustworthy company name behind them, access to in-house expertise, nice offices, and a basic salary so everybody feels secure.

Too high a comfort level is precisely why in-house ventures fail more often than independents. Everything is too easy for them. The path of least resistance is to just keep on tinkering, keep spending more money to make sure you have it right, keep analyzing. Above all, they avoid taking the big risks.

In contrast, entrepreneurs don't have access to endless capital. They borrow a little from a relative, or from the old American Express credit line. Once they do get capital, it costs them an arm and a leg and part of their ownership—so they take it seriously. They can't afford endless analysis, they can't afford high-powered secretaries, plush offices, and extravagant specialized expertise. They have to watch every penny. They have to be creative and innovative and consider new and better ways to do everything!

Isn't that what entrepreneurship is all about?

Companies are spending too much money on seminars and information systems to get people to become more customer-oriented, to be more creative, to work in teams, to visualize success, and to find their inner selves and motivating spirit. The best way to become an entrepreneur is to be put in a structure that forces you to be more intimate with customers, more action-oriented, and more accountable for your actions. This is the best way to learn, period! Companies spend too much money on endless motivation and training, but don't make simple investments in information systems to create the real sense of being a business for their employees and teams. We must structure our work teams to operate like businesses and teach them to think like businesspeople.

Seven Essential Qualities of High-Performance Businesses

Quality 1: A real business is focused

The highest-performance businesses and teams are small and focused. You should continuously strive to break your key business processes down into the smallest possible process teams within each of your larger business processes.

We return to the principle of strategic focus, but now at the micro level. Every unit and team must be made into a clearly defined business unit, the smaller the better. Don't worry about excessively fragmenting business processes for now. The key is for you to break something down into smaller teams or units within a larger process. If a team or unit can be responsible for an entire end product or service that is valued and used by an internal or external customer, do it. In other words, force every team to produce something you can sell to someone, but at the most focused level possible.

I have seen many examples of companies taking a larger factory or production process and splitting it into many small production processes. This is not a duplication of the assembly-line process that broke processes into many individual functions, tasks, and activities. That approach removes the team concept and the idea of a whole process. No, I'm talking about breaking a larger process into multiple microprocesses, each of which can be handed off to a team.

Here's an example at Leegin Belts: Have small multifunctional teams produce a narrow line of belts from beginning to end—an entire process. Prior to the reorganization of Leegin, teams focused on only one stage of production for all belts, like fastening belt buckles or cutting the leather. The new teams now have an end product and can be responsible for the quality, costs, and customer satisfaction with that product at every step of its design and manufacture. But the narrow lines can be handled by small, intimate teams of cross-trained, multifunctional people. Each person now has to take on, say, seven or eight related steps instead of one.

As to team size, you need the minimum number of people with the best mix of skills to make an informed decision in order to build your team. If you get too many people on a team, you create a new bureaucracy. As a general rule, teams of five to eight, even up to ten or twelve, are optimal. Once you get more than twelve you start to become a full-blown bureaucratic committee. Tom Peters suggests that fifty is an optimal size for a larger business process or unit, and some companies find that up to two hundred is okay as a maximum. But such process sizes are only feasible if you can break fifty-person business units into seven or eight teams of six or seven people. Just remember to focus on the skills of the people and the complexity of the process.

Don't dilute the focus of your best people

Here is another one of my pet peeves. I've watched many companies, large and small, ruin their best people and departments by overloading them with functions that aren't directly related to their strategic focus and highest skills. A new MBA comes into a critical department and transforms that department into a highly profitable and customer-happy operation. What is his or her reward? Upper management starts noticing other department and functions that need turning around. They place those departments and functions under the new superstar's responsibility. At first, improvements are made in that department. But then the inevitable sets in. Now the superstar no longer has time to focus on the highly critical value-added function he or she was originally hired for. An important area of the company starts to fail. When the superstar bounces back to the critical area that is now failing, other areas start to falter.

> **You kill your best people by diluting their strategic focus! Eventually, when you've diluted all your best people, you kill your company.**

Form strategic alliances at the micro level

Bring the principle of strategic focus down to the micro level of every department and team. That means forming strategic partnerships at the micro level with suppliers and subcontractors to which you outsource. Convert every outsourcing relationship into an intimate partnership, and make teams responsible for initiating and maintaining those relationships. Your suppliers can become strategic partners in a network environment.

Seek true, cooperative partnerships with win-win outcomes

You want your suppliers and consulting services to know your operations and strategies well enough to come in occasionally and say, "If you would just do steps A and B differently and pass step C to us, we could save 20 percent of the costs. We can pass on half of the cost benefits to the customer and split the other half between us!" This strategic cooperation offsets a potential for fragmentation caused by outsourcing. The efficiencies from it tend to be greater than the efficiencies of having many vendors compete for lower bids. You give a greater scale of business to one or a few competitors, which increases their focus and economies of scale and lowers their costs, and ultimately lowers the price they can charge you.

Encourage teams to form partnerships and alliances within

You also want to encourage your many business units to cooperate and form partnerships and joint ventures, and share information and expertise, with other internal units wherever possible. This is what happens out in the real world among businesses competing in the marketplace. You simply want to bring the forces of the marketplace inside of your company—into your microcosm.

We'll look at how such teams manage themselves later. The next natural step is to make sure every team that delivers an end product or result has a clearly identified customer to focus on and be accountable to.

Quality 2: A real business has customers

Make that clearly defined customers, those you identified via Principle 1, when you established a strategic focus for the company. Companies have customers, but most people and departments within organizations don't have customers. If they do, the customers are not clearly defined and formally acknowledged.

Customers for everybody

- **For salespeople** it is their front-line customers, and in the new customized economy, those end customers have to be defined more and more specifically according to specialized needs that the front-line salespeople have to focus on satisfying, like the kids' birthdays at Hallmark.
- **Your internal departments** have to be linked to front-line people who serve customers or other back-line units that serve the front lines. Example: The accounting department becomes an internal service that supplies salespeople with up-to-date information on costs, inventory availability, credit, and margins to help them better close profitable sales. The MIS department is a service group that

modifies the software driving the sales portable computer systems to their needs and mans a twenty-four-hour hot line to help them with any technical problems they experience in the field.

So internally and externally, make sure everybody has a customer and that there is a real tangible relationship there—an exchange of value. Write down the customer list. Get everybody to clearly acknowledge who his or her king is. Tell everybody: "Your team exists not to be a bureaucracy or a fiefdom. You are here to help facilitate the order process for the salespeople. If we don't book orders, we don't get paid either."

Structure your internal bureaucratic and back-line support and service departments just as if they were outside consulting firms. Make them sing for their supper. That's what consulting firms do. They put up proposals, they bid, they'll customize to meet your need. Why? Because if they don't do it, somebody else will get the business. That's how you want your internal departments responding to your front lines and your front lines responding to their customers.

Quality 3: A real business is self-managing

Self-management is achieved at all levels with cross-functional work teams. The whole company becomes a coalition of self-managed teams. The emphasis will be on new, small, self-managed, and self-directional teams.

Such teams make their own decisions in their own spheres of influence. They order their own materials and supplies, do their own scheduling and planning, monitor their own quality, make hiring and firing decisions for their team, decide the best layout of their office, machinery, and equipment, visit customers, and look at new product variations or ways of doing things. Although they are not making decisions at the top management level, they do need to have full access to their own operation, their own productivity, and their own ability to provide customer satisfaction. If they make their own decisions and monitor their own results, you don't need somebody in headquarters to check on them all of the time, maybe just some summary statistics that let you know they are on track.

Self-appraisal goes along with self-management.

An example from a consulting company I used to work for: Superiors give the employee an appraisal—but the results of that are combined with appraisals from the consultants on the employee's team, from research assistants below the employee, and from customers, and also with a self-appraisal. In the course of that multidimensional look, an employee receives a rounded evaluation that may direct him or her to personal changes and even to places in the company where he or she could be more effective.

Quality 4: A real business makes mistakes— but learns from them

The whole point of this exercise, no matter how you do it, is to challenge and nurture people so that they make their own decisions. Of course you want them to make better decisions for themselves than anybody from the ivory tower could make. You certainly hope they don't make the same mistakes over and over again. But you must surely know that the alternative to an environment that doesn't encourage risk-taking and mistakes is that rote bureaucracy we've been talking about shedding.

In the typical hierarchical company, somebody makes a decision and it just happens to be the wrong one. So the department manager comes in and gives the person hell for it. That sends the message: "You don't dare make a mistake in this company." That creates a climate in which it's much easier and safer to do nothing than to err.

What's important here is simply to acknowledge reality in your company. Learning results largely from mistakes—from successes, too, but more from mistakes. Tell your people: "It's okay to make mistakes. If you aren't slipping up once in a while, you are not pushing the learning envelope." Someone who can make decisions that affect the customer and the company is more likely to take pride and personal responsibility in his or her work.

Temper that outlook with this caveat:

It's *not* okay to not learn from your mistakes.

Employees or teams that keep making the same mistake should not receive support. In fact, they should be out of business, as an outside business would be!

Quality 5: A real business is well led

Every team needs a leader. Although most decisions may come from consensus or from the team's best expert in one area of skill, you need someone on the team who makes tough decisions in times when there isn't a consensus. You need someone who has a vision of the team's mission, who can keep the big picture and the focus on the customer in mind. You need someone who can motivate and pull the team together when needed. You need a CEO, just like any small business. Any effective team works just like the top management team of any company. I liken this to the well-known structure of an atom (Figure 8-1).

The CEO or leader is the proton—the positively charged, proactive, motivating force within the nucleus of the team.

But there is another part to the nucleus—the neutron. Every team needs an administrator, someone who establishes and maintains the systems, procedures, and controls that keep the ship afloat. It is rare to see a leader or visionary who has the qualities of both. The leader or CEO is like the right brain and the administrator or CAO in a management team is like the left brain. Both are necessary for the team to function properly. I have consistently found that this two-person mix of leader and administrator must be at the core of every effective company and business team. Small, everyday teams also need this mix, even if these functions are taken on part-time by members. This is where hierarchy comes into the new organizational structure, but note that it is put into the microcosm of the small team.

Quality 6: A real business requires multiple skills

This means the team must have the proper mix of specialized skills, not be overspecialized as in complex bureaucracies. Studies have shown that partners with different skills outperform single entrepreneurs in new business ventures.

Now we come to a discussion of the electrons in the atomic structure. You'll want teams of people orbiting around the center with enough specialized expertise to help make well-informed decisions. This means including a broader mix of people—perhaps a marketing expert and reps from production, R&D, and finance and accounting. The point is to have

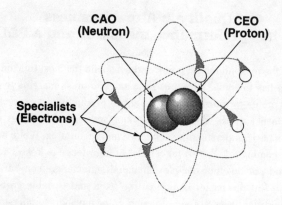

Figure 8-1. The atomic structure of business teams.

the smallest team possible for effectiveness and focus. Every team must be able to deliver results to the customer.

As a general rule you want the smallest number of electrons or team specialists that can accomplish the task to avoid bureaucratic tendencies and to achieve strategic focus for high performance. That means they have to be more multifunctional, just like the executives in the top management team. An entrepreneur is an extreme or a one-person cross-functional team, and is often appropriate for small-scale start-ups and highly focused or personalized roles like claims processing for an insurance company. The customer doesn't want to have to deal with a string of people in resolving a claim.

To minimize the number of people and costs, you often have to make trade-offs in smaller teams. In a small team or company you might have a leader (proton) who also does the marketing and sales (electron). You might have an administrator (neutron) who also does the accounting and finance (electron). Or, a single person may handle sales, marketing, and promotion (all electron functions). Remember, one of the principles of small teams, especially on the front lines, is that they must be much more multifunctional. Fast-learning, adaptable generalists work best here.

Quality 7: A real business
has performance measures and a P&L

This is the most important point, and I'll spend the most time on it. Every business has financial measures from sales to gross margins to overhead costs to profits to return on investment to productivity to assets and liabilities to net worth. You simply cannot make good business decisions without a basic understanding of finance and accounting. We're not talking about becoming a C.P.A. It takes a lot of knowledge to keep books accurately and put together complex financial statements. You have to be a *specialist*. But the basics of things like fixed and variable costs, profits, assets, and liabilities are simple enough for anyone to understand. Bear with me in this section. I'm going to give you the most important knowledge you will need of basic accounting and business financial decision-making, right here in the next several pages. Take the time to go over this until it becomes natural to think in these terms.

The main point: Everyday people at all levels of the corporation of the future will be making decisions and managing their own teams and operations. This means they must all learn the most basic financial tools for making business trade-offs and decisions.

In *The Great Game of Business*, Jack Stack tells how he turned around a fledgling division of a large manufacturing company after an employee buyout. His secret: He taught every employee "the great game of business." He taught people how to make a profit, to build a net worth, and to make a return on investment. Remember Customers "R" Us, where the plant manager holds weekly meetings and shares all of the financial statistics, costs, and performance ratios with every employee in the plant? This is the way smart businesses are operating. "Every employee a business," says Stan Davis in *2020 Vision*, or better, every employee a businessperson.

Measures of customer satisfaction

I stressed earlier the importance of every team or unit having a clear customer. What follows is that every team or unit have clear summary measures of customer satisfaction so that it and management know it is serving the customer and getting better at it. These measures will be as individual as the customers being served. They should be quantitative and qualitative.

Productivity measures

What follows from that is productivity. Every team or unit must have simple measures of its productivity—things like sales per day or units produced per hour—so they can gauge whether they are getting better at their strategic focus. Declines in productivity are great leading indicators of declines in sales and profits and customer satisfaction. That's why this is an important area to track. Each business operation might have a different gauge within a company. But in one respect everybody is the same: Everybody has a measure of productivity.

Two levels of performance measures

I have defined two levels of performance measures:

- **Summary performance measures.** The company's management needs only summary measures of each key level of performance. These will tell them whether the team is on track. Summary measures should not be so complex that they create too much information or generate a bureaucracy of their own. And they must never be allowed to handcuff your teams.
- **Refined performance measures.** Once management has established summary indicators of customer satisfaction, profitability, profit, return on investment, and so on, then it is up to the team to meet those summary performance targets and to develop more refined sets of measures and controls to run its business and meet the needs of customers on a day-to-day basis. The law of the microcosm requires that we put as much of the decision-making and complexity inside teams and business units for maximum simplicity and accountability.

151

Otherwise teams have plenty of leeway to decide how to accomplish their targets and to serve their customers. No one can do that better than the members of the team. Management can and should provide training, consulting, and guidance in these matters, but should expect the team to learn to implement such advice.

Profits and financial measures: the bottom line

Now we get to the most important performance measure for a business: profits. You don't even have to accept that making a profit is the main purpose of business. Satisfying a customer's needs and making a difference are what really motivate most people and businesses. Profits are simply the bottom-line measure of whether you're doing those things effectively and efficiently. In a free marketplace, with many competitors serving a customer's needs, the ones with the highest profit margins are generally the best at what they are doing. Only the best can serve the customer and maintain loyalty and patronage, but also do it at a price and cost that leave them enough profit to stay in business and invest in improving their employees' skills and their equipment and systems. It is the law of the survival of the fittest in business.

Profits, properly understood, are simply the costs of maintaining the business—paying investors for the capital you need, and constantly upgrading your people, technologies, and equipment to get better at what you are doing so you can preserve and perpetuate the jobs and structure that has been created.

Everyone in the company should want to see it be profitable. By measuring profits at the team level you force everyone to understand that principle and to see how he or she fits in. In this way you can diminish that idea that all companies are bottomless pits of wealth, which exploit every employee.

It's time Americans got over the idea that the game of business is one of companies screwing employees, thus it's okay for employees to beat the company out of anything they can.

So profits are an essential principle of business. Even nonprofit organizations have to sustain their people, operations, and technologies and, in effect, have to turn a profit to stay viable! If you're not making a healthy profit you generally aren't the best at what you do, though you may think otherwise.

Think of it this way: Profit is a reality test!

Revenues and costs

Understanding how revenues and costs combine to make a profit is essential to making everyday business decisions and trade-offs. Of course, your customers want the highest possible quality, but they won't pay any cost to get it. Your company and team can't afford to pay any price to give it without going bankrupt. So your teams must get used to making trade-offs, constantly living in that reality.

This understanding isn't usually so easy. Financial statements are typically constructed by accountants who are not entirely oriented toward making business decisions. Accountants tend to lean more toward legal and investor requirements. That has traditionally been their focus.

So I'll try to give you the basics of business in simple terms.

Sales

Every time you deliver goods or services to a customer, you get revenues in return. But here's the first key lesson. Out of every dollar in sales you take in, you must be prepared to make direct expenditures for costs of production and delivery. These costs include things like direct labor, materials, data purchased, energy, shipping, postage, sales commissions, order processing costs, credit checks, and so on—things that are *direct or variable costs.*

Direct or variable costs

Anything that varies in costs as your sales or volume varies is called a direct or variable cost. Don't mistake these for cost of goods sold on the typical accounting statement. Only a portion of cost of goods is variable. This is an important distinction. Every business needs to know the percentage of each sales dollar that goes to direct or variable costs, as this is the most critical financial variable in most businesses.

Let's say for your company the direct cost is 30 percent of each sales dollar, which is fairly typical. That means that every time a salesperson books an extra dollar of sales, the company creates 70 cents in cash flow that can go toward covering your *fixed overhead.*

Fixed overhead

Meeting your overhead is the single biggest short-term challenge for any business or household. Any good businessperson knows how much sales he or she must generate every month to cover overheads to the *break-even point.*

Visualize this by thinking of sales dollars flowing into a bucket. As sales increase, 70 cents on every dollar flows into that bucket called fixed overhead. This is called *contribution margin,* which is the percent of every revenue dollar that is available after variable costs to contribute to overheads and profits to keep you in business.

Break-even point

Your business is losing money until that bucket fills up at the rate of 70 cents per dollar of sales. When the bucket is full, your business breaks even. That means you have paid the bills and the payroll. You just get by. You have no money left over for emergencies, for investing in upgrading your people, or for new technologies. Here's the important point: Once you pass the break-even point, your *profits* accumulate at the rate of 70 cents on the dollar! Of course, you say, that is obvious. But few businesses and very few rank-and-file employees understand this simple principle. People would make very different decisions if they did!

A couple of myths about profit

The typical employee thinks his or her company makes higher profits than it actually does and that the owners put these profits straight into their pockets. The employee doesn't realize that something like 5 percent after taxes is a typical net profit and that until the business is sold or matures, few or no profits go back into the owners' pockets.

Most people also think that if profits are, say, 5 percent, every time you make an extra sale you are making 5 percent of it in profits. That simply isn't true!

Once that overhead bucket is full, every extra sale
contributes a full 70 percent to the bottom line.

Don't you think you would make some different decisions about efforts
in promotion and sales if you knew it meant 70 percent bottom-line profit
contribution instead of 5 percent? Don't you think you'd put a little more
value on the front-line sales efforts?

You can see why bureaucrats make bad decisions. An accountant sitting on the back lines thinking in terms of 5 percent profit margins can
just refuse to approve a discount of 10 percent to a customer, and have a
salesperson lose an order that would have brought 60 percent bottom line
to profits even with the 10 percent discount. The truth is, refusing the
discount may even cost you that customer altogether. You could lose a
stream of revenues with a potential 60 to 70 percent in profits for months
or years to come, maybe forever. Only the salesperson who knows the
customer and depends directly on the commissions for the business should
make such a judgment.

Most front-line people in companies don't understand this principle
and therefore make bad decisions every day. Just one example. I often go
into a hotel late at night and ask the room rate. The clerk quotes me, say,
$89. Then I say, "I'm just going to be here until 6:00 A.M., and I know the
discount hotel down the street is only $49. I guess I'll have to go there."
The clerk will almost always shrug and let me go out the door or say,
"Sorry, that's our policy."

What would a well-informed businessperson think? "He's willing to
pay $49 and maybe a little more because he's already here and this is a
better hotel. It's midnight and there is no chance of booking full tonight,
so the room will go unrented if he walks out the door. My direct costs of
servicing the room are only $9—$6 for the maid and $3 for supplies and
laundry. I could contribute $50 cash to the business if I get him to go for
$59. Even if I rent the room for $49, I contribute $40 to the business."

Does it take a genius to make that $40 decision? A C.P.A.? No, just
someone who thinks like a businessperson. Don't you think the hotel
owner, or your local dry cleaner, would have done likewise? That one
decision would be worth four to five times the hourly wages of the typical
hotel front desk clerk. Wouldn't it be worth it to train and reward people

to actually think like a business and make profitable decisions hour after hour for the company?

Figure 8-2 shows how a P&L should be roughly arranged for any business unit or process team to facilitate better decision-making. We start with revenues and then move to the first category of costs, which are *variable costs*, which we have already discussed. Variable costs are the simplest and most straightforward to manage. You simply identify them and constantly strive to get them to be a smaller percentage of sales so as to create greater contribution margin. Of course, there are also areas where you may increase variable costs to create greater quality and customer satisfaction. That leads to higher prices or more repeat sales or higher sales volume. The point is always to manage variable costs to maximize the total contribution margin to cover your fixed overheads and build profits.

Then there is a second important category of cost between variable and fixed overhead. I call these *strategic costs*.

Strategic costs

These include things like advertising, marketing, promotion, and R&D. These are not variable costs, although they are often lumped with variable costs because they tend to vary with sales or are discretionary, unlike the fixed costs below them.

These are, emphatically, strategic costs—expenditures that expand your sales, improve your quality, or lower your costs. These are the outlays that determine whether you grow and stay in business by educating customers and providing the right products and services to keep them satisfied.

Strategic costs are your investment in your future.

Strategic costs should primarily be measured on the return on investment they produce, not as a percentage of sales, or as a part of the necessary overhead you must meet every month to stay in business over the short term, or as a variable cost of getting out an extra unit of sales.

The typical error that comes from not understanding strategic costs is this: Product or department managers are seeing their revenues fall. So

Product Sales Dollars

(−) Direct Product Costs
  • materials
  • labor
  • utilities
  • shipping

= Product Contribution Margin

(−) Strategic Product Costs
  • advertising
  • sales promotion
  • R&D

= Product Controllable Margin

(−) Indirect Overhead Allocations
  • rent
  • management and clerical salaries
  • office costs
  • utilities

= Product Profit Margin (Bottom Line)

Figure 8–2. Basic profit and loss formula for self-managing teams.

they cut back their advertising or R&D to make budget or to hit profit targets. This is dreadfully important so they can pass the typical bureaucratic financial review of the month. But the truly dreadful part comes into play in months to come when they must face the crisis created by cutting into strategic costs. As a turnaround manager I have seen this mistake made over and over.

In time, these managers will likely see their revenues fall further, worsening their problem, not solving it. Chances are that the right decision would have been to determine that sales were falling because promotion and advertising efforts were either too low or targeted at the wrong media. The solution might better have been either to increase these investments in the future to solve the problem or refocus them in the most productive media.

Poor financial understanding and financial policies direct bureaucrats down the path of least resistance. That's why they usually respond with quick fixes instead of real analysis and solutions.

Back to the local dry cleaner. Watch how much these people value their investments in strategic costs. When you walk in the door for the first time, they're likely to ask you where you heard about them. They may not have a Cray supercomputer or even a portable Powerbook to crunch data. They simply mark another notch on the wall, the right side for customers generated from the yellow pages and the left for radio ads. They will keep close watch on every dollar they spend on promotion and how many new customers walk in the door. This will tell them to see whether they got their best return on investment. That's the way businesspeople think.

The expected lifetime value of a customer

Now let's relate this simple insight, measuring return on investment for strategic expenditures like promotion, and combine it with our other insight into variable costs and contribution margin and bring in a new concept. Let's say you put an ad on the radio for a week. It cost $200, and you counted nine new customers who came in and brought you their dry cleaning. What's the return on investment? First you do some homework. The first question you should ask would be missed by many M.B.A.s: What is the expected revenue stream of every new customer? You look back in your records and do some simple math to find that half of your new customers stay with you on average for twenty-four months. The average sale per customer is only $15 on the first visit, but over time it amounts to an average of $40 a month on dry cleaning.

Continuing your math tells you that 24 months times $40 equals $480. And what is the contribution to your company from that customer if your variable costs are 30 percent? Well, 70 percent of $480 equals $336. You won nine new customers off the ad. Half of them can be projected to stay with you for twenty-four months. Multiply 4.5 times $336 and you get $1,512! A really astute businessperson would adjust the stream of profit contribution over the twenty-four months for the cost of money and maybe get something like $1,400. The ad cost you $200—you just made a sevenfold return on your investment in real terms for the business! Do you think you'll be doing more radio spots? Shouldn't you be doing this regardless of your cash flow or fixed or variable costs this month? Borrow money off your credit card if you have to, but by all means start investing in radio.

It's sad that too many people couldn't understand this simple logic and make these calculations. Most people just look at their annual net profit margin of 10 percent. They would look at their revenues that week from new customers and measure that against the radio ad costs. Here's how the same situation would have worked out. Nine new customers who spend $15 each on their first visit times an average bottom-line net profit margin of 10 percent which comes to $13.50. That $200 radio ad was a poor investment indeed—that will be the last time we'll do that.

Fixed costs, or overhead

Next we come to perhaps the most critical level of costs: fixed costs, or overheads. In most businesses I find consistently that such costs end up being variable. They tend to increase in direct relation to sales, or in the worst cases, faster than sales. That's dangerous, even fatal. Most businesses get into financial problems or find themselves unable to compete because they do not manage their fixed costs. Some even go under.

Variable costs and advertising are more obvious in their impact on the business, but fixed costs are the least managed because no one is really responsible for them.

In most businesses, fixed costs are simply a big lump of costs that must be paid to stay in business. No one understands them fully or is accountable for them—except maybe Scrooge, the controller! People can't understand why the controller is always so uptight. It's because the whole burden of managing as much as 40 to 60 percent of the costs in the business are on Scrooge's shoulders. No one listens because no one cares. Everyone is too busy managing the costs he or she is responsible for.

The cure for the overhead dilemma

There is only one cure. Fixed office and overhead costs must be allocated to individuals, teams, products, and departments that use those services and facilities. Some consultants call this activity-based costing.

This is a splendid application for powerful information technologies as they become more affordable, and it may become the most powerful application for information technologies in the corporation of the future as the emphasis switches beyond reengineering to leveraging the power of small teams and individuals.

The corporation of the future will be able to instantly determine the bottom-line profitability of every order, customer, team, or individual, and every product, division, and department.

It's a relatively simple matter to program variable and fixed costs into software programs that allocate such costs fairly to every business unit in the company. You don't necessarily have to conduct a $100,000 accounting study to do this, although that may be worthwhile for larger companies with more complex cost allocation demands. It is mostly a matter of common sense. It can often be done with simple formulas that will give you results close enough to foster much better decisions. Take every overhead department and allocate it to the users or beneficiaries based on a direct or common-sense understanding of what drives costs in that area. Here are some examples of how to do it:

- **The accounting department** is basically a little factory for processing orders. Allocate costs by the number of orders generated by each sales team or unit, not by dollar sales volume.
- **Rent and utilities** are allocated by the amount of space each unit uses.
- **Top management's costs** may be allocated by the time spent with each unit, thereby rewarding highly self-managed units that can handle their own operations with little intervention.
- **Interest costs** are allocated based on the financial assets or inventories used by each unit.
- **Telephone bills** are directly monitored and allocated to each individual and team.

Fully allocating variable, strategic, and fixed costs to all business units, teams, and individuals forces every team into becoming a business—into making trade-offs in revenues and costs. By doing this you are providing your workers with information they didn't have access to before, data that can greatly improve their ability to make decisions and identify profitable opportunities for the company and their own teams.

That is what the Information Revolution is about: bringing information formerly only available to top-level people down to everyday workers and allowing them to make more and better decisions.

Once you start making such allocations, you will get plenty of feedback from your units. You can use this feedback to further refine cost allocations and make them more fair. Of course, you will get resistance to cost allocations, as people would prefer not to face the realities of what they do. Unfortunately, the tendency across our society today is to dodge responsibility rather than accept greater accountability. You simply have to incorporate it into your company's culture. You attitude should be: "We respect realistic feedback about such accountability measures, but we don't value people who complain and don't want to be accountable and pull their own weight. Never lose sight of what we're doing—we're giving everybody a chance to see where he or she adds value to our company. Those who can increase their value will benefit more than those who do not."

That leads us to our next dilemma.

Allocating revenue

To complete this consideration, we have to go back to revenues. The first task is to allocate costs. But you can't have a P&L without sales! It may be easy to identify a sales number for many front-line sales groups or product units that sell to an outside customer. But what about the internal departments that serve them? How can they become accountable as businesses without a sales number? The truth is that they can't.

The corporation of the future treats all internal units as businesses—as if they were independent outside contractors. This is where there is the greatest danger of inefficiencies and rising overheads that make you uncompetitive. Internal units not only get a full allocation of costs, but are allocated a fair market sales value for the functions or processes they perform. Then they can be accountable to a bottom-line P&L just like everybody else. If you retain your accounting function in-house, then determine through outside quotes or billing rates what an outside firm that does this every day for a living on competitive bids would charge. That becomes the sales or revenue number for your accounting department. Same for MIS, internal production departments, *and even management!*

Some firms see their top management more like venture capitalists: a group of professionals that provides funding, strategic alliances, information systems, and training to a portfolio of business units that have synergy in attacking a customer market. Therefore, the top management group's services from capital to information systems are charged out to all of the units. The top management gets a percent of revenues and an equity stake in the business units it spawns, funds, and supports. It can be fully responsible for its cost allocations and then be measured as a business specifically, not just on the performance of the entire company.

So the creative question here becomes: *What would we pay for this service if we did subcontract it to an outside vendor or a strategic alliance partner?*

Remember, you're supposed to be constantly considering subcontracting as one option in formulating strategic focus. Now you have both a means for evaluating internal competitiveness formally and for keeping internal units as accountable as outside vendors for efficiency and profitability.

You should be able to approximate the revenue or sales value for an in-house department by getting outside quotes from subcontract firms or by applying the billing rates of such firms to your internal services. In many cases, companies will price internal services or components at a discount to market prices both to encourage internal usage and to reflect the fact that marketing costs can be lower for in-house units.

Understanding value added: adjusting internal sales numbers

There is one more fine point you and your company need to understand about accounting to be a real business—then we'll leave the rest to the accountants. The sales numbers of different types of companies or internal units often aren't comparable to each other. In a network of internal minnows, everybody needs to speak the same language and be compared on apples to apples. Let me give you a quick example. In consulting I was often puzzled by the fact that distributors would seem to have typical profit margins of 3 percent, while manufacturing companies would be more like 10 percent. Why? The truth is they are not that different. It all comes back to the principle of strategic focus and value-added factors we have discussed.

The distributor sells a product to a retailer for $100. The sale recorded is $100. But that is not what the distributor is getting paid for—it is not its value added. The distributor only warehouses and ships the product. It bought the product from a manufacturer for perhaps $70. That is the manufacture's value added or contribution to this whole process at a fair market value. If you subtract the $70 from the $100 final price to the customer, you get $30. That is the value added or real sales number for the distributor. Now if you take the original 3 percent profit figure for distributors, or $3, and divide it by the real sales number of $30, you get 10 percent—just as for the typical manufacturer I described earlier. Figure 8-3 demonstrates how a typical company may focus on key value-added processes and then subcontract outside purchases and services to strategic vendors.

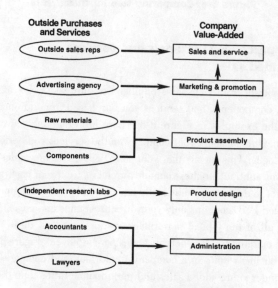

Figure 8–3. Company Value-Added Chain.

This brings us to a simple adjustment that must be made to our P&Ls as business units to give us a better understanding of our business and to allow the company to compare performance ratios across different business units:

	Consumer Division	Industrial Division
Sales	$ 2,045,068	$ 4,346,987
Number of employees	10	32
Sales per employee (Productivity)	$ 204,507	$ 135,843
Sales	$ 2,045,068	$ 4,346,987
Less: outside purchases	$ 896,345	$ 156,895
Value-Added Sales	**$ 1,148,723**	**$ 4,190,092**
VA Sales per Employee (Real Productivity)	**$ 114,872**	**$ 130,940**
Net profits	$ 102,460	$ 420,876
Normal profit margin	5.01%	9.68%
VA Profit Margin	**8.92%**	**10.04%**
Net Profits per Employee	**$ 10,246**	**$ 13,152**

Figure 8–4. Comparing two business units.

Sales – purchased materials and services = value-added sales

Simply subtract from your sales number the purchase price of any raw materials, components, and services you purchased from an outside vendor, like the examples in Figure 8-3. These are functions you chose not to perform. Only measure your company on the services you perform, your strategic focus. This means that your new P&L has a new sales number and that you subtract out these outside purchases from your costs as well—don't forget to do that or you'll really have a screwy P&L statement. Your value-added P&L contains only your direct revenues and costs. You then calculate all of the typical performance ratios based on these numbers, like profit margins and productivity (sales per employee). Figure 8-4 shows how two business units in a company would look and compare very differently under value-added sales and performance ratios than they would under traditional accounting methods.

In this case the consumer division sells the products of the company into retail consumer outlets and uses outside sales reps. It does not produce the products, but purchases them from the company's industrial division, which runs the plant. The industrial division produces its own products and sells them directly through its own sales force to its customers. Therefore, the consumer division is much more focused and has much more in purchased materials and services. In Figure 8-4, the bold numbers represent the value-added numbers. Compare them to the normal numbers. Big difference! Under the value added, the industrial division shows higher profitability and productivity, the reverse of before with the traditional measures.

Summary

To make every unit a real business and to provide information that helps teams make better business decisions, we must fully allocate variable, strategic, and fixed costs to all units. Either each unit must also have a fair-market-value sales number for the functions it performs, comparable to an outside vendor, or internal sales numbers must be adjusted to reflect the real value added of the business unit. There is probably no more important investment your company and your business team or unit can make than to make sure that the basic financial numbers you are getting are right.

This represents the most important information system that companies must invest in, to foster effective schools of minnows within and to increase the accountability of small, diverse teams. This is, likewise, the most important basic business skill that workers at all levels need to master if they are to become businesspeople operating in self-managing environments.

For some people, this may be the most technical and difficult section in this book. But it is important that you learn these basics of "the new accounting" and take them into account when restructuring your company or business unit.

The bottom line is: If internal units can't compete with outside vendors and there isn't a critical strategic reason otherwise, front-line units have the right to go outside the company to get a better deal for their client. Internal functions that can't compete are subcontracted outside. In fact, the best firms will purposefully outsource any internal functions that don't have clear strategic or cost advantages just on the principle of maintaining strategic focus.

The opportunities are endless when every unit is a business

You'll have to make an investment to allocate costs and revenues to all business units—even top management.

If you are an accountant or an accounting consulting firm, maybe you've been wondering how you will survive in this time of automation of clerical tasks. Wonder no more. Just think how many opportunities exist in helping clients restructure their information systems to allocate revenues and costs fairly to units at the micro level!

I'm not going to go into endless financial iterations and examples here. It's important to let you know that every team is going to become increasingly responsible and accountable when measured just as an independent business is. We are all going to be working in small business environments in the future. In the successful companies, everybody is going to have to acquire basic business skills, regardless of his or her particular customer or focus in life. Many managers, professionals, trainers, and consultants are going to be able to profit from transferring the simplest aspects of these measurements and skills to us all. The information age guarantees that! That is the subject for the fourth and all-important principle: real-time information systems. We not only need the right information, we need it quickly and in a timely manner so that we can learn faster and survive in this fast-paced new world.

9

Link Everybody in Real-Time Information Systems

Software is the only true promise we can look to
for the realization of the future's business axiom:
Every customer a market and every
employee a business.

Linking Your Teams and Partners

Creating a school of minnows that is so well linked every individual moves
together instantaneously in a coordinated network: That is the ultimate
principle, Principle 4. What is so amazing about a vast school of minnows
is that they can all turn or change direction in a split second. Does that
sound like the opposite of our largest, most bureaucratic organizations?
You bet! But how do you achieve such a thing in a real-life complex
network of business processes?

Let's retrace our steps for a moment. According to Principle 1, we made your company into a minnow by focusing only on its best skills and capacities. Then we talked about integrating your company into a school of minnows through strategic alliances to best compete and serve customers. According to Principle 2, we set in place the steps for organizing from the bottom up, linking all of the processes in your company with customers and the front-line units that serve them. According to Principle 3, we set out to break all of your company's processes into the smallest, most focused units that can operate like a school of minnows within, with every unit having the accountability and responsiveness of a small entrepreneurial business.

Now in Principle 4 we examine the final and most powerful organizational principle:

Real-time information systems are the lubricants that allow a vast school of business units inside and outside of your company to move together with a minimum of bureaucracy.

Your ultimate goal is to create a free-market environment within your company that can approach the efficiencies of the free markets outside.

Software is the key

Remember that in computer systems, software is the customizing principle. Any standard piece of computer hardware can be customized almost endlessly by simply switching software, which can be done almost instantaneously. Software is the organizing and directing tool. It tells the hardware what to do. You must have information systems that make the most critical strategic and financial and customer information of the company available to anybody who needs to use it. Software lets you report across the entire spectrum, from goals and performance measures to checks and controls to expert systems to customer information.

The meaning of real time

By real time, I mean information becomes available as it happens, or at the least, as soon as possible after software programs analyze it. The term implies immediate accessibility, so everybody in a company can see critical information by accessing a computer or video screen. More people will be making more decisions in the customized economy as we increase the numbers of people who interface with customers and as everyone becomes part of a self-managing business unit. These decision-makers need feedback on their decisions as soon as possible so that they can learn faster and make constant adaptations to meet their customers' needs better than anyone else. They need feedback immediately, not a month and a half from now when the accountants close the books and reconcile everything in accordance with accounting principles.

Real time is one of the essential differences between operators in the future and bureaucrats of old.

In a bureaucracy the top people see the bulk of important information. They decide what people below them see. A bureaucracy is the channel, organized in a specific sequence from top to bottom in a hierarchical, sequential manner—as in left-brain functions.

In a network, the front-line operators see the most and dictate the reactions and decisions in your company, just as your right-brain and sensory systems dictate your actions and reactions in life. This company "brain" is a holistic, simultaneously functioning, random-access organ— a vast network of sensory neurons in parallel-processing mode. Anybody in the company for any reason can know how the customer is feeling and reacting, how the customer is doing, how somebody else is doing, what goals are being met, what costs are, and so on. Anyone can make decisions, make deals or alliances with other units, at any time without coordination from above—at the sensory level, or point of contact with the customer. It is a true free-market system like the New York Stock Exchange and InterNet, which we discussed in Chapter 1. These real-time information networks are capable of extreme degrees of responsiveness and are user- or customer-driven, not management-driven.

Highly evolved right-brain network organizations are a reality today in cases such as these that are pure information systems. Our organizations will evolve increasingly in this direction as computer and software technologies progress. Greater proportions of what all businesses and hardware manufacturers do will become even more information- and service-driven.

Using real-time information systems and pinpoint controls

Ultimately what we need to accomplish in our organizations is a free market network—that school-of-minnows-within concept. This notion allows teams of different size and shape with very different skills, functions, and customers to exchange information, products, and services freely. Teams will collaborate freely to meet customers' needs, just like a network of businesses in an industry or a local region. This can occur without total chaos only if you have real-time information systems that allow easy communications between teams and levels within the company and high levels of accountability for performance. Critical information must be available to chains of business units that require simultaneous access to cooperate and interact effectively and efficiently. Management must know who is performing or not.

Five Simple Rules Driving Real-Time Information Systems

Just the thought of infinite numbers of small business units all making decisions simultaneously seems too chaotic and overwhelming to most left-brain-oriented managers and workers. But remember, such systems already work fluently in many organizations, establishing their own order out of apparent chaos. The truth is, it's not chaos, but just rapidly changing customer needs. Most important, the rules driving network or real-time information systems in businesses are simple. Here they are:

Rule 1: Let software manage the bureaucracy and details

Take bean counters out of the equation. Put your performance targets, goals, controls, checks and balances, and policies into the software and expedite the disappearance of details and bureaucracy.

The more you minimize the need for human intervention and human "report-to-higher" communications outside of business units, the better off you'll be.

We talked about this subject in previous chapters. In practice, controls on discounts are programmed into the front-line portable computers of salespeople. Every business team has its clearly defined customer satisfaction, productivity, and profit goals. As long as these controls and goals are met, a business unit will not be bothered. If there are exceptions, the computer sounds an alert, or, in the case of serious departures, the alarm. That's when human intervention and negotiation are required. But that should be the exception, not the rule. And the teams should be able to react fast enough that the problem has been solved by the time management asks: "What's going on?" Otherwise, all types of left-brain expertise and formulas and models are accessible through the software systems to business teams across the organization. They can access information and expertise, making more decisions without intervention from experts and managers.

More power isn't always better

This is one of the points George Gilder makes in *Microcosm*, in explaining the unprecedented productivity of information technologies. The secret to simplification is in moving everything possible from the "macrocosm" or visible, outer realm of objects into the "microcosm" or invisible, inner realm, where the laws of science are very different. By making transistors and other components smaller, computer architects can achieve leaps in efficiency compared to larger-scale computer methods and designs. Remember, the more small, low-powered, slow-switching-speed transistors that can be miniaturized and fitted on a single semiconductor chip, the more powerful the chip becomes at lower costs. Efficiency simply cannot be accomplished with larger, high-powered, fast-switching-speed transistors because they take too much space and create too much heat and resistance.

Our organizations have tried to increase the power of their slumping organizations by infusing them with more highly powered decision-makers at the top to constantly reorganize and reengineer and orchestrate high financial maneuvers like LBOs and so on. You can see it in the migration of name CEOs from one corporation to another. It simply doesn't work in today's microworld of customized products and services. These people have a tendency to waste their high-power skills in mergers and acquisitions, buyouts, and the latest wave of reengineering, training, and motivation efforts that rarely solve the problems of large companies.

What we have to do is use our highest-powered people to design the logic and to shape the vision for our software and organizational systems. They become more like computer and software designers than big deal-makers, more leaders of people than managers.

In that way we can bring more and more low-powered everyday people into decision-making and pass more of the management, control, information, and complexity into the microcosm of small, self-managed business units.

A company's top managers and professionals must be transferring their expertise and decision-making processes to front- and back-line units. In turn, back-line units transfer as much information and expertise as possible to front-line units. Why? So they can make more of the decisions and handle more of the increasing complexity. This will free up top management to build the organizational network, inspire people throughout the network to its highest vision of strategic focus, and define a mission or cause that makes change worth going through.

Top-level and back-line units should not be working to protect their power bases and their indispensability. These types are missing the paradigm shift in business organizations.

Your first priority should be to find companies that are inclined toward shaping themselves into corporations of the future. Vote with your feet for the right companies, because you're not likely to change upper management's philosophy.

Rule 2: Keep corporate goals and controls simple—*minimize!*

Use summary formats for setting goals and establishing controls. Avoid so many details that people have trouble keeping them in mind. You don't know how many times I have had CEOs say that they have instituted high levels of accountability and controls for small teams and can't understand why they created even more bureaucracy. The first question I ask is: How many goals and measures did you have for each unit? Twenty to thirty or more is typical. My answer: You've just created a new bureaucracy! Every unit should have at most a handful of key goals and performance measures.

It is also a central principle of a network that information is available but people or business units are generally not required to use it. They use it when and how they see fit to achieve their goals and to satisfy their customers—as in the New York Stock Exchange. Company management might insist that teams contribute certain input that other teams need to make decisions. There will be some critical information and systems that you require everybody to use and process, because they are considered so critical to the company's success. McDonald's franchisees do not have the option of experimenting with lower cooking temperatures, dirty bathrooms, or menus.

Minimize rules for how to use information. Minimize reporting requirements, while maximizing the demands for performance and results. Hewlett-Packard is stellar at this art of network management.

An optimal management control system would have one key customer satisfaction measure, one key productivity measure, and a P&L target for each business unit. Units are left alone as long as they meet or exceed these measures. The higher a team's performance, the more capital and assistance it gets from top management and the network.

It's as simple as that.

A model of simplicity

Led by its CEO, T. J. Rodgers, who is also author of *No Excuses Management*, Cypress Semiconductor is a pioneer in real-time information systems. Cypress is a complex, fast-growing specialty semiconductor maker controlled with simple targets and software systems. The central control comes from the requirement that every employee post and update key weekly goals. This is not merely to formalize the important process of goal-setting for individuals. It is more critically the link that glues together a diverse organization.

If a project is off schedule, any team, manager, or individual anywhere can track down precisely who has fallen behind in the relevant goals.

Cypress can get to the heart of a problem quickly with no bureaucracy or formal channels. Anyone anywhere at any time can access the goals of any employee at any level.

Imagine that kind of open access in a traditional company. No wonder Rodgers called his book *No Excuses Management.* Imagine these possibilities that such a system permits:

▪ Flexibility

Forget for a moment about the notion of fixing responsibility. Think of the flexibility this system allows. You might have diverse teams of marketers, production engineers, chip designers, and more, working on many projects in unison but from different locations. If a chip design team falls behind in its goals, the teams in marketing and production will be updated immediately—again, with no formal human communications. Without the need of meetings and rancorous finger-pointing, they can adjust their priorities simply and quickly. Then, too, there's instant feedback. Customer-changed requirements addressed at the front lines will be quickly reflected in the readjusted goals of front-line teams and individuals. These changed requirements are allowed to ripple upward through the company and horizontally. It sounds a lot like the New York Stock Exchange, doesn't it?

▪ Minimal detail

I continually hear complaints from some Big Eight accounting firms about the excessive bureaucracy accruing because clients require accounting consultants to keep detailed records of time and goals for billing and time management. That's the error of too much detail being required at a central level. T. J. Rodgers claims that the typical employee spends only half an hour a week updating goals. As a CEO he spends only an hour a week reviewing key goals and performance measures.

▪ Accountability

Rodgers keeps his system simple, but he is adamant that everyone meet the simple requirements of posting goals and progress. Everyone else at Cypress depends on real-time information. If people fail to update, their software systems will shut down until they do. Obviously, this almost never happens, as workers' software systems are critical to their performance in a high-tech company. But it shows how serious management is about this simple information system.

▪ Continuity and competitiveness

Rodgers says he is most proud of what he calls "Killer Software." Cypress finds every way to incorporate useful expertise, controls, and guidelines learned by management and its best professionals throughout the organization directly into software. This helps teams and managers at the microlevel to make better decisions by avoiding mistakes that have already been made and by applying valuable new lessons learned across the board.

For example, in performance reviews and merit raises, a difficult and much avoided area for most managers, the Killer Software requires managers to rate each employee formally on objective and qualitative factors, which generates a scored rating. A formula or "curve" in the software forces managers to reward their highest-rated performers and to penalize the lowest-rated. The software simply won't approve merit raises and bonuses that don't fit the curve. Yet the system is not so inflexible that one human being, face to face with another, cannot argue exceptions. This is something many managers tend not to do by nature. It is hard to confront low performers. But in a competitive industry where high-performance people are everything, you can lose your sharpshooters in a second to a competitor right down the street. Cypress knows it can't afford to neglect rewarding its top performers.

Similarly, Killer Software forces managers to document the steps the company has found critical to hiring and retaining the best people.

T. J. Rodgers claims, "We never miss budgets," owing to the software. Flexibility and changes en route are allowed, but nobody is excused from meeting agreed-upon goals. Killer Software ensures that the company remains lean and mean.

The importance of this is simple. There is almost no bureaucracy or politics at Cypress Semiconductor. People do complain that there are too many controls and too much performance pressure. There is some evidence that this may be a problem in the company. But there's no denying this:

> **Tight controls and high performance are maintained without middle managers and a bureaucracy of policemen. It's all in the software, it's all automatic, and the exceptions can be handled humanly when they occur.**

Rule 3: Link vertically—put smaller, highly focused process teams into larger business processes

Always strive to share key information among all participants in a larger value-added chain from suppliers to producers to distributors to retailers to end customers. Make sure your software connects business process teams to higher levels of management and broader business processes, including customers and outside suppliers.

We've already discussed breaking every business process into the smallest, most highly focused microprocesses and teams that can produce end products or services for internal or external customers. Here is where we link them back into the larger processes they naturally belong to.

This is critical. In technology terms this is called electronic data interchange or EDI. The aim here is to get all of the players in the value-added chain on the same information and transactions systems so that changes, especially at the customer level, are instantly reflected to everyone in the chain. As in the Cypress example, changes can be updated and dealt with without unnecessary bureaucracy and human communications.

The classic example comes in Peter Senge's book *The Fifth Discipline*. Senge shows how a temporary rise in demand for a product at the retail level can cause exaggerated rises in orders and reorders all the way up the chain to distributors and manufacturers as everyone panics and ups orders in response. If such a rise is temporary, everyone will gear up and produce or stock inventories far in excess of needs, costing everyone in the chain, except the retailer who was the first to see that it was only a temporary surge in demand. The time lags between the value-added stages were the culprit.

However, this won't happen if everyone in that same chain is linked to the same information system as the retail store. When a surge in sales is recorded via bar code information systems, everyone from distributor to manufacturer to all subcontracted components and materials suppliers can see changes as they happen. They can respond appropriately without intercommunication and without acting blindly. Everyone can have "just in time" inventories to minimize costs while maximizing the ability to respond quickly as changes occur at the retail level.

A caution:

Decide what information is critical, or else the expense and complexity can be prohibitive in setting up such systems.

Rule 4: Link horizontally into peer networks

Link peers throughout your companies so that they can network and learn from each other and even spawn new business opportunities. Professionals, technical people, salespeople, managers, production workers, software designers, and so on should have the ability to stay in touch. Make these systems voluntary and allow the users to drive the system, supporting their needs as seems productive for the company. Such a system maximizes peer learning and collaboration.

Use peer networks. Example: You may have broken out your salespeople into very small specialties by customer types or regions all across the world, but they are still salespeople. They still have to sell and close. They still deal largely with the same products or services and similar challenges with customers. You want your salespeople to learn from each other. Establish a bulletin board where they can post their successes and failures every day. Let them ask questions of other salespeople.

This doesn't mean you will sacrifice the face-to-face human dimension. For example, you will still want to bring sales staff together once a month regionally for a party so they can all kibitz and once a year worldwide for a major conference.

Do everything to encourage dialogue between peers
who can learn from each other.

This circuitry of endless possibilities for dialogue is why the network is so powerful. This is why the Internet grows. It is simply a means for peers around the world in all types of arenas to communicate and learn from each other. Create an Internet within your company and hook your people into it.

Here's another principle of a network: When you add somebody to the network, it's not a burden, as in a bureaucracy. It's just one more option to learn, someone else to talk to, another resource for the system. Why? Precisely because people aren't required to use it as a bureaucratic procedure, but only when it's productive.

As in all network information systems, these are generally voluntary systems. People use them however they choose. Some people may go out of their way to track all of the comments Fred makes because they think he is the best salesperson in the company. Other people may ignore Fred because they think he is an old-fashioned blowhard.

Rule 5: Link to experts and expert systems

One of the key challenges in network structures is bridging communications between the two new classes of workers—the *specialized generalists* and the *generalized specialists*.

We'll look at each of these types in detail in Part Four. For now, all you need to know is that in the front lines you'll find multifunctional generalists who specialize in knowing their customers better than anyone else. These are the specialized generalists. In the back lines you find generalized specialists, who provide specialized information or expertise on demand to the front-line teams.

Establish expert linkages to pass information down

Part of the art is linking your information providers to your information users. You want your front-line people to have access to experts. Traditionally, only top management has access to the accounting firm or business strategy consultants, while front-line people don't. In the corporation of the future, front-line people are making most decisions, so they need specialized information and expertise. They need access quickly and easily without having to navigate through a bureaucratic obstacle course. Front-line teams should be able to pick up the phone and call the lawyer and get advice on an urgent matter just as easily as the company president. And, of course, they'll be billed directly for it, but get a company-negotiated discount.

That's another reason why Principle 3, making every unit a business, has to precede real-time information systems. You can't have people accessing and using information and expertise when they aren't trained in making decisions and cost/benefit trade-offs, and certainly if they are not accountable financially for those real costs. Otherwise allowing anyone to call your lawyers indiscriminately could result in a cost explosion.

To make this system work, management must set up flexible relationships with outside experts and consultants. Front-line people often have short time frames for decisions. They aren't typically addressing five-year plans. They deal with daily challenges in serving customers.

You must provide your front-line teams access to consulting services that can take a call and intervene on short notice, providing practical solutions without a lot of jargon. On the front lines, teams can't afford to make an appointment weeks ahead—customers are demanding answers *now*.

Your teams won't give a hoot about the marble offices and Van Gogh paintings, since they will rarely come into the office and probably wouldn't care if they did.

They also need more training and software systems they can use on the spot to relieve them of the time, costs, and complexities of having to deal with too many experts. So you must . . .

Expedite linkages through training and software

Increasingly your back-line generalized specialists will migrate more toward the training and software business instead of direct consulting. Demand that they educate your people to make decisions and inform them so they can handle 80 percent of the simpler, everyday decisions that specialists used to make, as in the care pair in the hospital example. Have them go to the specialists only for the 20 percent of decisions that are too complicated for them to handle.

The best expert system is the software that has the expertise of R&D or accounting or management built in so you can ask questions and get answers. For example, a menu-driven software program should allow a small business owner or unit manager to decide whether it is better to legally structure as a corporation or an S-corporation without taking basic questions to the office of a tax lawyer. A software program would prompt you to ask the proper questions and score your answers. Then it would give you a recommendation and then spit out the legal boilerplate customized with your name and information ready to be signed by you or reviewed by an actual lawyer, if necessary.

Everyone Should Practice the Four Principles

Now that we have outlined the four basic principles of organizational change that will drive the work revolution, you should have a better understanding as a manager or professional, or as a front-line or back-line employee, of how your company is likely to change in the future, how to participate fruitfully in those changes at every level, and how to identify the companies that have the right stuff to invest your time and career efforts in.

In Part Four we will look at how this new concept of organization will change the key skills required of employees at all levels—and they are going to revolve much more around principles, behaviors, and right-brain skills, not the nice, predictable left-brain functional skills we are used to and that are still stressed in our increasingly obsolete educational institutions. Yes, Virginia, being a nurse or an accounts payable clerk is no longer sufficient in the new economy. You have to have a personal mission and embark on a never-ending process of continuous learning to achieve that vision.

PART FOUR

New Skills and Career Paths: How You Fit In

CHAPTER 10

Points out the nine skills you and everybody else need to excel in the new economy.

CHAPTER 11

Examines the role of the *specialized generalist*, the front-line decision-maker and information user.

CHAPTER 12

Describes the role of the *generalized specialist*, the new breed of back-line expert and information provider.

The Nine New Skills Essential to Success in the New Economy

Computers will easily replace people who perform left-brain systematic and clerical functions, but no machine will be able to replace people who fortify the most valuable trait of all, their *humanness*.

You Can Adapt—You *Must* Adapt

Like everybody else involved in a revolution, you can expect to be forced to evaluate your own skills and your adaptability to skills that will be essential to career success in the coming boom—otherwise, you'll follow the dinosaurs to extinction.

This chapter examines the personal career skills and career opportunities that will be most prized by corporations of the future.

Let me kick off this discussion by saying that the most valuable skills will *not* be those of the technical computer jock, despite the obvious fact that such people will continue to do very well in the information age. I won't be discussing the typical functional skills of the past in terms of whether you should study biology, chemistry, accounting, or finance in college—although strong up-and-coming fields of study will include biology, business, medical specialties, and computer sciences. And I won't be talking about jobs in the traditional sense of whether you should decide to be a registered nurse or a lab technician. No, instead, I'll be talking about doing what should come naturally to you: being a human being in service to others and using the innate skills that a computer is decades, if not centuries, away from duplicating.

The essential skills for tomorrow

I've relied heavily on my own experience in organizational change and on the advice of consultants who specialize in reengineering and front-line self-managing teams to order my own thinking on how you can prepare to function in the new economy. Gerry Faust in San Diego is just such a consultant.

To put it as simply as possible, the new, self-managing work environment demands two basic arenas of focus:

People skills

These are the basic human skills required to interface with and create value for the customer. We've already seen how the work revolution is driven by powerful new technologies that give us the ability to delegate most left-brain, rote functions to the computer. That means we will need more and more people who can interact effectively with other humans—customers, team members, and strategic partners closer to the front line. Communication and relational skills will be at a premium.

Problem-solving skills

The second critical arena of broad skills development is good old basic problem-solving and trouble-shooting. At the most fundamental level, this means that people must learn how to think, how to ask questions, how to diagnose problems, and how to spot opportunities for initiating constructive change. Managers need to get good at asking questions and teaching, not

184

giving orders and answers. Everybody must constantly be considering new solutions to solve problems rather than passing difficulties up the chain of command to someone else.

Perhaps the most difficult challenge for you in the new economy will be that you must learn to speak your mind and take responsibility—and not take offense when others speak up.

That means we can't just pigeonhole people into limited functional boxes. More than ever, people need to be given the bigger picture and the broadest company perspective. Managers of the future have to make sure they can impart the mission of the firm, the core competence of the company, the policies for treating customers, the basics of profit and loss, and so on. Everyday workers at all levels are going to have to learn to make the same trade-offs and face the same business issues that managers and professionals have in the past. The changes here are the greatest at the lowest levels of the organization as front-line people become responsible for decisions that used to be made almost exclusively by managers, professionals, and supervisors.

Managers and professionals should be the best people to teach this to front-line teams, because they already know how to deal with such issues and trade-offs—that has been their functional focus in the past. Whenever someone comes to a manager in the old habit of looking for an answer or an order, the response should be to involve the messenger in solving the problem, perhaps by asking, "What do you think we should do about this, and why?"

The new focus for developing your skills

Beware! If you are primarily considering the question of your new career in terms of "Do I want to be a doctor or a lawyer?" or "Should I take biology, or physics, or accounting, or finance?" you've got the wrong focus for this age. You'll need to change your perspective.

You should first consider: What do I really want to do for people? What am I good at? What type of role have I played successfully in the past? Where do I have strong interests to learn and grow? What is it that I do that makes me feel best? What do I do that I enjoy so much that it comes naturally and requires no strain? Do I want to work on my own? In a smaller company? In a large corporation?

In other words, decide what business you want to be in and are most likely to be qualified for. You need a personal vision and mission. This is no more than a personal inventory along the lines of a business defining its strategic focus as we discussed in Chapter 6. Once you identify what you can do better than anyone else, you can narrow your educational search to areas of skill and functional expertise that will be required.

The most important thing you can do in the new economy and job market is to get a clear vision of what you could do to make a difference for a select group of people or businesses or customers.

Vision, rather than functional skill, is the driver of the creative or entrepreneurial process that will increasingly dominate our information-driven, customized, right-brain economy of the future.

The creative process

You will find a direct relationship between the creative process of entrepreneurship and the vision we've already discussed. In *The Path of Least Resistance*, author Robert Fritz describes how the essence of the creative process is driven by a strong, compelling vision of "what could or should be." Such a vision stems from the unique experience and motivations of an individual. So the dynamics of the creative process are driven by the natural tension arising between this vision and the current reality—the aspects of the vision that do not exist and are thus unacceptable in light of your strong vision.

Maintaining this vision is the hard part for most people. For many, it's too easy to compromise or give it up when the struggle and discomforts of the current reality set in. But successful creative people and entrepreneurs are capable of adhering to their vision. Stick-to-it-iveness forces them to continually resolve the tension created by the current reality in favor of the vision. The tension between what is and what could be forces them to deal with the obstacles to their vision.

At its basic level the creative process is simply
the solving of problems that stand in the way
of attaining a dream.

The serendipity of success

Can you plan and project your own creative process? Probably not. As you pursue your vision and reduce obstacles in the resolution of tension, you will discover an unplannable process unfolding. The process is neither linear nor predictable. It will proceed in a way that only later you realize was probably the best path for getting there—better than you could have planned. In other words, the vision drives the process far better than any ten-step process or five-year plan. The vision will bring you to the problems, the skills, the flashes of insight, and the necessary tasks to best accomplish the vision—if you stay in the tension of the current reality. That is only possible if you have and hold to a compelling vision.

It is just such a vision that attracts other people to cooperate with you and follow you. This is similar to a term Adam Smith used to describe free markets. He talked about an "invisible hand" that guides the economy to the most efficient solutions without anyone actually planning and running the overall economy according to a master plan.

The vision game—anybody can play

It's unlikely that we can all become radical entrepreneurs spawning breakthrough innovations with the impact of something like the personal computer. But we will all become more entrepreneurial and more involved in this creative process as more of our left-brain skills are automated and we are moved into individual and small business team work environments. One point I stress to people:

Everyone has a vision of something that could be better or something that should exist—but doesn't. All you need to form such a vision is your unique desires and experiences.

Visions do not just belong to the Steve Jobses and Bill Gateses of the world. It is not the size or the span of the vision but your intensity and passion about it that matter.

You may see that the customers you serve could benefit from an improvement to your company's product that allowed them to better adapt it to their needs. You could see that the layout of the machinery in your workshop could be changed to reduce time and costs substantially. You could see that kids prone to crime in your neighborhood could gain some self-esteem if you formed a group to show them some respect and give them training on weekends to improve their skills. Yes, these everyday aims involve vision, dealing with realities, and persistence to accomplish them—every bit as much as the achievements of Jobs and Gates.

And no, these everyday things will never materialize without the passion necessary to overcome obstacles of all sizes—just as Apple and Microsoft would never have materialized without passion.

Without passion your vision amounts to no more than idle daydreams.

How you can specialize in solutions

Tomorrow's work environment demands that we build a new set of skills on top of our older set. We must acquire skills that serve the creative process, skills that amplify our human, relational, sensory, and problem-solving capacities. We will continue to need formal training in countless areas of specialized functional skills like nursing, bookkeeping, draftsmanship, carpentry, contract law, software programming, and good old reading, writing, and arithmetic. But that kind of functional specialization and left-brain learning was the primary focus of specialization of labor in the old economy. Now it is becoming secondary to right-brain skills and a focus on the customer and results—a *solutions specialization*. The question is, how do you get there from here?

Here are some steps you can take to acquire the skills you need to achieve an orientation toward a solutions specialization:

Begin by acquiring information—pump up on knowledge

Try to learn a customer's particular needs better than anyone else in the field. Develop your understanding of a product or technology application better than anyone else in your industry. Examine an important cause for change in more depth than anyone else in the world. All types of specialty magazines, books, newsletters, and associations will help you acquire information. Accumulate expertise by experimenting in volunteer or part-time work experiences. Attend seminars related to your area of interest or by building on work experiences with further research. Talk with experienced people in the field. Model the behavior of people who have succeeded. These activities will help you decide what business you are in at a personal level and how to proceed.

Look at this issue in terms of a hypothetical example. Assume you are already trained as a nurse. You foresee an opportunity to change your role to become a consultant to other nurses as the new economy brings on the work revolution. You strongly believe you can develop a program to help others expand their skills and responsibilities so they can take on more of the functions of physicians and increase their earnings and job satisfaction. You might even want to help other nurses start their own outpatient sub-contract businesses or home health care services. You know from your own experience at work that nurses could do more for their patients if only the education they received in nursing school had prepared them to expand their roles.

You start by identifying other organizations that have developed to educate or assist nurses in their careers. Determine why they failed or succeeded. Find out how they built their organizations and marketed themselves to nurses. Examine your educational and work experiences to identify additional functional skills you would have needed beyond normal nursing courses. Then commit yourself to learn more about the education and functions of doctors. Here you're trying to ascertain which of their functions nurses could learn and take on effectively—without attending a lengthy and expensive medical school course. You find cases in the United States and around the world where nurses have demonstrated they can take over a doctor's functions cost-effectively. Of course, you would need to understand more about the "softer" skills of how to tend patients so as to make them feel good about your services. So you might attend some practice management seminars in customer service. Then you will likely need some courses in marketing if you are going to have some feel for how you could promote this new idea to nurses.

Then you would have to consider what other skills you'd require to pull off a consulting business. You'd have to decide whether to master them yourself or hire experts. You might consult finance and accounting experts, a curriculum expert, and a management expert. You'd decide whether to hire people full-time or just consult with them occasionally. In other words, you begin to think like an entrepreneurial businessperson. You are designing a front-line team to solve a specialized customer need and determining the backup expertise and resources this team will require. Once you've educated yourself you'd be ready to . . .

Exploit the information you gain—take action!

You could either consider these possibilities in one of three ways, exploiting your knowledge to:

- **Start an entrepreneurial venture** for yourself. Set up a training program and counseling service for nurses that you run as a business, starting small and lean at first and then building up into a certified curriculum over time.
- **Suggest a new market opportunity** an educational institution might use to expand its established, certified curriculum. You, of course, would demonstrate how you could help the school launch and manage its new programs.
- **Develop a reengineering strategy** for your present employer or another medical institution. Show the organization how to create better value for its patients through an in-house training program that allows it to delegate expensive specialist medical functions to front-line nurses and other care providers.

What are you doing if you're the nurse in this example? You're using information to help you design new products and services, organizing human and informational systems to make your program work, and, of course, debugging those systems. You're becoming an entrepreneur, using skills as if you were a creative software designer.

We'll all have opportunities to become "career fashion designers" in an increasingly entrepreneurial world. Those with customer contacts on the front lines

will be known as information users. Those on the back lines with expertise to serve them will be known as information providers.

We'll look at information users and information providers in the next two chapters. For now, let's identify and discuss skills that will be required in both arenas.

Nine Behavioral Skills You Must Cultivate in the New Economy

In my experience, people skills and problem-solving skills can be divided into nine more specific behavioral skills for succeeding in the workplace. Because these skills originate in the right side of the brain, they are more like behaviors than functional skills as we normally think of them. Nothing wrong with that. The smartest managers I know hire their people based on behaviors that have proved to be effective in their best employees in the past, not as much on functional skills or résumé check-offs. In Stephen Covey's best-seller *The Seven Habits of Highly Effective People*, note that he uses the word *habits*, not skills, which is more behavioral in nature. *Fortune* magazine described the new worker in terms of the behavioral traits required: "empathetic, flexible, informed, articulate, inventive, and able to work with minimal levels of supervision." For you to avoid job shock in the world of tomorrow, you will need:

Problem-solving skills
    1. Become results-oriented.
    2. Be proactive.
    3. Think creatively.

People skills
    4. Know yourself.
    5. Become sensitive to the needs of others.
    6. Increase your tolerance level.

Integrative skills
    7. Expand your ability to communicate.

8. Sharpen your business skills.
9. Get a grasp on information technologies.

Let's examine each of these skills in some detail starting with:

Problem-Solving Skills

1. Become results-oriented

On a personal level this ties in neatly with the idea of organizations developing a strategic focus on things that matter most to customers and doing only what they are best at. The new workplace is fundamentally concerned with creating real value and organizing around front-line results. It's not about being paid for activities that don't make a difference.

The orientation here is to the customer and to running a successful business process, not toward the segmented functions and bureaucratic fiefdoms that grow out of hierarchies. You can't define this skill in functional terms. It is a much broader requirement. You must be willing to do whatever it takes to make something happen for the customer, to create the desired result.

That may mean stepping beyond your normal boundaries, or breaking a few rules, learning something new—perhaps even becoming an expert at it. It means that you "live for the customer," as Gerry Faust says. When you master this behavior, there's no question that you value the quality of your results and integrity of your craft above all else.

Remember the Customers "R" Us account specialists in Part Two? They were home office staffers serving field sales reps. They demonstrated this quality when they went down to shipping to personally get a product out the door. The customer had already suffered a delay from an internal mistake. The account specialists knew they shouldn't force a customer to wait even one extra day until shipping department personnel could get around to the extra requirement.

That is an everyday example of being results-oriented. What's remarkable about it is that it's such a simple thing when your credo is: *Get the job done.* Simple but important—and in the functionally specialized bureaucracy, so seldom done because the lament of the bureaucrat has become a different credo: *It's not my job!*

This skill also has its rational aspects. A results orientation means that you are willing to be measured on the results you create for your customers. You therefore expect to be rewarded accordingly. Nobody expects bureaucratic entitlements for just being a loyal employee who has put in time. Success is defined not just in your eyes but in the eyes of the customer.

When you master this skill, you define success in terms of your ability to make your customers happy. In fact, you define your own happiness in terms of making customers happy.

2. Be proactive

For Stephen Covey, this is the first of his *Seven Habits of Highly Effective People*. In my own scheme this is a skill that is every bit as valuable as the first. But it must necessarily follow a results-oriented focus on the customer. You must develop a desire to take responsibility and make decisions. You must become a participant in the action, making things happen instead of watching others as a spectator. If you don't understand this one, just go to a Tony Robbins seminar and watch the audience. They may look at first like a bunch of crazy, hyped-up people, but what is really going on is that people are learning tools for changing their lives, learning to step out of their normal habits of thinking instead of merely reacting. They are identifying the obstacles to changes and obliterating them. They are learning the creative process of harnessing a strong vision and owning it. Most of all, they are learning not to blame others for the failure to achieve their goals and dreams.

People who have "a bias for action," as Tom Peters puts it, learn more and achieve more. This bias differentiates the true performers from the cool analysts and bureaucrats who procrastinate forever while waiting for the perfect shot.

Proactivity implies adaptability and a willingness to do three things:

- To accept a certain level of risk
- To take an action
- To observe the response, to react, and to change as necessary

193

A new twist on the meaning of *Ready . . . fire . . . aim*

Ready, fire, aim is anathema in the realm of functional hierarchy. To functional specialists it means going off half-cocked without the benefit of vast amounts of data, laborious staff work, and detailed projections about the prospects for success, including a step-by-step plan for implementation, timetable and all.

In the economy of the future, *Ready, fire, aim* will dominate and take on a very different connotation: Move fast, acting on the best information you have, taking manageable risks to achieve positive results on an ever-changing landscape, and learning from your mistakes as you go along.

Functional specialists prefer to get ready and aim ever more precisely, even if it means never firing, which can be risky. You will learn a lot faster if you start firing and reaiming based on where your bullets hit rather than waiting forever for the perfect shot. In tomorrow's economy a product may be obsolete by time you take that perfect shot.

To make anything happen you simply have to be willing to change, grow, and learn. And that can often be painful. Know what you want. Consider the best strategy for achieving it. Follow that strategy. Change that strategy when it doesn't work. Tony Robbins likes to say, "It is in your moments of decision that you change your destiny." Real decisions demand clear action and leave no alternatives. Learn to make and commit to the decisions that will effect your customer and your career.

I like one of Gerry Faust's most important principles: Practice solving problems. Don't pass problems up to supervisors, sideways to peers and team members, or downward to others. Cultivate the people whom you work with and supervise to do the same.

Solve problems as they occur—don't pass the buck or avoid them.

Reevaluate your natural inclination to delegate everything possible. Delegation simply is not all it's cracked up to be. Sure, it's a valuable technique for focusing your best talents and getting others invested in your results, but it can also add time and complexity to problem-solving. Over time, delegation has mutated into the watchword of the bureaucracy, which expends enormous efforts defining lines of delegation and standard policies and procedures. In the time it takes to delegate some tasks, you could do them yourself and be on to the next problem. Within the teams of the corporation of the future, we're sure to see less delegation and more of an effort to take responsibility for one's own business and the customer's needs. That's because we're going to see the very nature of decision-making diffused. We'll have more teams of decision-makers.

More people will be making decisions, thus there'll be less occasion and even less need to delegate.

Even if you have to go outside your team to solve problems, hold on to the responsibility until your customer's problem is solved.

Being proactive hits at one of the key themes in this book: restoring responsibility, accountability, and initiative to the individual and small team.

3. Think creatively

The world is moving at too fast a pace to rely entirely on left-brain, linear solutions to problems. To keep up with the pace of the new economy you are going to have to develop your more creative, right-brain faculties.

Thinking creatively requires you to adopt some habits you may not be accustomed to. To begin with, you must:

- **Look at problems from multiple, differing—even opposite—points of view.** Take into account the views of other team members, customers, suppliers, and outside experts wherever possible. These will help you to gain a better-rounded picture before coming to conclusions. Allow yourself to go to extremes and argue both sides of an issue. This also allows you to gain a broader perspective and to see the most potential options, instead of just one. For example, you are confronting a problem at work and you say, just for grins: "We've always done things this way—what if we did them the opposite way? How would that create new problems? And what benefits would come from doing things this way?" Ask your suppliers or customers if any of those new benefits would be more valuable to them, and if solving any of these new problems would be easier. Of course, you don't want to fall into the trap of getting ready and aiming forever, never firing. You can gather good information quickly and maintain that bias for action throughout this process.

- **Consider sweeping, radical solutions** rather than just incremental evolution and modification. This is a time of paradigm shifts, so always ask, "Is it possible to effect a revolution here instead of just an incremental improvement? Could we start from scratch and come up with an entirely different approach that would work much better?" Don't worry about costs and restrictions at first, just allow yourself to fully consider more creative approaches. Don't be too quick to dismiss the more radical ideas that come from some of the "crazy" people in your work environment. It is precisely the offbeat types who frequently come up with breakthrough solutions. They also come up with the most harebrained approaches. Remember that when dealing with this mentality, a little eccentricity goes with the territory.

- **Think in terms of potential new solutions and opportunities,** not just about present problems and how to fix them. Most people, especially in America, are into searching out problems and obstacles and then eliminating them. True, that can be useful. But often a better approach is to visualize new solutions and opportunities first. Is there a better outcome we could create for the customer that would transcend the present problem? Is there a new way to do this that is inherently better? Then you can focus on the problems such new solutions create. Here you are willing to create new problems in return for new solutions—the mode of the entrepreneur.

- **Learn from solutions in different areas of expertise** and not just your own arena. Often when it is hard to come up with new approaches to a problem, creative people look outside of their own fields of expertise to see where a similar problem may have already been solved in another discipline. Insights from another field may help you in solving a problem in your own. You might consider how best to organize your work team and be reading an article on how chimpanzees order themselves for picking and shelling nuts and see

196

how you could incorporate aspects of those principles into your work team.

- **Learn to rely more on your intuitions and perceptions** to make decisions even when you don't have all the facts and expertise necessary to solve the problem. Why? A late solution that is near perfect may be no solution at all in the new economy. Timing and speed are everything. To get comfortable with this it is best to simply start observing the everyday little flashes of intuition you have about things, whether they tend to be right or not. Don't act on them at first—just observe and notice how you then tend to override them with rational left-brain thoughts. As you start to see areas where your intuitions are consistently right, like whether certain people can be trusted in business dealings, then start acting on them. The more you practice, the more your intuitions will be refined and the better you will get at cutting out left-brain blocks to these intuitions.

- **Systematize and automate non-right-brain processes.** Our right-brain intuitive faculties are often superior to left-brain analysis. But don't get me wrong—I'm not suggesting you should abandon left-brain processes. Anytime you can reduce a problem to linear analysis that leads to quick, reliable, and consistent results, do it. Then systematize it and automate it so that it doesn't clog your more creative functions. In other words, whenever possible, let one of those powerful, wonderful computers do the job. But don't forget—more often than not, problems in the new economy will be too complex, too fast-moving, or too humanly complex to permit developing a systematic answer.

- **Get comfortable in being wrong.** When you make intuitive judgments you will often be right in your response, but you will also sometimes be wrong. Being wrong will require some getting used to. You'll have to move quickly to reexamine your assumptions, perceptions, and results. Then you have to act creatively and quickly to make the proper changes. The point is, right or wrong, to keep learning and developing your intuitive capacities.

Creative skills are just like your body's muscles— the more you exercise creativity, the more creative you become.

Now let's go on to the second set of skills essential in the corporation of the future.

People Skills

4. Know yourself

To excel in the coming economy, you must capitalize on knowledge of your strengths and weaknesses, your internal values and beliefs that drive your most important decisions—your unconscious ones. Most people are not aware that most of their decisions and actions are generated unconsciously and subconsciously at a deeper emotional level. It's only later that we rationalize these decisions with our more conscious, left-brain faculties and then argue we did something for that rational reason.

In coming to know yourself, remember that we are not primarily rational beings. Just ask any savvy advertising executive who makes a living by understanding how we respond to communications about a product and make decisions to buy it or not. In advertising it's an adage that people make decisions emotionally and then build the rationale to justify those decisions. We have to become aware of our unconscious presumptions about life in order to gain control over our lives and decisions. Most of these presumptions were established in childhood to protect us from fears. Trouble arises when we continue to shield ourselves into adulthood, creating blind spots to reality.

Acquiring self-knowledge is much more difficult to do than to say, because most of us have been practicing just the opposite skill for so long.

As youngsters we develop simple presumptions about life, people, and ourselves. We may have felt we didn't get enough attention at a critical time and assumed, "People don't really care about me—they won't help me out when I really need it." These assumptions become unconscious filters that determine how we see the world and deal with problems. With such a predisposition, you may go through the rest of your life not even asking other people to help you when you need it. You're probably not

198

even aware of what you are doing, let alone that such an attitude stems from when you were two years old. Your presumption therefore becomes a self-fulfilling prophecy. Your only observation is that you don't ever seem to get help when you need it!

There's nothing wrong with this natural process. Simplifying the complexities of life helps youngsters deal with reality by avoiding the most unpleasant truths when they aren't equipped to deal with them. Later in life, however, if these filters are left in place, they can be damaging. They can short-circuit options that could help us solve problems better or maneuver more creatively. They also block our ability to learn in more effective ways. In other words, we have to grow up and take greater responsibility for our fears, presumptions, values, and beliefs as we age or we can't become fully effective adults who can shape our own lives. We remain essentially childlike, letting others determine our destiny. Most of us are largely unaware of these unconscious impediments to our ability to determine our lives and achieve our goals.

As we age chronologically we need to mature in the art of self-observation.

The new workplace will demand that we all acquaint ourselves with self-help and self-understanding practices, both as leaders and as individual team members. I know of many seminars and methods for learning about yourself, not to mention personality tests of all types. Anyone who has practiced the art of self-knowledge or self-observation will testify to the power it has to change things and create results by starting with the person in the mirror.

Until you have time to enroll in a seminar, here are a couple things you can do to improve your self-knowledge.

Evaluate your assumptions and behaviors

This is a simple self-inventory. Ask yourself questions like: What are my underlying assumptions about life and business, especially at the unconscious level? How do others see my behaviors based on those assumptions? What consistent actions and results do I obtain? What assumptions and beliefs might be driving those results?

You may think you are very sensitive to customers' or team members' needs. However, others might think you are constantly ignoring important needs. You may not even be paying attention to feedback you've been getting from coworkers and customers who do not feel you are sensitive because you unconsciously block out these inputs. Listen to and solicit objective feedback from customers and team members. Learn to observe if people are responding to you or not. If most people's feedback and behavior toward you suggest that you are not being sensitive, then assume you are not sensitive, and probe for reasons that may be causing you to be insensitive.

Maybe it is time for some blind self-observation about a quality that is becoming more indispensable all the time. Maybe you should reverse field altogether and assume that you are totally insensitive and examine yourself from that point of view.

Ask yourself: What unconscious presumption or blind spot is keeping me from being sensitive? What do I gain from this presumption or blind spot? Is it worth it, considering the adverse effects it is having on my relations with customers or team members? If not, then you may need to work on further observing and retraining yourself out of this presumption or behavior, perhaps with the help of your team members, until you demonstrate a new behavior that is felt to be to the benefit of your customers and team members.

Maintain your grasp of reality

The art of entrepreneurship and achievement requires you to maintain a tension between reality and your vision. Dealing with reality keeps you from flying off into fantasy land while tending to move you toward a resolution in favor of your vision. This is a highly creative process, as opposed to the left-brain process of setting goals and solving problems in a linear sequence. A true vision simply cannot be mapped out in a linear sequence, as a general rule. It is more likely to be realized by going with the flow, adapting to changing situations brought on by heavy doses of reality and occasional flashes of insight. It is necessarily more entrepreneurial, thus flexible and fast-moving. This is why vision and leadership are so valued in today's information-based economy, in contrast to the emphasis on management and analytical skills in the old economy.

Maintaining your vision while staying in touch with the realities it brings you in contact with will force you to develop your capacities of self-observation. The process will tend to bring you the same problem over and over until you see that you are the cause of problems rather than some outside force. This is one of the greatest rewards of the creative process. It forces you to mature in the art of self-observation as your vision is driven by your beliefs and values and depends entirely on you for its achievement. It's a process that won't allow you to go for long assuming that you can blame the world or others for your situation.

5. Become sensitive to the needs of others

Sensitivity may be the key word in identifying critical people skills. The new breed of worker must be able to understand the needs and perspectives of customers and coworkers. This is the reverse of self-knowledge. We could call it "other-knowledge." We simply cannot meet the needs of individual customers or work closely in teams and with networks of partners of all types if we don't connect with the needs and personalities of others to learn how they process information. We must become capable of resolving the natural disputes that will arise among coworkers and customers in more intimate environments.

My thinking on the workplace of the future is exactly the opposite of the conventional wisdom.

I don't foresee a time when the workplace will be dominated by robots, computers, and highly technical people like computer programmers. A few good programmers and experts can create effective software that allows everyday people—people with well-developed acumen for other people—to better serve the human needs of customers.

I envision a future where computers and robots will become all but invisible. Our bureaucracies and paperwork are literally going to disappear into the software while computers become smaller, less visible, and more friendly to people. Most people don't realize today that the great majority of microcomputers are already invisible, imbedded inside products you already use—your car, your video recorder, and other items.

I'm not denying that there will be robots. In fact, they will proliferate like computers. But they will also become increasingly smaller and invisible, doing the dirty work behind the scenes or late at night. The point:

Our work environments will only become more human and dominated by human interaction. Therefore, we are going to have to invest more time in understanding the needs and behavior of the customers we serve and the people we work with. This means observing how they are different, and how they learn and process information. It means finding out what is important to them and what unconscious assumptions drive them. It may often mean sitting down and taking personality tests with coworkers or having discussions in your work group moderated by a trained counselor.

In a magazine company I once managed, the editorial department staff took a basic personality test that identified things like key driving motivations, behaviors, strengths, weaknesses, and factors that would provoke stress. Afterward individuals first reviewed their own scores. Later everyone met and shared test results.

One remarkable case of self- and other-observation occurred during the group session. The newest member of our team seemed especially bright and eager to work. She was highly regarded by everyone around her—that's why people were so shocked at her test results. Her scores identified her as someone with a low sense of self-esteem working under high levels of stress. She felt she'd made hardly any contribution to the group. Her team members brought a very different picture to her attention, saying how they really felt the opposite of her self-appraisal. They truly wanted to know why she felt so inferior. She simply did not feel qualified for her job and thought she wasn't contributing that much.

Her unconscious predisposition to assume that she wasn't competent had nothing to do with the reality that she was well respected and liked by her coworkers. And of course, her feelings of inferiority were impossible to maintain in the midst of across-the-board praise from the team. She was forced to confront her unconscious presumption and was quite taken aback by the team's praise of her work. I asked her to take the test again the following week. She scored much more positively, indicating her presumption of herself had been changed. But so had the team's. We now knew more about how she saw herself and how we had to interact with her to take into account that presumption and help counter it.

Personality over skills?

From the broadest perspective of working in a more humanized workplace you could say that a new dimension is emerging. As Gerry Faust says:

> **"Having a personality is becoming fashionable again in the workplace."**

Southwest Airlines, the most profitable major airline by far, ranks personality as the most important trait it looks for in hiring new employees.

You can expect to see a much greater emphasis on personalizing and humanizing everything you do in the new economy, in which customization to individual needs will be the biggest single consumer trend. Computers can give you useful information or can run systems to help you accomplish this, but only human beings can bring the human dimension to business and work.

The human dimension

Bringing that human touch to business will occur in two ways:

- **Human beings design systems**—software, management, and hardware—to help deliver personalized service to customers.
- **Human beings deliver personalized service,** often with the aid of such information systems.

An understanding of human needs begins with the fundamental perception that every individual is different. Again, this is essentially a corollary of Skill 4—*Know yourself.* Self-knowledge necessarily comes first, because you can't hope to have knowledge of how other people's conscious and unconscious presumptions affect their needs and behaviors if you don't understand your own. Skill 5 requires us to study the way other humans operate so we can be sensitive toward them.

> **What people say they want can be quite different from their actual needs and from what their behavior indicates.**

Remember, everyone has assumptions resulting from childhood, ethnic background, gender, and so on—the things that create filters and different perspectives. That's why everyone sees things differently and values different things. To make it even more complicated, most people are not even conscious of what they really want or value.

The good news is that we can compensate for each other when we work together. What may appear to be either complex or emotionally charged to one team member or customer can be very simple and intuitively obvious to you (dealing with a customer) or to fellow team members (dealing with you). That is the magic of intuition, a capacity extremely well developed in people but only advanced to the most primitive stages in computers.

I know you have seen time and again how certain people in your circles can quickly recognize the unconscious assumptions and needs that drive someone else's actions. For every person with a blind spot resulting from excessive intimacy with a situation, two or three others can analyze a situation more clearly. They can even point out evasive strategies of the individual with the blind spots.

In the future, we are all going to have to learn to listen more and become sensitive to the needs and differences of others—the customers you serve, the team members you work with, and other experts and resources inside and outside of your organization. Creating the personal touch in business interactions may be the most important value creation process of all.

6. Increase your tolerance level

An obvious extension of the principle of sensitivity is tolerance, which is growing in importance in today's global economy. With the world shrinking day by day via sophisticated communications technologies, we are all going to be working with and serving people from increasingly diverse backgrounds and mind sets. That means we all have to learn the art of tolerance—cross-cultural as well as cross-personality.

Tolerance begins with accepting this simple reality:
There is no one best way to be or to do something.

Differing cultures and differing experiences cause people to approach problems and work relationships differently. We all have to learn to respect those differences. There is a practical reason for this that I have learned thoroughly: You can seldom change someone's basic character and values.

In fact, such changes only tend to occur in times of extreme personal crisis—a time of personal failure or self-observation so great as to force someone to examine and change a fundamental belief, value, or presumption. Therefore, unless someone is ready for it, forcing people into a mold or behavior that is uncomfortable to them just isn't fruitful. Trust me on this one, as I've had about as intense a background in change management as you get. We must allow people to do things their way, to tolerate a diversity of approaches, and let the *results* be the judge, not the method. Tolerance is a necessary ingredient for getting along in a highly individualized age and world marketplace. Tolerance also opens the doors to learning from others and their different values and approaches. It doesn't mean you have to change your values or ways of doing things, except where you find it fruitful for your own strategies and goals.

Tolerance versus equality

I don't think most people actually accept true tolerance as a requisite in today's world. The popular notion is that people are basically equal and that to make distinctions between different races, genders, and ethnic groups leads to the evil we call discrimination. My own feeling is that such an idea of equality is actually the enemy of tolerance and explains why we have seen so little real progress emerge from thirty years of the civil rights movement in this country. A true understanding of the high level of diversity in personalities and ethnic and cultural backgrounds demands the opposite.

We need to become better at discriminating in the original sense of the word—observing and learning the real differences between various personality, race, ethnic, and gender types. What's wrong with differences? What is important is understanding those differences in a way that allows us to communicate better and to work together effectively without requiring that we change each other's most prized values, beliefs, and cultures. Such an understanding takes the ability to stand outside our own values and beliefs and to understand those of others without judging them or reacting to them. This is obviously not easy for most people. Our unconscious beliefs and values emerge out of fears, and we seem like bigger bigots than we imagined we could be. It is a natural survival process to fear and be suspicious of people who appear to be different for any reason. What is unfamiliar is scary for most of us. Only by becoming more familiar through human interaction and an open examination of other cultures and personality types can we get past fear. Other approaches that do no more than allow us to feel tolerant are just cop-outs.

The last thing we need is the homogenizing of the world into one bland culture that loses the very richness and innovation that stems from diversity.

Individualists versus team players

Another great misconception I hear all the time suggests that teamwork is the only proper mode for business organization for competing in the new economy, especially with the Japanese. This line of thinking says that Americans are basically cowboys—individualists who don't work well in teams. I say *Hooey!*

Don't buy any argument that diminishes the individualist, entrepreneurial nature of Americans or workers anywhere. It is our greatest strength in this new economy.

The new breed of cross-functional, self-managing teams I portray in this book has nothing to do with putting together a bunch of conformist wimps that go along with the team at all costs and sacrifice their personality for the good of the whole. It has everything to do with combining very different skills and personalities—hence the need for sensitivity and tolerance.

Think of this in terms of a top-notch basketball team. Imagine a team with talented, individualistic players, each of which has his or her own special skills to add to the mix. Each person also understands the special contributions of everyone else on the team and knows how to function to create a unit superior to any of its individual members. We need strong, highly specialized, individualistic workers who can understand and communicate with different team members and who can tolerate conflict and resolve disputes when necessary. Most important, we need teams and companies with individuals from different cultures to successfully attack the customized world marketplace consisting of many different cultures.

Resolving disputes

This brings us to one of the most critical skills in the new world of self-managing teams. You simply cannot operate in the me-versus-you mode. As Stephen Covey says, you must develop a win-win disposition. Whenever someone on your team or a customer or a supplier appears to be acting irrationally or behaving contrary to your point of view, do not automatically assume that that person is stupid, is out to get you, or is violating an agreement between you. Instead think: Could there be a misunderstanding here? Could this person have misread something I said or see our agreement differently? Is this person simply approaching things from a different direction that makes it appear that he or she has a different intention from mine? Or am I misreading something or making an assumption based on my prejudices and preferences that may not even exist here?

In other words, resort to self- and other-observation, from a disposition of tolerance. Then from that point of view seek to resolve the apparent conflict in a win-win manner. Simply approach the other team member and say that his or her behavior seems to be in conflict with your understanding of what is supposed to happen. Then listen to the other person's assumptions and rationale before making judgments. You may have to probe to see if the person misunderstood something that you said or if you miscommunicated something or didn't make something as clear as you could have. The point: Always first assume that disputes and conflicts are arising out of differences in perspective and communication and how people process information and not out of bad intentions or malice. Always try to clear up those perspectives and come to a common understanding.

Diversity adds power

Diversity is strength, especially in today's world economy of customized products and services in a highly individualistic age with powerful information technologies affording us the ability to deal with diversity. Pretending that people are all alike and equal is a cop-out for not dealing with one of the most important issues today in the marketplace and the workplace. One of the greatest single issues is that of gender—men and women. I would like to see the person who could stand up and convincingly argue that men and women are not different. I have never seen two more opposite human systems than men and women. How they perceive things, react to things, process information, relate to people, and yes, down to very basic biology—these are different animals. The most intelligent books and training programs I have seen educate men and women with these differences in mind so they can better communicate and interact, not require each other to change and lose their gender identity or to become alike within their gender. Far better we stop communicating to members of the opposite sex as if they were exactly like us. That is the key to good relations both in the bedroom and in the workplace.

Here are two examples of generalizations put to good use—remember, a generalization doesn't apply equally to every individual in a group:

- **As a rule, women have an easier time with the new roles** in a self-managing workplace that favors coaching and facilitating. Many more men feel comfortable with traditional command and control environments. That means women can be a real asset in situations that require coaches and facilitators. Men may still be stronger in the command and control functions that survive in the corporation of the future.

- **Members of Latin and Asian cultures** are much more concerned with getting to know a person before even considering doing business. It's suicide to ignore this cultural tendency in dealing with Latin and Asian individuals and cultures. Who is to say that establishing a relationship personally before getting into a deal is less effective than the American approach of going straight for the deal and getting to know each other later? In fact, most of the world favors the relationship-first principle.

By studying other cultures we can learn new approaches that we may find more suitable. Men who are trying to become better at being coaches and facilitators may do well to study the habits of women in these roles.

The point is: Take the time to learn differences between people as individuals and between races, genders, cultural backgrounds, and so on. Knowing how people are different, how they process information and experience, and how they learn and communicate is vital to working successfully with or serving people who are different from you. And, face it, everyone *is* different to some degree.

Integrative Basic Skills
in the Coming Work Revolution

7. Expand your ability to communicate

We've just discussed one of the key principles of communications: making sure others understand what you think you said or agreed upon. That is a constant process in life, because we all perceive reality differently depending on our own beliefs, values, and experiences. Some futurists have called this the communications age rather than the information age. I agree that we are all going to have to get better at communicating, building on previous principles of sensitivity, tolerance, and self-knowledge. These principles help people communicate better.

Communicating well in the past meant mastering basic writing and speaking skills. Of course, these are still important. But tomorrow's requirements go way beyond that.

> **H**ow artfully you send your message will be
> dependent on your ability to read how it was received,
> understood, and acted upon.

What is most important in the organization of the future is to be able to communicate in ways that are effective with your customers, co-workers, vendors, allies, back-line staff, and so on.

Key concerns in sending your messages

- **Adopt a straightforward and trustworthy approach.** The more sensitive and individualistic people become, the less they will accept messages that are slick and manipulative.
- **Avoid professional jargon** that doesn't make sense to people outside your field or culture.
- **Learn to use the entire range of communications capacities,** including body language, facial expressions, emotions, and gestures. Good communication means learning to read those qualities in

209

others. Some people are more verbal, others more visual, others more sensory and experimental. Some are more left-brain-oriented, some more right-brain-oriented. Some people learn to change fast, some slowly—and by the way, that doesn't mean that slow is not as effective. Slower people often learn much more thoroughly.

- **Use more graphic symbols, pictures, and images,** not just words. This is made increasingly possible by new technologies that even allow us to edit our own video images at home. We say a picture is worth a thousand words. Why? Because of the superior processing capacity of our right brains and sensory systems that allows most people to learn better through visual means.

- **Use your best intuition.** Most of all, communicating will come to mean mastering the more right-brain elements of communication and taking advantage of the supercomputer powers of human perception that are far from being mastered by computers. Human beings learn and grow primarily through associative learning. How our educational institutions and people have taught us to learn is not how we best learn and communicate. People learn better by doing, not analyzing or reading instructions. People learn by associating new ideas or images with things that they are already familiar with. The people who unlock and master those associations will have the head start into the future.

Pleasure versus pain

Tony Robbins emphasizes in his seminars that the key driving factor in our lives is what we associate with pain and pleasure. There's no rocket science to this—people move toward pleasure and avoid pain. Of the two, do you know which is most influential? In fact, most people will go to much greater lengths to avoid pain than to seek pleasure. Like most elementary principles, it is a powerful one, especially when you understand how two people might have opposite associations for exactly the same circumstance. Let's see what we can learn about the dynamics of pain and pleasure.

Take stress brought about by change, for example, since change is what we're talking about in this book. I find the stress of most change stimulating. However, when I go into a company to try to introduce a turnaround—by definition, a change situation that often involves stress—I often encounter stiff resistance from different quarters in the company. That's because many people are threatened by change and find it very stressful and disconcerting. In one company, I was introducing the concept of self-managing teams and the marketing department's response was: "It's about time!" That kind of response is much in line with my own. The accounting department, however, was virtually paralyzed by fear of such a notion—its members were perfectly content to remain in an unchanged company following orders, because they valued security. Ironically, they would accept a status quo that really meant the worst form of change, slow but certain disintegration into oblivion.

Somebody paralyzed by the perceived menace of looming changes is not going to receive the message I'm trying to communicate—this person associates change with pain. No amount of my enthusiasm for exciting improvements will move somebody in terror. As a communicator of future trends, I will be better off to learn how this person makes associations to pleasure. In most cases, somebody fearful of change derives pleasure from a feeling of security. For example, I often find that people opposed to change are more open to improvements that can be explained in terms of how they will solidify the company's market position and stabilize the company's jobs, profits, and growth. They actually take pleasure in seeing an even more stable status quo.

To communicate effectively in the future you'll have to understand what other people associate with pleasure and pain and how they process information. Then you'll have to tailor your messages to them.

You may think this simple reversal of your point of view, in moving from what causes pain to what causes pleasure, is too simplistic. Not at all. Simple, but not simplistic. Direct, not obtuse. Honest, not devious. What's wrong with things like simplicity, directness, and honesty? Nothing, of course. People are far more likely to connect with messages built on these qualities than their alternatives.

The bottom line in communications for the future? You have to understand other people better to be better understood by them.

8. Sharpen your business skills

We will increasingly be working in small team environments like a family business. If we accept the even more radical standard that every employee is a business in the new economy, the need for this skill becomes self-evident. We will all be making more decisions and will therefore have to learn more about the business implications of those decisions.

Running a typical small business does not require a Harvard M.B.A. It does require a heap of common sense and a grasp of basic business principles. You can expect to be required to master terms and realities like revenue, expenses, fixed overhead costs, variable costs, strategic costs, return on investment, assets, liabilities, product life cycles, S-curves, negotiation skills, marketing segmentation of your customers, market positioning, the time value of money, quality control, and basic measures of productivity.

But don't be overwhelmed. I am talking about things that can be learned in simple seminars or by reading a few good books like Jack Stack's *The Great Game of Business*. We outlined some of the basic financial skills in Chapter 8, and I covered a broad variety of business decision-making and forecasting tools in my book *The Great Boom Ahead*. You won't have to take an entire college curriculum. If you're going to specialize in high levels of management, perform as a generalized specialist trainer of management skills within a company, or be a management consultant from the outside, then you will probably need the M.B.A.

Most people in front-line teams will need to learn only business basics and then develop a mastery by consistently applying those skills in their everyday work to their customers' needs.

Most of the decisions and trade-offs we have to consider in everyday business are simple, mostly based on right-brain judgments about common-sense principles. I think it's a relatively straightforward matter of educating ourselves by identifying the business emphasis we wish to begin to pursue. After that we need only tailor our education programs. Later we can continue to expand on business skills in much the same way we expand our other multifunctional skills. Perhaps the greatest responsibility of managers and business professionals will be to impart the basics of business and decision-making to employees—individual businesses—at all levels. Such skills should certainly be incorporated into our school systems.

9. Get a grasp on information technologies

Too often you hear this particular skill touted as the one of highest importance in the information age. One study, by Alan Krueger, a Princeton economist, estimates that people who use computers in their jobs earn 10 to 15 percent more on average. Despite this, I feel the human skills we have emphasized are more critical. Still, the ability to deal with and understand information technologies is simply a must.

You'd be wise to stop chasing technology and place your emphasis on acquiring and sharpening your _human_ skills—let the information technology come to you!

This means deciding what you really want to specialize in and then assessing the information technologies and skills that could help you achieve your goals. It is much easier to learn new technologies when they relate directly to achieving something you value.

Several factors will make it easier for you to absorb and use the new technologies.

User-friendly software

Computers and information devices have become much, much easier to learn. With the first personal computers, software seemed to be written for programmers. Just to learn the early word processors required days of training, reading, refreshment, and memorization. Nowadays any child can sit down to a computer and use the mouse to open and manipulate files of all kinds. Elementary-level children are teaching themselves typing on gamelike programs. They're even writing, editing, and publishing books on today's computers, in which the more sophisticated the software, the easier it is to use.

But dabbling in a piece of software is not mastery of it. You must be prepared to spend a good bit of time to master any items of software,

213

including today's word-processing programs, before you can work effectively with them. Remember, software programs are like bureaucrats— they do only what they have been programmed to do, and there is no point trying to reason with them. You must understand the logic of the software program or you will get locked into situations you can't even figure out how you got into, let alone get out of. So working with computers today can still be frustrating.

But you also have to remember that computers and software will just get better and more user-friendly. We've already seen handwriting recognition in the hand-held electronic notepads and are now seeing the very beginnings of effective voice recognition, although fully effective voice recognition by computers is expected to be about a decade away. This is why I always stress that information technologies will only become easier to use. Not being a technically trained computer type will be less and less a disadvantage in the future, unless you want to work as a software programmer or computer technician.

Intelligent software

Jobs such as software installation and troubleshooting of hardware once required systems specialists. No longer. Because of the advances in power and software, anybody can point with a mouse and click. Software practically installs itself. Programs check out the hardware and tell you step-by-step instructions for making repairs. By putting a bar code reader into a wristwatch, Timex and Microsoft have combined to create a system for downloading calendars from a computer to a watch. All you have to do is pass the face of the watch in front of the computer screen. You don't get much more user-friendly than that!

For now, the trend in software is toward user-programming. Software designers are building more powerful object-oriented software—standard blocks of software code that can be mixed and matched. That will allow you to choose broad functions and desired results stated in plain language. From menus of choices and subchoices, you'll make selections that will already have the detailed code programmed into invisible segments. More and more you will be able to use simple commands to have your computer designed to meet your specific needs without the complicated intervention of programmers. I've given this a name already, remember? This is just another manifestation of the move toward personalized, customized performance in the new economy.

Education software

The information technologies of the future from personal computers to fax machines, cellular phones, and answering machines will be complicated computers on the inside but easy to use on the outside. And all new machines in the future will come equipped with software to make use easier than ever. No doubt you've already seen the television commercials touting a variety of voice-activated conveniences such as programming the VCR and dialing numbers simply by speaking the name of a person into the phone. Imagine the convenience, flexibility, and power you will achieve when you can educate yourself in any field at your own pace and schedule. Once this technology catches on, perhaps the biggest revolution accompanying the work revolution will be that in public education.

Steps you can take

What you need to do is to find opportunities in leisure and work to get used to information technologies from computers to portable communications devices to fax machines to TV shopping and banking programs. If you haven't already, find one application in your business or personal life and learn a computer and software program to deal with it. And then find more. Learn video and computer games—anything you can to get comfortable using information technologies. Learn how to type, even though the keyboard may increasingly be eliminated by voice recognition devices.

Most people find it difficult at first to get used to computers and their bureaucratic logic, but end up wondering how they ever got along without them.

Summary of the Importance of the Nine Skills

We will all continue to have to learn specific functional skills, but we will do more mixing and matching to fit our specific career and business objectives and find ourselves engaged in continuous education. The most important skills will be the ones we add to this old set of functional skills—

these new behavioral, more right-brain skills. True, they are fuzzier skills, not the linear, spelled-out, checklist steps you'd find in a manual for programming the VCR. That's because we are in the earlier stages of understanding these skills. But there are numerous books, tapes, and seminars from Tony Robbins to Ken Blanchard to Stephen Covey to Paul Hawken for helping you to master these skills in relatively short periods of time. Our educational system will have to evolve to become more customized and flexible and to gear toward continuous learning. More of our learning will be self-designed or provided by our companies in shorter formats and seminars—more interactive and more experiential.

In the next chapter we will look at the predominant growth category for careers in the future, the front-line-oriented teams and individuals who serve the customer: specialized generalists.

11

Career Path One:
Become a "Specialized
Generalist" or
Front-Line Information User

You must strive to become more multifunctional.
Constantly search for and acquire new skills as the
focus changes to customer and customer needs on
the front lines.

Specialized Generalists—
New Workers for New Work

Since the biggest trend to come in organizations and jobs is automating,
eliminating, and redeploying indirect, bureaucratic jobs, it follows that the
largest growth in jobs will be in direct, value-added front-line and front-
line-support jobs. This means we'll see expansion in arenas like sales,
service, production, design, and all related front-line business functions
from quality control to necessary technical and clerical functions related
to these areas. It will take more people on the front lines to deliver
the levels of service and customization required to compete in the '90s.

Everything that can move forward will move forward to achieve the all-important customer-focused and multifunctional emphasis the new economy will demand.

I have coined a name for the people performing such jobs. I call them specialized generalists or SGs.

The specialized generalist defined

Specialized refers to the focus on meeting customer needs and solving customer problems. This is the most critical overall shift in work specialization that we described earlier from hierarchical, functional specialization to team-based, customer specialization. The specialization is in knowing your customer needs better than anyone else, not in being the best accounts payable clerk on the payroll.

Generalist refers to two things: first, that functional skills specialization has become secondary to customer and solutions specialization; and second, that all successful front-line workers will become more multifunctional, having to master a broader range of related skills. Remember, I'm not suggesting that specialists will become obsolete—we'll discuss them in the next chapter, in fact. It's just that workers on front-line teams will have to sharpen and broaden their functional repertoire to become more helpful to customers, and will have to adopt a solutions orientation. As the weight of the company shifts closer to the customer, most front-line workers will represent some arena of specialized expertise on the team. Teams will need people who can master the intricacies of marketing, promotion, sales, production, accounting, finance, and management, to name a few. But they will also develop broader expertise in those general arenas of specialization, because such focused teams can only afford a few specialists who must handle a broader range of tasks within their area of expertise.

There simply won't be room for high numbers of overspecialized workers in self-managing front-line work teams.

The trend in the coming work revolution will be to pull professional, managerial, technical, and clerical workers into front-line teams or into support groups that are closely linked to them. Remember the example of Hallmark. Artists, writers, production coordinators, and so on were pulled out of back-line functional departments and put directly onto front-line teams responsible for particular holidays and occasions in the life of consumers. That is a perfect example of moving back-line people into front-line teams. Those people became both more customer-focused and more multifunctional as former specialists cross-trained in the skills of teammates.

Remember, too, the account specialists at Customers "R" Us. That was an example of clerical back-line jobs that were converted to front-line support teams—to serve the needs of the salespeople and to handle follow-up orders from customers. Although you might be tempted to describe these teams as back-line support, look again. They are really a direct part of the front-line operations situated back at the home office, where they can more easily access information needed to help the sales staffers close in the field, where they are the ones with eye-to-eye contact with customers. After all, account specialists also deal person-to-person with customers and work as a direct extension of the sales force.

The scaled-down back-line staff will then be made up of more highly specialized functional experts who provide information on demand to such direct-value-added and front-line people.

Front-line teams make the decisions and are information *users*. Back-line experts are information *providers* and no longer make decisions or even set policies and standards as the bureaucracy did in the past.

This idea of moving the decision-making power forward in a company is crucial; it distinguishes corporations of the future from most companies of today.

An entertaining case of multifunctionalism

The best example I have seen of a high-performance, dynamic, multifunctional front-line team was one I encountered when I was traveling in Australia to promote my last book. I had heard a lot about an entertainment miracle, the Circus Oz, and decided to see it. Much as I enjoyed myself, I couldn't help being captivated by a sense of how well this new wave circus performance fit the picture of the corporation of the future.

Here was a group of performing artists that travels constantly, staying truly close to new customers to sustain itself. However, the group can't afford to cart along the huge caravan of specialists and equipment you'd see with a traditional circus.

During the excellent show, I could have sworn there were fifty performers involved in Circus Oz. By the time it was over, though, I could count no more than fifteen. Key actors changed roles, constantly showing off new talents—singing, acrobatics, comedy, and gymnastics. That was the versatility. But I could identify patterns of specialization too. One fellow did most of the physical feats requiring strength. Another segment of players did more of the theatrical skits and comedy. Another collection of the troupe showed off a broad range of acrobatics and stunts.

The musicians changed the look and sound of the show a dozen times. One played six stringed instruments from guitars and bass to violin. Amazed as I was, I saw her playing keyboard instruments as well. Two people played the entire range of horns from sax to flutes to trumpet. One person did every keyboard I could think of and a few I'd never seen. Next thing I knew, some of the actors were filling in on the drums, percussion, and guitar. Finally it occurred to me that even the ticket vendors and food and drink barkers at intermission were the actors and musicians. What's more, after we left, everyone in the show had to contribute to the takedown of the show and equipment and help with the setup at the next venue. I'm sure someone also took on some of the bookkeeping functions on the road.

Was this a practical arrangement for the circus? Heck yes! Think of the wages and travel costs if the circus required even as few as fifty people to travel from city to city, not to mention the management complexity. The break-even costs are far lower than for a traditional circus. Hence, they can appeal to smaller, more finely targeted, and more profitable audiences.

Did I feel cheated by the smaller-than-expected number of performers at Circus Oz? On the contrary, I was dazzled. I saw a high-quality performance at a reasonable price—a win-win proposition.

That's the way it's going to look in business in the new economy, folks. You're going to love working in such a setting full of the excitement of multifunctionalism and the intimacy of making things happen as part of a team.

Imagine the ability of such a group to ad lib and innovate in response to audience reaction. You'll be doing the same thing as you read your customers.

I've also seen many companies assign teams of managers and professionals to launch new products, just like an entrepreneurial start-up, or to focus on a very narrow set of products. A visionary leader from management, a marketer, and a finance person may be charged with testing and launching a new product. They would operate much like a small partnership in the entrepreneurial world. They may even work in a small outside office or from their homes. Again, the point is that they are highly customer-focused and must be broadly multifunctional. The marketing person has to handle every aspect of marketing, promotion, advertising, customer analysis, and segmentation. He must also handle and coordinate any outside services in his arena. I tell management and middle management people who are afraid of being laid off to consider moving forward to become a leader or key player on a dynamic front-line team that could grow and become a major breadwinner. Learn in the new economy to grow horizontally by exploiting increasingly better front-line opportunities rather than climbing the hierarchical ladder. There simply isn't much of a hierarchical ladder anymore. And, remember, there are plenty of front-line high-RBI hitters and low-ERA pitchers who make a lot more money than coaches and managers. The same will only be increasingly true for front-line leaders, salespeople, and entrepreneurs.

I've seen brokerage firms put brokers into their homes to be responsible for very small local markets. These people are one-person front-line teams. I've seen insurance companies put one person in charge of processing all claims from certain types of customers, with specialists accessible to them when difficult issues or questions arise. These people are one-person front-line teams, totally responsible for meeting the needs of the customer and being the primary point of contact with the company.

Remember our discussion about the atomic structure of teams in Chapter 8. For now, it's enough to summarize by saying that teams will need leaders, administrators, and specialized skills, with some team members doubling up on functions to maintain focus and the efficiency of small-team sizes.

The career path of the SG

The career path of the specialized generalist is characterized by being:

- **Customer-focused.** The SG career path is for people who are more people-oriented, who like working with customers in an ongoing relationship, who like making people happy, who enjoy relationships.
- **Decision- and action-oriented.** Front-line teams are decision-makers. They are in charge of their customers and of making the decisions and taking the actions necessary to solve their problems, like small businesses. They have a bias for action, not for bureaucracy and analysis. Such teams will be self-managing, as we said earlier, meaning they will make daily decisions on things ranging from hiring and firing to ordering materials and supplies as needed.
- **Longer-term as regards employment continuity and security.** The emphasis here is on developing intimacy with a narrow group of the company's customers and adapting continuously to meet their needs. Loyalty from customers requires loyal front-line employees. Thus, companies are going to value and reward long-term employment and loyalty here. In the future it will be self-evident that the front line is the wrong place for a company to casually shift or downsize and lose the loyalty of its key workers.
- **Multifunctional.** SGs enjoy constantly learning new skills. As we've said, they may specialize somewhat within their team structure, but they have to learn whatever is necessary in their arena of skills to keep up with changing customer needs and to keep the team as small as possible. As people learn and grow, they may even find themselves taking on new roles. Maybe the marketing person grows into the leadership role. Maybe the accounting specialist on the team grows into taking on new finance and quality-control functions, allowing the team to save the cost of replacing a member it just lost. If this should happen, of course, the profits gained and expenses saved would accrue as benefits to the small business that the front-line team has become.
- **Composed of direct-value-added work.** The roles on front-line teams typically involve a high proportion of value-added functions that the customer feels directly and a low content of more bureaucratic, non-value-added control and measurement functions. It's more about "doing" than "how to do."

- **More right-brain.** These jobs will generally require more right-brain, sensory skills like reading customers' and team members' needs, going with the flow as things constantly change, coming up with new, creative solutions to problems on the spot, and so on.
- **Flexible in leadership roles.** Although every team needs a leader, most fast-moving teams have people in specialty roles take over temporary leadership roles when the problem to be solved requires their expertise. So, you have to have the ability to shift into a more communicative leadership role when the team needs you to.
- **More likely to value experience over education or credentials.** Since results and ability to know and meet customers' needs are critical here, businesses will be looking more for demonstrated people skills and a track record of successful experiences with teams and customers, and for people who have been able to solve problems for customers. Education and formal training are important, but less critical.

Is being a specialized generalist for you?

Carefully review the list of work traits above and those in the next chapter for generalized specialists. Do your skills and behavioral traits fit that of an action-oriented, customer-focused individual or team? Or are you more of a knowledge-based information expert or training type? If so, check out the next chapter.

If you are a specialized generalist, your first priority is to identify a set of customers whom you want to get to know, solve problems for, and serve. You need a disposition to live for the customer, much like a local business proprietor. Your commitment is to the customer. Your skills and what you would like to learn more about will determine your position on the team that will serve such customers, but the customer focus comes first. Are you primarily a people person?

Summary

More of us are going to be working in environments resembling very small entrepreneurial businesses. In some cases, we'll stay inside larger companies working on an independent team, which is a business within. Some will be on the outside serving customers directly or selling services or components to larger companies. Either case means learning to operate in faster-moving environments. It means operating in more intimate situations. It means becoming more of a generalist—multifunctional in your arenas of interest or expertise. It means getting closer to the customer and specializing ultimately on knowing a customer's needs better than anyone else. It means learning how to analyze information and make decisions. It means better communications skills to deal effectively with team members and customers. It means we must all go back to Gerry Faust's two basics: people skills and problem-solving skills.

You are best able to decide whether your skills and behavior patterns and interests are better suited to being a front-line specialized generalist or a back-line generalized specialist. These are two very different career paths. It won't easy to switch from one to the other. Few people will be qualified to do both. Front-line people are generally more action-oriented, more people-oriented. They generally like to learn and experience a greater number of things. To them, human skills and the customer come first and technical expertise in their craft or profession second. As we'll see in the next chapter, the opposite is true of the new breed of generalized specialists.

12

Career Path Two: Become a "Generalized Specialist" or Back-Line Information Provider

Computers will ultimately automate as much as 80 percent of what today's experts do. Don't think of this as a disaster. Look to the explosion of opportunities for a new breed of experts.

Generalized Specialists— New Roles for the Experts

The generalized specialist (GS) will take an entirely different career path from the specialized generalist. In the customized economy we will need more back-line experts inside our companies and far more outside consulting services to replace in-house and government bureaucrats. Both groups will provide front-line teams with the specific and timely expertise and training they need to make decisions for their customers—call it "information on demand." These new experts will be the prime facilitators of the real-time information systems that keep the minnows moving together in a flexible, coordinated fashion.

Generalizing and specializing— a division of effort

I hear a constant debate among experts in the job market. Some are saying that you have to become a generalist to make it in the new world of work. Others claim just as vehemently that only the specialists will survive. The truth is that both sets of experts are correct.

You can choose either career path. The new breed of back-line experts in some sense represents the path of the past—functional specialization—but taken to a new extreme. To prosper as a GS you do have to become even more specialized in your expertise.

I said the SGs in the previous chapter would have to become more multifunctional while specializing in customer results. That means that they necessarily can't have the detailed functional skills and expertise required to make every technical decision effectively. That's why they need GSs. Here's a rule of thumb that perhaps points out the division of specialization between the two roles.

The 80/20 rule

SGs operate on an 80/20 rule, learning the 20 percent of critical information in a field that allows them to get 80 percent of the results and focus most of their time on knowing and responding to the customer.

The new GSs have to know an increasingly narrow arena of functional expertise better than anyone else. They must be able to maximize that specialist focus by being capable of applying it in broad arenas. They must know the other 80 percent of the information in a field that brings the remaining 20 percent of the desired results, but that is necessary to fully understanding that field and critical to problem-solving on the front lines. This specialization takes greater functional skills and focus in expertise. You can do the math yourself on this simple illustration: The 80 percent contribution of the SG plus the 20 percent contribution by the GS add up to 100 percent solving of customer problems and, ideally, 100 percent customer satisfaction. This specialization also means that there will be more jobs for more people in SG roles because of the greater contribution in the customer's perception of service.

Qualities that distinguish the GS

I have been in both roles in the past. As a consultant in strategic planning and finance to large and small companies, I was a true GS. But when I moved into turnaround management, I had to become the CEO of these small companies. In managing day to day and in dealing with employees and customers, I was acting like an SG. Along the way I learned about some key qualities within me that helped me decide which role I preferred to play.

People versus expertise

As we've seen for SGs, the key motivation and satisfaction come from dealing with people and creating results—a relationship orientation. SGs are people people.

> **F**or GSs, the key motivation and commitment is
> to the profession, the skills, and knowledge
> for its own sake.

As a consultant for change management and corporate turnarounds, I found that I loved expanding my field of expertise and creating real results for the customers and companies I worked with. You have to be customer-oriented to succeed in almost any endeavor these days. But when push came to shove, I was more committed to mastering my field of knowledge and research than I was to pleasing any single customer or team I was working with. If a customer was not interested in working in the manner I had found was most productive from much experience, I would prefer to find a customer who was interested. I clearly preferred to be the best at my profession, assuming that would ultimately make me the best adviser to the type of clients who needed me the most. I am now a GS who focuses on understanding the complexities of business change. I translate these complexities into simple tools that can be used in any industry and at different levels of companies and workers, to help identify opportunities for growth and implement effective solutions.

The primary reason a customer, often an SG, comes to you as a GS is that you know your field of expertise better than anyone else. Customers are looking for quick and effective answers to their problems, not necessarily for an entire solution to provide for their front-line customers. SGs will determine the end result, and GSs will help them by filling in key gaps in expertise or information.

Big picture versus small picture

In this new fast-paced economy with new paradigms in all areas of business and work, creative solutions to problems are needed. GSs who specialize in a given area of expertise but who apply that expertise in many industries and companies have a broader perspective. Often they are able to see more ways to apply their expertise. They are more likely to come up with a creative solution than someone inside the industry or customer area of focus who suffers from tunnel vision. Front-line teams running a business are so busy with implementing and doing that they often lose the big picture and miss creative alternatives.

The biggest advantage of GSs is that they allow you to maintain your strategic focus at the front line. They take on tasks that are not key to the customer or that are too complex to be moved to a front-line team.

They are information providers and subcontract product and service providers.

Let's further examine the distinctions between the roles of SGs and GSs.

Opportunities for the GS

The range of specialized functional skills is endless. On one extreme you might have a one-person company operating out of a home office calculating payroll taxes and filing quarterly returns for other small companies. At the other extreme you might have a consulting firm in a plush downtown office that helps Fortune 500 companies at the highest levels to gauge the impact of global warming trends on their twenty-to-fifty-year strategic plans.

Between those extremes you will find the in-house corporate GS team that trains managers and advises on human resource issues.

Typical Examples of GS Fields of Expertise

- Advertising agents
- Architects
- Auditors
- Book writers and editors
- Bookkeeping services
- Business strategy consultants
- Computer programmers
- Computer systems designers
- Computer training experts
- Environmental impact consultants
- Estate planners
- Graphic designers
- Headhunters
- Health and benefits specialists
- Lawyers and legal specialists
- Legal research database specialists
- Motivational experts
- Newsletter mailing house staff
- PR agents
- Secretarial services
- Seminar trainers and speakers
- Speaking agents for seminar trainers and speakers
- Tax specialists
- ZIP code marketing database specialists
- And on and on

GSs specialize in their expertise

Note in these examples you find many people who do not create end products for customers. In most cases they provide only expertise that helps companies and front-line teams produce the product. As a GS your key is to specialize within a field of expertise so you can better meet the needs of your clients and know your arena better than anyone else! That is your strategic focus.

GSs always have to consider where they should focus to maintain a competitive edge. For example, look at health and benefit plans for smaller, family-owned companies. There is a great deal of difference in the scope of such plans and the decision-making process for small family-owned companies versus larger corporations. That creates an opportunity to focus in a niche. A tax lawyer might specialize in charitable remainder trusts for deferring taxes for wealthy individuals. A computer system designer could look at specializing in designing and installing systems for midsized distributors dealing with consumer retail stores, or in bar code sales and information systems for small retail stores. You could cut it even finer and focus on small, boutique, upscale consumer retailers that want a lot of information and user-friendly systems for personalizing their services. Now go one step further, cutting it even finer, and specialize in upscale clothing stores only!

The front-line emphasis in GS services

The new breed of experts must understand that a new approach to expertise and consulting services is needed for the customized economy. The whole point of the new organization is responsive, front-line decision-making. This renders obsolete the current method of having consultants come in and evaluate a problem, then recommend and implement solutions for top levels of management.

A quick example. Traditionally, if you're a typical high-level manager with a legal question on hiring and firing an employee you would be expected to make an appointment with a lawyer and discuss the question in the firm's marbled-floored office.

The new work environment cannot afford this formal and high-overhead approach by consultants. Front-line teams need to be able to call and get a consultant who will answer questions right away and do it from a low-overhead office at more reasonable costs.

If the key goal on the front line is to be responsive to customers by making more decisions faster, then the role of GSs is to facilitate speed and accuracy for the customers' sakes.

The days of company experts being exclusive advisers to top management are over.

The job of the expert GS in the corporation of the future is to transfer as much knowledge as quickly as possible to front-line people, to coach and facilitate them so they can make more decisions without delay, and be accessible to deliver expert advise on demand as needed by front-line decision-makers. I repeat, the emphasis is *downward*, to the trenches, not upward to the executive suites.

That means that you as a GS will make fewer decisions and implement less and less. It means you have to involve your front-line clients in the analysis and process and lead them to come to their own conclusions.

You should see yourself as in the business of providing software, decisions support systems, and training. Your job is to make front-line people better decision-makers and to help management and professional experts within a company do the same for their front-line employees.

In short, the generalized specialist is an information provider to information users on the front lines.

How you can refine methods supporting the front line

Let's look at several areas.

Knowledge

Ask yourself: What is the 20 percent of knowledge in my field that I could train my clients in, so they can make competent decisions in the 80 percent of applications that arise day to day?

An accounting consulting firm might see that the basics of fixed and variable costs could easily be taught to front-line teams and built into their computer feedback and decision systems. This skill, critical in day-to-day decision-making, must be built into the front-line team. So the consulting firm develops a team that focuses on this mission in relation to needs of front-line teams serving customers needs.

On the other hand, auditing and preparing financial statements for the company are high-level tasks, certainly too broad and perhaps too complex to be delegated to either front-line teams or even the company's top-level accounting staff. But the firm finds that certain aspects of auditing can be incorporated into the in-house accounting staff's functions to streamline the process and cut accounting costs for the company.

Here's another question to consider. Can you back up your training with user-friendly reference guides or software systems that allow front-line teams to answer questions or solve simple problems on the spot? The short answer is yes. For example, one of the most important things to understand for day-to-day decisions in accounting is simply the relationship of fixed costs and variable costs. In the case of teaching front-line teams how to understand fixed and variable costs and their impact on break-even and profitability, a GS might develop a seminar with simple handbooks that instruct front-line managers and employees on how to make simple break-even and profitability calculations. It is the GSs who should be writing the software systems that can calculate on-the-spot profitability of an order or customer. These systems should have enough flexibility to take into account changes in discounts, volume, or product specs.

GSs become order *facilitators*, not order *preventors*.

Responsiveness

How can you be more real-time responsive as a GS?

You could establish a hot line. Use it to diagnose problems or answer questions as needed by companies and their front-line teams you serve.

Or develop simple menu-driven software that the front-line users can query and get answers. For example, a tax firm might develop software that would allow front-line managers to assess the risks in hiring temporary employees. The software might also help decide whether to classify new hires either as temps or as independent contractors for tax and payroll processing. The manager answers a series of true-false questions. The system then rates the candidate on a scale of 0 to 10, with 7 or higher meaning a very low risk of IRS rejection and fines, 5 to 6 a medium risk, and 0 to 4 a high risk. With this as a guide, a manager can decide whom to classify as independent contractors. Then the system might go further to print the boilerplate paperwork to either start the person as an employee on payroll taxes or to produce a simple independent contractor agreement.

What the tax firm has done here is to simulate the same line of questioning its best experts would use in a face-to-face or phone conversation. This can be done effectively in decisions that are highly systematic in nature. After all, the IRS uses computers and formulas to select audit candidates. Why shouldn't you use a similar system to rate your chance of getting audited? And why should you have to travel to the marble-floored offices to get your answers?

The point is that the front-line decision-maker can get answers immediately and at a very low cost compared to a $200-an-hour consultation!

We hear a lot of talk about expert systems invading the workplace. This is a simple example of such a system. They needn't be complex computer models. In fact, the great majority should be these simple "rule and rating" systems.

The typical accounting firm would say, "Why should we set up a software package that will eliminate so much hourly billing?" The answer is simple: If you don't do it, a competitor or an independent upstart will. You will lose the hourly billings anyway. Most important, you'll also lose the trust and confidence of the client, who will ask, "Why didn't you come up with this solution?"

And of course you must never forget that the less you have your highly trained experts dealing with repetitive tasks, the more time they can spend creating new, better, more valuable and thus more valued services, which in turn will generate higher-quality billings.

Minimize job shock

One way GSs can help the work revolution proceed with a minimum negative effect on workers is to ease the transition of people from the back lines forward. An example is the administration of personality and other tests to examine the profiles in behaviors and attitudes that match performance on the job. These instruments developed by GSs can give managers the ability to evaluate new hires and transfers. This helps greatly to increase the effectiveness of hiring and transfer decisions at a low cost and through an easy-to-use system that is instantly accessible.

Clean up your language—no more jargon

One more critical new dimension to the world of GSs lies in communicating with people who aren't technical types. All back-line experts must learn to communicate to front-line people without relying on jargon. This means your oral, written, and software messages have to be user-friendly. Remember, in the past, consultants tended to work with upper management and with back-line in-house counterparts—the computer systems consultant worked with the MIS department. In that case the tekkies spoke the same language.

There will be a premium on professional, technical, managerial, and training experts who can communicate in everyday language to broader-trained, more action-oriented front-line workers.

Continuing your GS education

I have to stress perhaps the largest area of opportunity for GSs: adult education! Since we are in a period of high change in skills and in the workplace, and since education is becoming a continual process, the biggest area of growth for back-line experts will be in education.

Already we are seeing a whole new mode of education emerging: books, audiotapes, videotapes, workbooks, software programs, seminars, lectures, and so on. This is an entire education system outside of the formal one in colleges and public and private schools. This new system will predominate and move into the formal school systems in the future, because it is flexible—it can be customized. People get to learn the specific skills they need as they need them from whomever they respect in that field. Finding ways to educate workers, consumers, and companies in your specialized expertise should be a high priority for you.

Get into educational services and training both because it will be profitable and also because it is a great way to promote your expertise and services.

I wrote my first book in part to establish expertise in my field and to attract consulting and speaking business. Now, when I speak, I have the opportunity to educate others on the trends I see in change management and the tools of the futurist. In turn, every time I give a seminar I get exposure that leads to other seminars and consulting work. The whole point is to then charge your highest rates for your most complex and human or right-brain services.

The formula for success for the generalized specialist

To succeed as a GS you must:

- **Commit strongly** to a specialized field of knowledge that can help front-line people make better decisions.
- **Constantly refine** your specialization and update and refocus your knowledge base.
- **Differentiate** between aspects of your expertise that can be transferred to your clients through education and training and the aspects that will require your intervention and experience.
- **Clearly communicate** to your clients how you can streamline their decision processes and reduce their costs by offering software and training systems that allow them to make the decisions and save money.
- **Simplify.** Companies will grow increasingly distrustful of consulting firms that try to maximize their services rather than focus and minimize them.

Don't compete with computers

Since computers will ultimately automate 80 percent of what experts did in the past, a GS should coopt this trend rather than battle it. Help your clients to save money, overhead, and time by assisting them in turning the systematic, left-brain aspects of your knowledge into effective software, expert systems, training, and educational materials. Then identify and educate your clients as to where your personal services are required for more complex decisions with high payoffs.

Charge a healthy fee for the right-brain,
more complex and human services where you don't
compete with computers.

GSs also have to be aware of the other trend that threatens their fields. Companies are going to benefit from moving more expertise and personnel to the front lines. Overall, I expect the ratio of front-line, value-added people to rise versus back-line, non-value-added bureaucrats. Your jobs, roles, and services will be highly scrutinized. You have to make sure that you are adding high value and be willing to transfer functions to the front line when such transfer is in your client's interests. However, because of the high skills and specialization required of many GSs, I expect that salaries will continue to be higher on average than for SGs.

As we will see in the chapters ahead, the greatest growth in GS jobs will tend to come with one-person, home-based specialists. These will be people who carve off very narrow functions and perform them for companies—often starting with their former employers. They will operate with much greater focus and flexibility and with much lower costs and overheads than consultants of the past.

On the other end of the scale you'll find service firms that take very complex information systems, creating and sharing enormous databases and modeling or diagnostic systems across many companies. The best examples that come to my mind are the ZIP code computer modeling databases. These allow small and large companies alike to define their most profitable customers by lifestyles and demographics. Then they are able to find the households and neighborhoods that contain these customers and target them as directly as possible. Large companies lease the entire software and hardware system, as they have the scale to then do their own analysis. Smaller firms can simply purchase a report by lifestyle or ZIP code as they need it for their marketing efforts, at very reasonable cost.

Career differences between the GS and the SG

Should you look toward the path of the generalized specialist? Here are the traits that characterize the GS. Notice how they contrast with the traits and roles of the SG. You can identify a GS because:

- **Their first loyalty is to their profession or field of expertise.** They have to be customer-oriented, but their most important contacts may be other experts in their field whom they learn from and network with on projects. These people tend to be more technical-oriented than people-oriented.

- **They are the true knowledge workers.** These workers primarily deal with knowledge and information and its application to improving all aspects of business. When futurists refer to the new class of knowledge workers, this is the primary group they are referring to—not that all of us won't become more knowledge-based in our work.

- **They are more temporary and project-oriented in nature.** Their functions are often outsourced or hired on an as needed basis. Since these workers possess highly specialized expertise and apply it across broad applications, they naturally move from project to project, or information need to information need. Therefore, they will tend to deal with many customers and types of assignments within their fields of expertise. This is how they learn.

- **They are more specialized.** As we saw earlier, these people have to become even more specialized to compete in the new economy, and yet have to be on guard to the danger that their roles will become either automated or outmoded by technological and marketing change. If you are a specialist in information systems for distribution companies, you might find most such middlemen being eliminated by advancing technologies. Your specialty may become obsolete as well unless you can update your knowledge and switch your focus, say to information systems that connect producers directly with retailers.

- **Their work is indirect, non-value-added.** Their functions more often than not involve functions that don't directly add value or are not visible to end customers. This is the reason such people are naturally expertise-oriented.

- **They are more attracted to left-brain, systematic functions.** More of the right-brain functions naturally occur on the front lines, and many of the back-line functions provide highly specialized or automated left-brain expertise to support the front-line-teams. Of course, since left-brain functions are being automated by information technologies, such workers have to learn to help their clients automate many of their functions and constantly move into more complex left-brain and right-brain functions to compete, as we saw earlier.

- **Their education and credentials are critical.** Many entrepreneurial people may be able to succeed as SGs in front-line teams, but it is very hard to be considered an expert GS without strong educational credentials and continuous learning and updating of your skills. GSs must be more serious about obtaining the right formal education and the appropriate updates in professional and technical credentials.

The best of both worlds

One final consideration. You could find any number of exceptions to these two clear-cut career paths. Some people will combine both of paths in their functions. The most obvious example would be the top management teams, especially of larger companies. These people clearly have to be customer- and results-oriented, exhibiting strong people and leadership qualities, more like an SG. But they also have to have a very high level of technical and professional mastery in their fields of expertise, whether it be management or marketing or finance.

High-level executives tend to have to be a blend of GS and SG. The same can be said for entrepreneurs and one-person consultants who have to be both highly technically inclined and also multifunctional and customer-oriented.

In Part Five we will take a look at the options for entrepreneurialism in the new economy and how many more people from all fields, GSs and SGs, will be able to have opportunities to run their own businesses and achieve greater control over their lives and their earnings capacities. Remember, the status symbol of the '90s is control over your own life and time.

Leveraging the New Entrepreneurial Climate

Part Five shows—from high risk to low risk— the options available for independence in the great boom ahead.

CHAPTER 13

Looks at the changing nature of entrepreneurship.

CHAPTER 14

Deals with the riskiest option for prospective entrepreneurs.

CHAPTER 15

Examines entrepreneurialism within companies.

CHAPTER 16

Tells how to duplicate the successes of other entrepreneurial operations.

CHAPTER 17

**Reveals how you can build your own low-risk
business as the coming new wave of
entrepreneurialism takes hold.**

The Entrepreneurial
Lessons of the Past

You can start a boom business and prosper in the
new economy—*if* you have what it takes.

Are You Ready for Ownership?

The best solution to job shock and all of the endless changes and downsizing within larger companies is to start or run your own business. Millions
of people have done this in the past decades, and many more millions will
do so in the coming decades, because new opportunities will abound. We
can learn many lessons from entrepreneurs of the '80s, even as we watch
the nature of entrepreneurialism changing in the '90s and beyond. And
what will those changes look like?

First, we will see a shift away from radical and breakthrough types of innovations and high-risk garage start-ups toward more incremental innovations. If we go back to look at the Generation Wave cycle in Chapter 2, we can see that most of the radical innovations and early-stage business concepts already came during the Innovation Wave between the '60s and early '80s. Most of the growth products, services, technologies, and industries for decades to come have already been established.

Everything from the battle for dominance of the information highway to the superpremium ice cream wars will be fought between larger and larger companies, both old and new, as these markets move into the mainstream with the Spending Wave of the baby boomers. That means it will be harder for entrepreneurs to start radical new ventures, although this will always occur to some extent in our economy, as we'll see in Chapter 14. Increasingly, innovators will take trends and products already established in their growth patterns, enhance them, and extend them into broader markets. Figures 13-1 and 13-2 show how innovation and products change over their life cycle, moving along the path from radical to incremental innovation.

Look at how desktop computers fit these innovation and evolution paths. If desktops move into most households in the coming decade, as my tools predict, then there will be a growing need for local tutoring and training services, repair, new home applications of software, new ways of advertising into the home via computers, new services that can be accessed by computers, computer user clubs, and so on. Notice, these aren't breakthrough innovations. Instead, they represent clear opportunities, many for

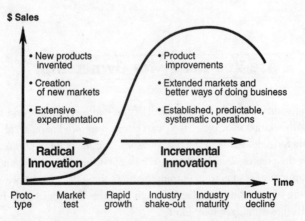

Figure 13–1. Radical versus incremental innovation.

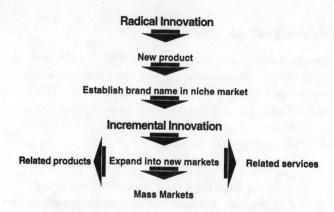

Figure 13–2. The evolution of new products.

individuals and small businesses. The chance of your starting a software firm out of a garage that could compete with Microsoft is nil at this point in the Generation Wave and business cycle. However . . .

You will find far more lower-risk opportunities for entrepreneurship and owning your own business in the next phase of the coming economic boom.

The basis for an entirely new entrepreneurial climate

The biggest dimension of the change in the growing entrepreneurial climate is based in the Power Wave of the baby boom generation. Of course, that's the work revolution we've been addressing all along in this book. The four principles in Part Three are going to force all types of changes inside and outside of organizations, large and small. That's what will create entrepreneurial opportunities in the boom ahead. When talking to businesses I stress that they must use these principles to define entrepreneurial opportunities by asking: How can we extend our products or services to help our customers employ these four principles to win the race for leadership in their markets?

Entrepreneurial Megatrend #1

Prospective entrepreneurs! Take a good look at any industry or market you know and look for opportunities to extend emerging new products, services, and technologies into broader markets and applications. The best opportunities will come from networking small, local businesses into broader networks and from subcontracting functions that companies choose to outsource in honing their strategic focus.

One of the biggest opportunities I see is for networking small, independent businesses together like schools of minnows. Finding ways to tie companies together so that they can share regional, national, or world-scale promotion, PR, purchasing, information systems, databases, distribution channels, basic R&D, and so on will become an industry itself.

This will be like the example I pointed out in Chapter 1, the networking of bed-and-breakfast inns into a national chain with a national advertising campaign, an 800 number for reservations, and quality ratings people can trust. The original idea of a bed-and-breakfast was a radical innovation. Now the concept of B&B is moving into mainstream awareness as a highly customized and experiential travel option. This networking twist is an incremental innovation that can help these inns both reach a broader market and lower their costs—without losing their essential, unique, individual identities. That is practically a redefinition of what it takes to move mainstream.

The possibilities here are endless. I saw a company the other day that coordinates home delivery of takeout meals for a city's upscale gourmet restaurants. It's just another way to network what already exists and to extend it into new markets. You can't tell me these opportunities don't exist in cities and industries near you.

I see huge opportunities stemming from companies outsourcing their nonstrategic functions, as we discussed in Chapter 6. Small businesses and home-based businesses are growing out of this trend in everything from secretarial services to graphic design to advertising and public relations to training in team building to economic forecasting to career counseling to accounting services.

Instead of seeing downsizing and reengineering of companies as a threat, I see it as the entrepreneurial opportunity of a lifetime.

Prospective entrepreneurs! Keep your eyes open. Ask yourself: How can I make a business out of the jobs and functions that are being eliminated and automated by companies? Many people can perform these functions for a number of companies at a variable versus a fixed cost and at much lower overheads while gaining more control over their lives and schedules. All that's needed is the initiative to seize the available opportunities.

Remember that this first megatrend revolves around the inevitable, predictable path of customization moving into the mainstream economy. If you but look, you will find endless opportunities to take any product or service and apply it to another need, or to a more specialized market niche. Again, this doesn't involve a radical innovation—starting a whole new product from scratch—but merely taking a growing product and finding new niche markets to adapt it to. The Dove Bar was a good example of an extension of the superpremium ice cream trend. If people will pay $3 for a pint of high-quality ice cream, why not turn the old ice cream bar into a superpremium product? Why not turn candy bars into ice cream versions, as Snickers did? Why not take the old-fashioned ice cream sandwich upscale, as Ben & Jerry's did? These are all incremental innovations and extensions of the once radical superpremium ice cream trend, which began as a mere niche, high-end market back in the early '80s.

The leaders in most emerging new markets will be established by the top of the current economic boom, around 2007. That means that the next decade is the most powerful time for business innovations that can pay off far into the future.

Entrepreneurial Megatrend #2

Prospective entrepreneurs! Watch the population shift already underway. As we saw in Chapter 2, the next great population migration will have its effect in the coming decades: from the cities and suburbs to the exurbs and small towns and cities. As many as sixty million to eighty million people could shift outside of major metropolitan areas in North America. These new towns will provide growth opportunities for everything in the way of infrastructures: restaurants, houses, office buildings, all types of business services, and home conveniences. Such boomtowns will provide ample opportunities for individuals to start one of the "cookie cutter" businesses we discuss in Chapter 16—transplanting a successful business idea from the cities and suburbs to a similar area of consumer demographics and lifestyles in a growing small town. This is a prime way to be in business while improving your quality of life and lowering your cost of living at the same time!

Let me give you one of the best examples of a brilliant, yet simple, low-risk business opportunity I heard of recently. It combines all the important principles of the coming boom: customization, incremental innovation, networking many small businesses, leveraging information technologies, and exploiting the growth of small towns. Edward D. Jones has introduced a new way to grow in the crowded field of brokerage and financial services. The strategy is simple. The company sets up one broker in a highly visible Main Street office in smaller towns that don't have a Merrill Lynch office or Charles Schwab or any other "name" brokerage service. Most people in these towns either stow their money in a low-yield bank account or have to travel to the big city to establish a relationship with a broker. So the Edward D. Jones offices have virtually no competition yet. But they are positioned in towns that are likely to grow much faster than metropolitan areas.

But here's the best part. Each office has a satellite dish that is hooked up to the main office in St. Louis. At regular intervals the home office will sponsor an expert over the satellite, someone who can talk, say, on the benefits of variable annuities for IRA and retirement savings. As many as three thousand brokers each can bring in three to ten clients and deliver the best leading-edge information into small towns. This is a spectacular idea—I mean, *you can't even get this at a major brokerage in metropolitan areas!* Then each local broker can discuss the concepts in more depth, customizing the pitch for each client, and, of course, closing sales.

Think about what is new in this concept. Is it brokers? No. Brokers already existed in larger cities for anyone who felt capable of investing via long-distance telephone. Is it the existence of smaller, discount brokerages? No. Discount brokers have been growing for some time now. What Edward D. Jones has added is a slice of the biggest growth market in the industry, customized financial planning. This requires more than just writing orders. It means educating clients and adapting investments to individual needs. This company does all of the above, at a low price *and* in small towns with no competition.

That's the game of the future, folks. Get used to watching it happen. Better yet, get out there and make it happen yourself!

Learning from the '80s

Before going much further into our discussion of the future of entrepreneurialism, it wouldn't hurt to glimpse into the past to see which lessons will apply to the future and which won't. We've seen a lot of entrepreneurial companies succeed in past decades, and in all markets. But we've also seen a lot of them fail in the '80s and early '90s as competition has intensified in emerging markets.

Through the media we hear dozens of stories of entrepreneurs who followed their dreams, took risks, and beat the odds to became millionaires and even celebrities. We don't often hear the millions of stories of people who had their dreams and started their own businesses only to fail. Or even that many of the successful entrepreneurs failed or went bankrupt many times before succeeding. In working with entrepreneurs I've seen plenty of them founder and fail, so I can tell you without fear of contradiction:

For every entrepreneur who has succeeded, ten more have failed—and for every one of those ten who failed, ten more would-be entrepreneurs never got far enough off the ground even to be noticed as failures.

One of the most critical traits of successful entrepreneurs and creative people is what we have already stressed: the ability to have a vision so compelling as to enable you to work through the painful realities and formidable obstacles of entrepreneurialism with unwavering persistence. Believe me, the realities and obstacles are almost always much more daunting than you dream.

Therefore, you have to be very realistic about what you are capable of doing and what you are willing to sacrifice to have your own business. The more radical, the higher the risk, of an entrepreneurial venture, the more it is going to require of you in skill, perseverance, capital, and sacrifice. Underestimating the level of risk can ruin your life. I have seen it with many entrepreneurial clients.

Radical innovation and breakthrough entrepreneuring is highly risky, and only something like one in a hundred of us is qualified or "crazy" enough to pull it off. So don't be naive. But the good news is that the next stage of our ongoing economic boom will hold many more lower-risk opportunities. These are opportunities that have a much better balance between quality of life and financial rewards. You may not become a multimillionaire with many of the options we present in the coming chapters, but you might just become a millionaire. You may earn yourself time to spend with your family and favorite leisure pursuits. And you may not have to risk everything you own as the entrepreneurs of old have had to do.

The new economy will bring a greater degree of entrepreneurialism to all jobs, not just to business opportunities. So you can learn from the coming chapters even if you don't decide to start your own business. You will eventually be running your own business within most companies anyway. The most important thing you can do is evaluate what level of entrepreneur you want to be and are qualified to be. The next four chapters outline the basic options for entrepreneurship so that you can get a better feel for where you fit in.

We start with radical innovation in Chapter 14. Are you the heroic type? Then in Chapter 15 we look at being an entrepreneur or "intrapreneur" within an existing business. In Chapter 16 we look at how you can start a business with lower risk by buying a franchise or copying a business that already works and transferring it to an area that doesn't have it. Then we look at the lowest-risk option in Chapter 17: taking your present function within your company and turning it into a business that performs that function more flexibly and efficiently—from your home if possible—for the same company.

For the Heroic: Radical Innovation—Strategies for Creating a Breakthrough Start-up

The traditional heroic start-up involves rejection, failures, and endless chaos in its early stages—making the occasional, eventual success the sweetest of all possible prizes.

Breaking New Ground Virtually Under Your Feet

In this chapter we talk about taking the highest risks of entrepreneurship: radical innovation. By radical, I mean achieving something that hasn't been done before. Steve Jobs of Apple, Bill Gates of Microsoft, and Anita Roddick of the Body Shop are three of the more dramatic examples of radical innovators.

But don't count yourself out of the company of these big-name innovators just because you think there's no more room for another personal computer, a superior operating system, or another line of natural beauty products. It's very likely you have the potential for lucrative breakthroughs right within your grasp.

I have seen many radical innovators spawn breakthrough ideas and products at an everyday level. Take Tom Chesus and Kathy Maxwell at Ascent Cash Flow in San Rafael, California. Over a decade ago they observed that most people did not know how to save money systematically and to achieve their most important goals in life. So they came up with a vision of a radical new idea: personalized budgeting and savings systems. They started off with a well-honed counseling session that forced people to articulate their most important priorities in life, to compare those priorities to where they were actually spending their money, and then to figure out how much saving was needed to meet their goals and the shortfall versus what they were actually saving. Later they came up with workbooks and systems for building the various levels of savings families needed, down to the annual savings for car repairs and taxes. Then they developed "The Financial Valet," an automatic bill-paying and savings system for people who want to lessen the stress of making payments and to ensure that they accumulate savings despite their tendencies not to.

Word of mouth spread, and Tom and Kathy had a growing business. Are they multimillionaires? Probably not. But they have built a rewarding business. They exercise adequate control over their lives. And they enjoy the satisfaction of making a real difference in the lives of their clients. They have also written a book I recommend to you: *Richer Than You Dreamed, Poorer Than You Think*. They are just beginning to move into their real dreams, public speaking and consulting to companies that want to help their employees get the most from their finances. This is occurring even as their high-end counseling business has peaked and their bill-paying service is beginning to be threatened by advances in home financial software. As for most leading-edge entrepreneurs, change is a way of life for Tom and Kathy—they'll adapt and look for new opportunities to exploit.

If you were to talk either to Steve Jobs or to Tom and Kathy, you would hear much the same thing about entrepreneurialism: that it is a very exciting and self-fulfilling path—but not an easy one. They all have gone through hell before they got to heaven, and they all recognize they could end up back in hell again just as they finally thought things were where they wanted them. Steve Jobs saw the pinnacle of the success of Apple crowned by his ouster as chairman. I heard Steve in an interview once talking about how you never heard about the Apple I because it was a flop.

But you did hear about the Apple II. Same with the Lisa (flop) and the Macintosh (raving success). Now he says the same about his latest company, NeXT (flop), and that he's ready to make another comeback in object-oriented software.

One of the facts of life in radical innovation is that you simply have to be willing to deal with high rates of failure.

Remember this phrase I once heard someone utter: "Success is going enthusiastically from failure to failure."

If you're considering launching a radical innovation at work or in your own company, here are some realities to ponder:

Get used to rejection

Do you know how many restaurants Colonel Sanders pitched to license his famous chicken recipe before he got his first deal? One thousand nine—that's 1,009—before he got his first yes, meaning he heard 1,008 nos in a row!

The most difficult reality to face, one that will almost always clash with your vision, is that most people just won't see what you see until it becomes more tangible. People can generally only see something that already exists. Although everyone has a vision or is capable of it, no one has *your* vision. Stores or distributors will not want to try something new from a company with no track record. Banks won't even look at you. Even friends and relatives will tend to pooh-pooh your project—though probably not to your face. Radical new innovations live off the unwavering persistence of the visionary entrepreneur. It is your job to nurse your vision like a newborn child until it can walk on its own.

Thoreau wrote in *Walden:* "If one advances confidently in the direction of his dreams, and endeavors to live the life which he has imagined, he will meet with a success unexpected in common hours."

Therefore, it follows:

Get committed

This means much more than taking rejection in stride. It means plain old going it alone for many years before you finally get support or financial backing or even before a retail store gives your product a try. It is a lonely road, one that you cannot appreciate until you have been on it. Are your commitment and vision strong enough to tolerate years of no support and little positive feedback?

Most important, you can't take a lack of support from others, even from customers, as a sign that your vision isn't worthy. Most people simply won't see the practicality of your vision until it has been further refined. Such a lack of support can be useful in showing you where you need to make modifications, but you simply can't give up. Giving up too soon is perhaps the biggest single reason I have seen entrepreneurs fail, even those who had promising products or innovations.

On the other hand, you can't be foolish and pursue a dream that has no merit. Here's what to look for to judge if your vision really has worth in the early stages of rejection. First, always review your own experiences, analysis, and convictions. Continually reconfirm to yourself that what you see is needed in the marketplace and possible to accomplish. Then look for positive remarks and comments amid the overall rejections—can people see something great about your vision, even if they don't get it altogether? But most important, communicate or market your vision or new product first to leading-edge users or other innovative or entrepreneurial people. Look for at least a few of these people to see your vision and to give you support and helpful feedback. Expect at least one other visionary person to understand what you see and give you an objective stamp of approval.

Here's a brief account from James V. Smith, Jr., an entrepreneur and writer who worked with me to write this book:

"I sold my first book based on a rejection letter that said, 'Although we don't have a place for the book on our list, I find your writing lively and compelling—the story really jumps with excitement.' I sent out a copy of that very rejection slip with my next set of submissions. The rejection earned a sale that has led to a writing career publishing five novels and three books of nonfiction. This was on an initial manuscript that I believed in but that had been rejected fifty-three times. I never lost faith that I could sell it, but it required a lengthy, painful search to finally find somebody who shared my vision of the story. Of course, I became discouraged, but I took faith in an encouraging rejection from that editor who bought the vision but not the book."

Heroic entrepreneurial ventures typically require
three times the capital and twice the time
of your best estimates.

As your vision collides with realities, you will consistently tend to find that things will take longer, and therefore you will need more capital or have to make more personal financial sacrifice than you thought. It is very important to conserve capital in a radical new venture. You can't afford to underestimate on these issues of time and capital. Here are some guidelines that might help keep you out of trouble:

A Do and Don't Checklist for Your Start-up

☐ **Do not rent an office,** or hire a secretary, or splurge for anything fancy unless you absolutely have to.

☐ **Do everything possible yourself** to minimize your financial needs and the complexity of involving too many people.

☐ **Don't start a business just after you or your spouse has had a baby.** Babies are the only other thing as consuming as a break-through venture—don't force them to compete if you don't have to.

☐ **Do keep the lowest possible overheads and costs.** The longer you can last on the least money, the higher your chances of making it through that critical early period of rejection and refinement of the product.

☐ **Do lower your capital needs.** Capital is scarce and expensive for a radical new venture. Venture capitalists typically look for at least 30 percent returns on capital, whereas banks will lend capital to stable established businesses at a prime rate of perhaps 8 percent. A little capital will cost you a large percentage of your equity, so conserve it and try to provide from your own funds or from a close relative. Even credit cards at 10 to 18 percent interest are a bargain compared to venture capital. Just don't tell Visa how you're using your credit line.

☐ **Do have back-up plans for capital** and customers to approach when things inevitably do not go as planned.

It follows from this checklist that:

You must be multifunctional and learn whatever is required

As a general rule, you won't be able to afford to hire others or to retain expensive outside services. That's why the best entrepreneurs are one-person cross-functional teams. It's also why so few people are qualified to launch a breakthrough start-up. The fortunate start-ups have partners who can share the load.

I saw a woman with a very good new line of flavored teas fail after achieving initial success in gourmet stores and supermarkets, two tough outlets to crack. Unfortunately, she had no skills in finance and brought in a partner who also had no skills in finance but thought he did. He made all of the classic mistakes, including building high overheads. He also milked the company's cash flow to help fund another failing venture. She was a great innovator, marketer, and salesperson. But she didn't understand finance. That single blind spot cost her everything.

A new venture requires a solid, cross-functional skill base just as a front-line self-managing team does. It's just that the restriction in capital often means you have to have all the skills yourself. This is another big reason I have seen entrepreneurs with good products fail. You have to make sure you have access to all of the skills needed to launch a new product. If you don't have the skills and can't afford to bring someone in, then you are simply going to have to master the skill yourself before expecting to achieve any kind of success—whatever effort that takes!

Prepare to live in constant chaos

The demands of an entrepreneurial undertaking require constantly changing your plans. Launching a radical new venture is the epitome of the creative process. You learn that you can't plan through chaos, but that you must go with the flow. It's like the punch line to the joke about dancing with an eight-hundred-pound gorilla—you stop dancing when *it* wants to stop!

You have to be willing to deal with realities and obstacles, and I can tell you in advance, you will not be able to anticipate most of them. If you're doing something radical, chances are a carefully crafted ten-step plan might last a week or two before you've hacked it to death and have a whole new plan. That's a sign of progress. The entrepreneurial process is so powerful precisely because failure and change come so fast, and hence learning is magnified.

Any soldier involved in battle planning at any level, from international theater commands the size of Norman Schwarzkopf's in Desert Storm down to individual squads, will tell you to expect everything in the best-laid plans to go to hell the moment the first shot is fired.

But that's not bad for you! I tell you, Americans are better adapted to ad-libbing through chaos than any other culture. It's what we do best! And lucky for us, too. Remember what I told you about the nature of the corporation of the future—you may be better off to stay in a continual mode of *Ready, fire, aim!*

Too much capital early on will kill you

You may wish you had this problem, but be wary of raising or spending too much capital in the early stages of your venture. Not having capital forces you to be creative and find inventive ways to do everything. The shortage of cash is a too little appreciated stimulus to the creative process. It's also hard to resist using money to ease the pain of the current reality. It's too tempting to get an office and other trappings of success just for comfort or to make it look as though you're making progress. During the initial phase of developing, refining, and promoting the product until you have an initial success, limiting your capital is usually a plus.

But beware . . .

255

Too little capital later on will also kill you

When the product begins to succeed and attracts competition, then you typically need enough capital to move fast and roll it out before a faster competitor runs away with your success story. After the product has shown success in initial niche markets, the risks are greatly reduced for investors and the vision is much more obvious to competitors and customers alike. Now you can get capital at more reasonable rates, and without giving up all of your equity. This is not the time to be overly greedy. Don't give away more equity than necessary, but it's very important that the product expand fast enough in this stage—especially if there is the threat of strong competition. And why wouldn't there be if you're succeeding? I repeat, make sure you have enough capital at the stage where you must roll out the product or service and *deliver.*

Basic Rules of Entrepreneurial Success

I have seen some studies on new ventures, and so I'll pass along a few summary findings:

Venture capitalists bet more on the person than on the product

For many of the reasons we've just examined, the vision and commitment of the entrepreneur determine the likelihood of successfully overcoming the trials of getting the product developed and accepted in an initial market.

Cross-functional partnerships do better than one-horse shows

As I've suggested, many entrepreneurs fail because they simply can't cover all of the skill bases. Partners can share skills and pool capital and hence have proven higher success rates.

Entrepreneurs with business experience succeed most often

Business savvy is key. It's also critical to have experience in the industry where you are innovating so you can exploit contacts and know the ropes.

Women start more businesses—men start far more high-growth ventures

It seems that women have the greatest incentive to start new businesses, as they face discrimination in the workplace and often are looking to balance work and family. Women seem to prefer small, manageable businesses, boutique-size stores, gourmet food items, business services, and so on. When it comes to the Inc. 500, the fastest-growing firms, or to businesses that start small and expand rapidly, men primarily dominate them. Such businesses require ruthless focus and commitment. It seems more men go for that. But you would be hard pressed to find a more exciting growth business than the Body Shop, founded by Anita Roddick. In some sense she has rewritten the rules of business as much as anyone, with her radical strategies of revolving her business around environmental issues, operating with intensive in-house training and quality programs but with no advertising and promotion. We are likely to see more women enter the high-growth arenas in the future, but still expect areas of great risk to be more of a man's world.

Summary

Doing something radical or new for the first time takes a highly individualistic person with strong vision and persistence. There is no substitute for having and learning all of the skills for launching a business. Do your homework, study your potential markets, discover how other similar innovations failed or succeeded, and learn everything you can about what it will take and how long and what capital and what skills are required before you dive in. *Dive in* is the right expression, because from there on you are likely to live a life of rejection, failures, and endless changes of plan. If you get through it and succeed, there is nothing else like starting a business for putting you in control of your life and making you feel that you've made a difference and accomplished something truly worthwhile.

If this doesn't sound like you—and for most of us it shouldn't—then let's move into the next chapter and consider a second option. You can become an "intrapreneur," an entrepreneur within your existing company.

For the Creative: Become an "Intrapreneur" Within Your Company

Look for increased numbers of radical and incremental innovators to come from within established companies, an arrangement guaranteed to reduce the risks of entrepreneurial failure while providing a springboard for quantum leaps in creativity within the corporate ranks.

The Expanding Climate for Radical Innovation

A number of companies have found successful ways of fostering entrepreneurship inside their companies, in some cases encouraging radical innovation leading to true breakthroughs. The key to such success lies in designing structures in-house that closely parallel the dynamics of outside entrepreneurs and small innovative businesses.

Let's start with the obvious advantages here. Larger or more established companies have many resources at their disposal. These assets can reduce the risk and increase the odds of success in entrepreneurship. Established companies have access to capital at lower costs. They have credibility in and access to the distribution channels that have to give a new product a chance. They have basic R&D and other expertise, in areas like industry and market research. Often they can afford in-house specialists in esoteric areas such as packaging and shelf life. I saw one entrepreneurial cookie venture fail largely because of inadequate packaging for preserving freshness when the company finally expanded nationally.

A company acting as big brother to a new venture can give an inside entrepreneur support that outside entrepreneurs can only dream about.

The more I think about intrapreneuring, the more I'm certain it will become an inevitable major trend in business innovation. Intrapreneuring is a natural step in evolution for our corporations. In fact, I invite you to think about it in evolutionary terms. Our present entrepreneurial and venture capital system resembles the primitive reproductive system of a frog. Millions of frog eggs are spewed out into the stream and left on their own, with only a few tadpoles surviving the turbulence. Meanwhile, higher mammals tend to have few eggs and to care for their young better, to the point that most humans nurture one infant and enjoy a very high survival rate.

Does it make sense for new ventures to start virtually on their own without the guidance of an existing business that knows the ropes and can lend a helping hand where necessary? Of course not. How would we have done as kids with no parents?

Does it make sense that independent entrepreneurs should be developing many similar products when there is only shelf space for a few? No. So it makes perfect sense for the corporation of the future to develop units within its network that can have the culture to spawn radical innovation while tapping the resources and expertise of other units and cultures within the bigger family.

I expect to see more and more outside entrepreneurs and established companies working in joint ventures to launch new products, to mutual benefit. I also expect to see more radical innovators within established companies working in new structures just like the joint ventures with outside entrepreneurs. This represents an approach to new product innovation that can significantly reduce the risks of failure and increase the chances of breakthrough success, which currently run about one in ten in the venture capital world.

But first, established companies must learn to counter the disadvantages they often bring to the arrangement. These can outweigh the advantages. The broader culture in a more mature company will tend to resist such new ventures and see them as a threat to its cash cows. If new ventures are put under the same management that oversees the cash cows and incremental innovations, then radical innovations have a low chance of being supported and succeeding.

Principles for running successful innovative ventures

The greatest opportunities for entrepreneuring within companies come from radical innovations. It's best if your company has a history of working with outside entrepreneurs so you already understand something about working with radical innovators, but of course, it's not a prerequisite.

Whether you are an outside entrepreneur approaching a company or an inside intrapreneur, you and your company should make sure that the following principles are followed to increase chances of succeeding in such a venture:

- **Set up separate structures** for managing newer or more radical ventures and products—separate them from more mature or incremental innovation products.
- **Start small in innovation projects** and aim for many niche markets so as to maximize the hit ratio, given that as many as 90 percent of efforts will fail.
- **Team up early in the innovation cycle** with outside entrepreneurs or inside intrapreneurs to maximize corporate help and minimize cultural disparity.
- **Make clear agreements** on the role and rights of the intrapreneur and the role and rights of the company.
- **Plan for and make clear the time frames and conditions** for management succession and control by the company. Don't forget to consider how you will manage spin-offs of the venture into a new division if an acceptable level of success is reached.
- **Appoint a qualified sponsor or manager** to lead, oversee, and counsel intrapreneurs and help them gain access to corporate

resources. This means someone who understands radical innovators, optimally with experience in venture capital or entrepreneurial activities. I emphasize the importance of good leadership. The disparity between a corporate culture and an entrepreneurial spirit will kill a venture faster than almost anything else.

- **Establish clear and minimal budgets,** but give intrapreneurs ample latitude to operate within budgets—for example, allow them to work out of their homes, to save money if they want to.
- **Establish discretionary funds** for the sponsor or manager to allocate as the person sees fit as opportunities arise for intrapreneurs, so that such opportunities can be exploited without bureaucratic intervention.
- **Establish clear parameters for performance** on which the intrapreneurs' autonomy and future funding rest to make sure they are accountable.
- **Allow intrapreneurs to source products and services** inside or outside the company as they see fit.
- **Concentrate** only in areas that fit the company's long-term strategic focus.

What we are doing here is outlining the principles by which a company can simulate the efficiencies and accountability inherent in outside entrepreneurial start-ups while harnessing the resources of the established company.

How launches of radical innovation are handled in real life

T. J. Rodgers, CEO of Cypress Semiconductor, has as good an in-house approach to launching new ventures as any I have seen. This is a high-growth, $300-million company that specializes in customized semiconductor chips. New products are critical to growth, as the company focuses only on the key steps of R&D and production that are essential to quality and innovation and subcontract out most other functions. Cypress allows company engineers and other entrepreneurial types who have a new idea to spin off new ventures. The advantages the company can offer are primarily capital, information, management systems, and an established sales force to move the product if the entrepreneurs can get it off the ground.

Individuals or teams can approach management at any time, but must prepare a formal business plan as if they were approaching a venture capitalist. A committee from Cypress, including the CEO, will review it with their extensive industry knowledge and rake the plan over the coals. Is it realistic? Is the product viable? Is there a market for it? Is the innovation team allowing for enough capital and time? Does it have the skills necessary?

If the plan musters approval of management, Cypress will offer capital and access to key resources in exchange for an equity position in the spin-off.

In other words, Cypress literally acts as the venture capitalist. The intrapreneurs get an equity position in the venture and an initial round of funding for their knowledge inputs and sweat equity. They aren't going to get top salaries, and they will have the same pressures as an outside entrepreneur to get the product developed within budget and time parameters. Why? If they don't, they will have to dilute their equity by soliciting another round of capital from the company. But if the project succeeds, ultimately they can end up forming their own division of the company.

Do you have what it takes to pull it off in *your* company?

You should consider if you have the qualities of a radical innovator and if you should approach your company or another company with a proposal to launch a new venture with its help. It's best if the company understands the entrepreneurial process and will set up structures something like those outlined above.

Approach your company with a well-thought-out plan showing how you could develop and test-market a new product idea at much lower costs by acting like an outside entrepreneur—taking a minimal salary, working largely out of your home or another low-cost, off-site location, and handling more of the subcontract tasks yourself. Then outline your expertise, the required access to company resources, and the time and capital you would need. Get the help of an expert and develop a solid business plan covering the product development strategy, the customer profile, the size of the market, competition, risks, sales and profit projections, and so on.

Here's where your research and communications skills come in. You are going to have to be persuasive if your company has not tried intrapreneuring yet. And to be persuasive, do your homework. Gather data on the company's past internal innovation efforts. If you know that nine of ten of their product innovations have failed, you have a standard to shoot at in your presentation. Know the costs of the typical innovation project. Demonstrate that you can beat those costs. Then, using your own vision, commitment, and knowledge of the venture you are proposing, convince the company that you will have a much higher chance of succeeding than previous efforts—even if you can only promise a success rate of two in ten you will have shown a 100 percent increase in past performance. As a sweetener, you may even propose to put up part of the capital yourself for an even greater share in the equity or a greater royalty if the product succeeds. With a little imagination and intensity you can make yours an offer the company can't refuse.

If you do get the company to accept your plan, then the last important step is to make sure top management pledges its support to your new approach. This means extracting an agreement and establishing a process for gaining access to company resources you need. It means management will help you fend off the attacks and resistance that will tend to come from the established sectors.

Incremental Innovation Within Companies

Thus far we have been talking about more radical innovations, new product ideas that can be envisioned but not really measured and analyzed well because they don't yet exist.

If you don't think that the radical innovation approach is best for you, take a step down the ladder of risk until you find your level of comfort as an intrapreneur. The next level of innovation would be to target incremental innovations within your company and find a way to turn them into a business for yourself or a team of partners.

Once new products are out in the market, moving from niche markets into broader markets, the nature of innovation shifts, as we saw in Chapter 13 in Figures 13-1 and 13-2. With an existing product you can conduct market research and anticipate the next group of customers that will adopt it and the next stores or channels of distribution it will move into. The process becomes much more incremental and predictable than we saw in the product's start-up stages.

We are entering a period in our economy when incremental innovations will dominate—innovations that extend the radical new growth products, services, and technologies of the '60s, '70s, and '80s into mainstream markets in the '90s and 2000s.

So how do you know how to examine an established product to see whether you can identify incremental product innovations? Start by asking questions.

Questions for identifying opportunities for incremental innovation

- **Who is buying the product?** If the product is selling to urban families with $75,000-plus incomes, then the next likely market is not rural families with $20,000 incomes, but urban families with $50,000 to $75,000 or suburban families with $50,000-plus incomes.
- **What related products or services would they buy** under this brand name or concept? Here you have to find out more clearly how your customers see your company. What do they think you are best at? What do they like the most in your products and services? What qualities and concepts do they naturally associate with your company, and what products or images don't fit for them? For example, a car company with a great reputation for value cars is not likely to be accepted under the same brand name with a new luxury car, because the two are seen so differently by consumers and upscale buyers wouldn't want to be associated with a value brand name.
- **What added features would consumers like?** Ask them informally or in formal surveys—they would love to let you know. Make sure you get both tangible, quantitative data and more intangible, qualitative views.
- **Who is the next likely customer group** to purchase this product? At what price? In what outlets or stores or sales channels? If, for example, a product has succeeded strongly in gourmet stores, the next place to try is the gourmet section of grocery stores.
- **What features or modifications** would allow this product to appeal to other buyers and customer groups? Interview other customers, but also study how similar products have made successful and unsuccessful forays into such consumers and markets.
- **How can costs be lowered** to make the product appeal to broader

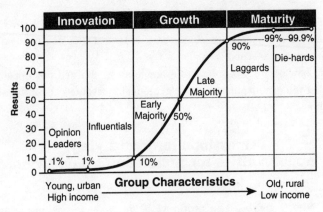

Figure 15-1. Consumer adoption patterns.

markets of customers? At what price range would successive customers and markets adopt our product? What are the time frames, volumes of production, and investments required to achieve those cost ranges?

- **How would we have to advertise and promote** the product to reach these broader segments? How do their values and lifestyles differ? What media have traditionally worked best for similar products in these markets?

This is how the incremental process works. You simply creatively ask questions and try to project the path of how a product will move into broader markets. That is just logical. Now let's talk about how consumers predictably adopt products and services. This discussion will help you understand the dynamics of customers as you ask your questions.

Consumer adoption patterns

It's as much a human tendency for consumers to resist new products as it is to resist new ideas. Any marketer will tell you it takes education and familiarity over the test of time to get most consumers to buy. What any marketer may not tell you is that this consumer adoption pattern follows the S-curve. That means we can predict when a product will take off.

There's no rocket science or economic mumbo-jumbo here in the graph in Figure 15-1, another refinement of the basic S-curve.

You see by the arrow in the graph that new technologies move from young to old and from urban to rural, and from higher income groups to lower income groups, as a rule. Think about it. In general, who are the first to adopt new products? For example, take VCRs. Usually younger people, and especially younger people with money, adopt them first, right? These early adopters usually come from urban or affluent suburban areas. Why? Because cities are where the numbers and the trend-setters are. The greater the concentration of a population, the greater the likelihood of finding more sophisticated consumers and specialty stores that can cater to them. Now a brief word about each of the categories on the graph.

Opinion leaders—1 percent

These people are professionals or hobbyists in new technologies, new products, and social trends. Who bought the first VCRs? Electronics buffs, of course. Movie freaks. Television junkies. Television industry analysts, critics, and employees . . . a small minority of technologically sophisticated insiders who knew the potential and excitement of such machines. Remember, industrial-strength video recorder-players had already existed for a long time in television studios in one-inch and three-quarter-inch formats. When VCRs became consumer items, only a few people had seen them used in editing, replaying, and storing of video images. These became the opinion leaders in consumer adoption. Opinion leaders start trends by being the first to adopt new products and technologies.

Influentials—1 to 10 percent

These people tend to immerse themselves in their world, keeping touch with new trends. The influentials know what's hot.

Influentials are the people who must own every kind of gadget imaginable—and *now!* They adopt experimental products, hang the cost. Then they launch their word-of-mouth networks. With the adoption of the VCR, you saw trade journalists, then high-tech magazines, then general journalism picking up the story. Eventually new products saturate their niche markets—sometimes called yuppie markets. That's the sign they are approaching the takeoff stage near the 10 percent point of market penetration. When the upper-middle-class markets start to show interest, watch out!

Early majority—10 to 50 percent

These upper-middle-class people, usually from the suburbs, have the discretionary bucks to spend on a product. They'll try to be the first to own one on their block. Mind you, they don't take the risk of buying until the product has proved its benefits and reliability in niche markets. And of course, they wait for the price to drop somewhat. In effect, they watch what the influentials are doing and follow. Their adoption of the product kicks off major growth in the S-curve.

Late majority—50 to 90 percent

These folks pooh-poohed the VCR in the beginning. Or they didn't have the discretionary income to blow on creating their own television reruns. Or the early technology seemed to be too confusing to them. The late majority is the true mass market, for obvious reasons. Once they follow the early majority in adopting products, they push the percentages up over 50 percent toward 90 percent. Products that arrive at this stage will be widely available in stores like Sears, Wal-Mart, and Kmart.

Laggards—90 to 99 percent

Laggards won't own the new product until their children buy it as a gift for them, or until their favorite older products are no longer available or cost more than the new product. These are usually not going to be sophisticated adopters. You've heard the stories of grandparents getting a VCR they now use as a digital clock (that sometimes stays blinking on 12:00 P.M.).

Diehards

These folks in the hills and hollows of the American outback may never adopt new technologies. It's a matter of principle, not cost.

So, you see how the S-curve and many of the tools presented in Chapter 2 and in my first book, *The Great Boom Ahead*, can be used to help you identify opportunities for innovation and entrepreneurship. Now that we have described the nature of both radical and incremental innovation, it is time for you to begin to decide which is the best entrepreneurial path for you.

Radical Innovators	Incremental Innovators
Tend to: • Rely on the right brain • Approach problems from new angles • Be loners • Love challenges and puzzles • Operate in messy environments • Be eccentric and moody • Have a strong sense of humor	Tend to: • Rely on the left brain • Approach problems systematically • Be social and competitive • Love results, progress, and feedback • Operate in neat, methodical environments • Be stable and measured • Be more serious

Figure 15–2. Radical versus incremental innovators.

Radical versus incremental innovators

Radical and incremental innovation are very different, as are the people who tend to be radical or incremental innovators. In case you are not clear as to which type you are, Figure 15-2 summarizes the difference between radical or original thinkers and incremental or creative thinkers.

Stranco, Inc., has learned how to identify and manage both radical and incremental innovators simultaneously and has a very intrapreneurial culture. It is a smaller company that has grown rapidly in industrial water purification systems by structuring itself to foster radical and incremental innovations internally. This company sees its history as having revolved around a few radical, breakthrough innovations. Its primary growth has come between breakthroughs during a time of many continuous, incremental innovations.

Stranco has a small cadre of radical innovators, including the founder, Frank Strand. The members of this cadre are left free to tinker and operate on looser schedules. They are given plenty of freedom to pursue projects, they come in on their own hours, and they aren't subject to constant daily deadlines, although they are expected to produce results in the longer term. The company respects the more temperamental nature of its innovators. The most powerful tool for stimulating them is to get them together occasionally in technical brainstorming sessions.

Incremental innovators in all departments are managed quite differently. They have clear short-term deadlines and budgets on a continuous basis. Weekly meetings keep them up on each other's progress. Meetings also help maintain a state of accountability and competitiveness and give incremental innovators useful feedback from each other and from outside inputs and expertise. These people are managed for incremental results, their strengths, and are clearly rewarded for them in their compensation and bonus plans.

Which are you—incremental or radical innovator?

Which of the Stranco environments sounds more in line with how you work best?

If you are more of an incremental innovator like most people, then you look for the opportunities to make small improvements to existing products, or to take an existing product into new markets, or to sell an improved product or an extension of a product to the same customers, or to find a more customized niche for it. If that's you, you might prepare a proposal to present to your company's management. Use the same procedures we discussed earlier in presenting the more radical innovation.

The difference is that there are a lot of options for being an incremental innovator in a company. You can propose that you and your team be put in a separate venture just like a radical innovator. You could have equity in the venture or a share of profits or royalties on the product if it succeeds. Or incremental innovation can simply be part of the normal goal-setting and performance-review process in the company, as it is at Stranco. Your rewards, raises, and bonuses come from meeting and exceeding goals.

Optimally, even for incremental innovations, you will become part of a self-managing team making your own decisions, pursuing constant innovations and improvements, and being rewarded with a share of your team profits.

Let me emphasize that I think it's always best that a corporation of the future allow its workers to run their own businesses using the support of company infrastructures and information systems. And, as you know, running a business always means you get rewards based on your performance as an individual or team. Most self-managing teams in the corporation of the future will be focusing on incremental innovations within their companies and will benefit enormously from being part of an established network that offers brand recognition, access to capital, access to distribution channels, access to technical and information networks, and sound management systems.

Chances are, your company is not operating in such a progressive structure yet. You have options. You can propose that the company adopt a more flexible structure open either to radical or incremental innovation. Or else you can find a company that is already nurturing innovative employees like yourself.

Of course, if working for a company as an entrepreneur doesn't give you enough freedom or you can't find a company that is suitable, you can move into one of the even-lower-risk alternatives in Chapter 16. You can buy a franchise that you can manage or start your own cookie-cutter business. Let's take a look.

For the More Systematic: Buy a Franchise or Start a "Cookie-Cutter" Business

There's room in the new economy for traditional corporate types to run their own businesses, bringing products and services to us as we move farther away from cities. Most of these opportunities won't require a life of endless risk, only accountability to and relationships with customers.

Established Success Formulas for Business

If you can't run your own business or spawn your own innovations within a company and feel the freedom and control over your life that you require, then look at running a low-risk company on your own—either a franchise or a concept you can easily study and translate into your own area or to a place where you've been wanting to move.

Let's look at each of these possibilities.

Franchises

Franchising has been the largest growth sector in retailing and business services for decades. It represents a means for taking advantage of the sophistication and world-scale economies of a centralized operation while simultaneously exploiting the motivation and accountability of a local, family-owned business.

There's one problem. A franchise for a McDonald's could cost you more than $300,000 just for the initial fee. The company prefers to sell franchises to large investors or groups that will take multiple locations. Most prominent mass-market franchises are like this. They work well for former middle managers who have substantial management expertise, a high net worth, and a handsome severance pay package from a large company. In fact, a substantial percentage of laid-off or fed-up middle managers and professionals have gone into franchises. Franchise operations are run by the book, and that fits their systematic skills perfectly.

As a rule, I tell people to forget McDonald's and other large, mature franchises.

They cost a lot, but have little growth potential in the future, except, of course, overseas. Everyone who likes Big Macs already eats them. A growing sector of the population is realizing that fried foods aren't so healthy. Heck, it's not even the lowest-priced when you look at Taco Bell— a franchise that follows the four principles of this book in a way that delivers better value for the money to middle-class consumers.

Your better bets in franchises

I tell people to look to emerging franchise concepts, ones that fit the mode of the customized economy. These offer higher quality, fresher, healthier foods, real time-saving services, and responsive, personalized service. These concepts are newer, have growth potential for decades, and are generally much cheaper to get into. Let's consider a few of these.

You can find plenty of quality fast-food concepts from Panda Express (Chinese) to La Petite Boulangerie (fresh baked goods) to Ben & Jerry's or Häagen-Dazs or Gelato ice cream parlors. But the list is endless. It ranges

273

from salad-and-soup bar concepts to mail and packaging stores to white-collar pool halls to home maid services to office services and copy shops to home delivery services for local restaurants to secretarial services to wine shops and tasting bars to ethnic family restaurants to video stores to fresh pasta cafés.

The new threat to McDonald's is not ultimately from Taco Bell, but from new chains of upscale, or old-fashioned, burger joints. Ruby's is growing rapidly in Southern California. I've also seen Taxis in San Francisco. These places typically have an old-fashioned '50s environment and serve big, juicy burgers and sandwiches and thick, real milkshakes, and for substantially higher prices. Is it healthier than McDonald's? In fat, no, but in freshness, yes. If you're going to indulge in a burger now and then, this is the place—except when you just want to stuff a Happy Meal into a kid's face to shut him up. You typically can't even get into a Ruby's much of the time, it's so popular. I've even seen them in the worst of locations, like in a Jaguar dealership or in a dead mall. They still thrive!

In pizza there's California Pizza Kitchen, which is exploding across America, featuring old-fashioned Italian wood-fired-oven pizzas. Sammy's Wood-Fired Pizza of La Jolla is looking to expand with a great new concept.

As baby boomers mature and move into their peak spending years and see the ravages of inflation recede, bolstering their two-income earnings, they will spend their money on higher quality and convenience, and less on the standardized, bland concepts of the past.

The niche concepts of the '70s and '80s will come down in costs and increase in popularity as the baby boom generation ages. These are the concepts to target, not only for people who can't afford a $300,000 up-front investment in a McDonald's, but for investors and professionals with more money to wield. Better to buy three Sammy's pizza franchises than one McDonald's.

Here's the best thing about a good franchise. Yes, you can run your own show, according to some rules, of course. Yes, you can build up your own equity and be rewarded directly for your own efforts. But many more people are going to get that satisfaction within companies in the future. In franchising there are so many different concepts that you can choose something you really enjoy, something that deals directly with customers. I would much rather be providing the best wood-fired-oven pizzas to the neighborhood than running a widget factory. Or if you're a movie nut, run your own movie franchise or store and talk movies all the time. The most profitable route is to get going with a promising new concept in the early stages, get in cheap, and then buy into multiple franchise locations out of your profits or ability to attract investors based on your track record.

If you don't have the money, consider teaming up with a friend or relative who does to form a joint venture. The most important point: If you can't come to a happy and lucrative business arrangement within your company, then do whatever it takes to start your own business. Your personal freedom and your control over your life are worth more than your health and retirement benefits and the security of your job, which are disappearing fast anyway.

> **The new status symbol catchword of the '90s won't be "Doing my own thing" but "Controlling my own time."**

Of course, there is another option if you aren't one of those crazy, even neurotic, radical innovators:

The cookie-cutter business

Now here's a simple concept: Find a great business someone else has started, study its nature, and transfer it to your own community or a community where you would love to live.

This brings me back to the small-town trend for a moment. I hear people say all the time that they would love to live in Sedona, Arizona, or Telluride, Colorado, or Fort Myers, Florida, or Waterbury, Vermont, or Whistler, British Columbia, or some enchanted place such as Hawaii or the Caribbean—but there aren't many jobs there. Take heart. There's always the possibility you will see your company relocate divisions or departments or individual R&D or phone sales people to locations like these, as many companies are doing. But even that's too chancy, isn't it?

The best way for you to live in the town you want to
live in is to find out what the town needs and open up
your own version of a franchise
or cookie-cutter business.

The last time my wife and I were in Hawaii, we saw Lappert's ice
cream shops. An older man had moved there to retire and just started up
a Häagen-Dazs type of place with local island flavors added. Not only is
he a millionaire with many shops in Hawaii, he is now expanding back to
the mainland states.

The cookie-cutter operation is the second great opportunity for exploiting the trend toward incremental innovation.

As I've said, authentic pasta shops and wood-fired-oven pizza cafés
are hot. Telluride, Aspen, Jackson Hole, and Hilton Head probably already
have one, but maybe Durango, Colorado, doesn't. Make a marriage between
something you would like to do and a place you would love to live. It just
takes a little creativity, and certainly some capital, but it's not the dramatic
risk of a breakthrough start-up.

Research is the key

Now comes the most important part of a cookie-cutter business. You must
invest the time to study that business you like. Who are the customers?
What are their demographics in income, age, lifestyle, and so on? What
are the key principles that seem to make the business work?

Interview customers. What do they like most and least about the existing business? Why do they go there? Ask the owners and employees.
Most people are happy to tell you why they do what they do and how smart
they are! How much did it cost to start up? How long did it take to reach
break-even sales? How much and where do they advertise? How much
inventory do they have to carry? What type of people do they hire and how
much do they pay them? What hours are they open and when do the most
people seem to come in?

These are things that you can learn through simple detective work. We
had neighbors who opened up a video store in a local community, the only
major town along our strip of the California coast that did not have a video
store. That signaled opportunity. The wife wanted a business she could

oversee from her home so she could stay close to her children. They started a video store that was profitable within its first year.

Here's how they did it. They talked to video stores outside of the area, with whom they wouldn't be competing, and learned all they could about the business, asking many of the questions we asked above. Then they found people selling video inventories from stores that had gone out of business. They lined up inventories of older videos at the lowest costs.

They then examined the procedures of the video store closest to their town. They tracked who came and went, comparing customer numbers to the total local population. They counted the number of videos people rented and noted peak hours. They studied the inventory a store should carry. They found out what rent the closest competitor was paying. They recorded many more facts. By the time they opened their business, they knew exactly what their costs would be and about how much business to expect in their local area. They knew what prices to charge and where to discount. They were ready!

A caution

One of the keys to marrying a business to a place you want to live is to carefully match the demographics of both. Just because wood-fired-oven pizzas take off in La Jolla, California, doesn't mean they are going to take off yet in Tulsa, Oklahoma. Check your demographics before taking the leap. The census bureau and many marketing services provide inexpensive data and reports on the demographics of different counties, ZIP codes, and even neighborhoods. The best marketing firms, from Donnelly to Claritas to CACI, provide analysis of which lifestyles live where. This last is often the most potent factor. Make sure that the business you are transferring to a new area fits the demographics and lifestyles of that area or that you can make the modifications that will transcend any differences.

Research is indispensable. It's the difference between a franchise and a cookie-cutter business. The central office of the franchise does all types of research for franchisees, offering a host of guidelines for using proven systems and procedures, quality standards, and demographics. They also offer sophisticated software systems, national and even international advertising support, and the purchasing economies of scale inherent in them. In a cookie-cutter business, you do those things for yourself. This means that you can often get into a business cheaper and keep more of the profits.

But the dangers are obvious. You don't want to start a cookie-cutter business and then have a franchise concept move in down the street. With its advantages in advertising and purchasing costs, it might kill your new business. The cookie-cutter approach works best when there aren't large economies of scale, when the principles for successfully running a business are fairly easily discerned, and in towns or areas where franchises are not likely to enter—at least not for a while. Our neighbors chose their town for a video store because they felt that it was too small for a giant like Blockbuster Video to enter. Finally, it wasn't difficult to figure out the basics of pleasing customers.

Summary

This chapter provides the best options to professional and clerical people who are laid off from larger corporations or who become fed up with the bureaucracy in the corporate world. Leverage your systematic skills and the severance package you might get from a larger employer into something you can thrive at: analyzing what worked in a business and running it by proven rules and procedures. We need more of our systematic people to bring us wonderful franchise and cookie-cutter products and services in the areas we are moving to. Most of these opportunities do not require you to enter a life of endless risk and danger, just accountability for what you create and a relationship with your customers. You don't have to play it totally by the numbers. You are free to innovate and improve your business because you own it and run it.

In Chapter 17 we will look at the final option for entrepreneurship and another one that will become widespread in the future: taking the job or function or service you now perform for your company and turning it into your own subcontract business. In some cases, you'll remain within your company, but, in the best case, you'll run your new business from your own home or place of business—which you might be able to relocate to Aspen or Hilton Head.

For the Homebody:
Turn Your Job or Function
into a Subcontract Business

Many changes in the corporation of the future are
going to come from the bottom up, from people just
like you who leave their jobs to contract their
services back to their former employers
and other companies.

The Office of the Future

Now we come to the form of entrepreneurship in which the greatest number
of people might be employed in the work revolution ahead. Using this
method, you restructure your present job or some variation of it into a
subcontract business working either from your home, from your own outside office, from inside your company, or even from a combination of all
three. This method is both a simple and powerful way to put you in control
of your life.

Unfortunately, companies continue to resist this trend because managers are afraid of losing control over their employees. Yet results have tended to prove the opposite:

Loosening control and focusing on results improves productivity. In the corporation of the future, you won't need to hire managers to look over people's shoulders.

American Express has seen productivity increases of 25 to 30 percent in moving their phone travel agents into home offices. Much of this gain comes from avoiding all of the distractions and politics at the office. Plus, the company saves office overheads. Travel agents save time and money usually spent on commuting. It's an entirely win-win situation!

Still, companies are slow to adapt. A friend of ours approached her company with a proposal that she perform her software programming and computer design work from home. Her reason: She needed to spend more time with her daughter. The company refused to approve her suggestion. So she quit. The company then acceded and reluctantly allowed her to work at home. Of course, it worked out great—or else I wouldn't be bringing it up, right? She was as productive as ever, and the company saved on overhead expenses.

It's always a surprise to me that companies will often pay fantastic fees to hired guns who drop in, perform a service—from outside the company— and leave after achieving the agreed-upon results. Yet those same companies won't allow their own people to take on similar arrangements that they might perform better than outsiders, and certainly can perform at lower cost.

If I could accomplish only one thing with this book I would choose to wipe out this unfounded corporate fear of being cheated out of time and services by their own employees.

Companies have nothing to fear but their own paranoia

Too many companies and people trained in traditional management are plain old afraid of the changes they're seeing. Change threatens their positions of power and their old modes of operating. They certainly don't want to aggravate their fears by introducing change of their own. Many other companies are adapting, but often slowly and clumsily. A lot of the minnowlike changes in the future are going to come from the bottom up— from creative people in all types of jobs who break off and do their own thing and take back control over their time and lives. Many more people in the future are likely to leave the company if they aren't allowed to create their own small businesses to help the business save costs and increase accountability.

We are simply going to have to get more aggressive and help save our companies from themselves. Many design, sales, and office jobs can be performed as well or better out of people's homes with the proper computer links and controls.

More people are going to be like my friend and threaten to quit in order to force the obvious win-win decision. I mean, talk about control— anyone working on a computer can be tracked far better by software than by some surplus middle manager looking over the shoulder. Software can measure dollars spent or earned, time, words, keystrokes, files created, results generated—you name the productivity or profitability measure. As companies become more operational in Principle 3 of Part Three, they will turn teams and individuals into self-managing, accountable businesses. Increasingly, it will be less relevant where people work or even the number of hours they spend "on the clock" as long as they achieve the best possible results for their customers.

Moving functions off-site

If you're a secretary, why don't you get together with the other secretaries in the office and come up with a secretarial services pool? Yes, for some functions executives require personal secretaries who work at hand. But much work can be pooled and farmed out to a group of off-site secretaries. Such a situation might require a coordinator who works primarily on-site to take in requests and farm them out to the network of secretaries. Members of the network stay at home or in a small office out near their homes if they must use specialized machines. First you analyze the present costs to the company, including all overheads and office space requirements. Then you demonstrate to management that you could do the same work cheaper than even outside services by allowing secretaries to work out of their homes.

Spinning off functions

For that matter, why couldn't the accounting department employees work out of their homes or in a neighborhood office or in a nice small town somewhere? Why not take a good group of accountants and open up a service that markets not only to your present employer but also to other employers in the same locale?

You can see why more of us are going to have to learn some business and accounting basics. To spin off and run your own business, you'll have to make convincing proposals to your company. You will need to have a solid business plan and other financial tools to prove to the company that it can save money, increase productivity, turn a fixed cost into a variable cost, or sharpen its strategic focus. You need to be able to present yourself in business terms. I hope the principles and explanations in this book clarify the big picture well enough for you to develop that business lexicon.

Teaching your special expertise to others

Another option: Take your skill, further develop it, and become a trainer, speaker, author, or consultant on your subject. Start by providing your service to your present employer and later branch out to others. Test yourself by taking on a training function within your company, formally or informally. Then show company management how you could learn faster and lower your costs to the company if you also served other noncompeting companies. Next thing you know, you're in your own business working out of your home and on-site with a variety of clients.

Becoming a one-person firm

One of the fastest-growing business categories is one-person consulting and service firms. They can be both highly specialized and focused (generalized specialists), yet flexible, with low overheads. The most important advantage from my point of view is that such an arrangement gives people a great amount of personal freedom and control over their lives, and also a simple lifestyle. There isn't much bureaucracy in a one-person business. I see great numbers of professional, technical, and clerical people moving into home-based services and into small subcontract firms in the future.

Other opportunities for independent subcontractors

Here are just a few examples of the types of functions that can be split into home-based or subcontract functions:

- Accounting and bookkeeping
- Advertising and promotion
- Art and promotion materials
- Career counseling and outplacement
- Editorial and writing
- Field sales
- Janitorial and maintenance
- Market research and analysis
- MIS, computer software and systems
- Personality testing and evaluations
- Phone sales and telemarketing
- Secretarial and office production services
- Tax and tax planning
- Training and educational materials

So get creative and get a little aggressive. Start fighting for the changes you can see would benefit your company, its customers, and your work and life situation. Do your homework. Present it in sound business terms. Make your company an offer it can't refuse.

Roy's Rules

Some friends of mine wrote a book called *Roy's Rules*, which I recommend to people who run small businesses or are thinking of starting one. Herb Henderson worked with many small-business CEOs as a consultant and as a chairman of The Executive Committee (TEC). TEC is a network of small-business CEOs around the world who meet monthly to help each other troubleshoot problems and to hear speakers who can update their skills. Herb was impressed with the talent among the many small-business CEOs he met, but he was especially amazed when he stumbled upon one who he felt had really made the successful transition to having a highly profitable business and a great lifestyle. He found that rare bird, an over-achiever who was not a workaholic! The man was Roy Jacobson, who lives in Paradise Valley (of course), Arizona.

Roy runs a profitable $5 million business, Southwest Apparel, which sells a simple, narrow line of clothing (cheap shorts, he calls it) to major retailers like Kmart. Roy was a sales rep who started the business with no real management expertise beyond what he observed in industry sales. In fact, he violates most of the accepted management rules. Here are five of his most basic concepts:

- **Don't hang around the office** or the plant. Get into the market-place.
- **Don't spend too much time on your personal computer** and spreadsheets. The important numbers must be in your head—all the time.
- **Don't even think about growing your business.** Think about serving your customers better.
- **A written business plan is a useless, even dangerous document.** Just say no to formal business plans.
- **Don't let your business run your life.** Business is meant to be fun.

Roy runs a 150-employee company with very little bureaucracy and few outside consultants. He is able to retain full control over the company because he stays small and focused. Since he is able to be firmly in control, the business stays on track and is profitable. He also can take time out to have a life. He runs the company from a home office and is a family man and an avid skier. We could learn a lot from this example of small, extremely narrow concentration within the market.

Small is beautiful

Find a small need that is not being filled or a product or service that could be improved. Stay focused only on what you do best. Stay small so that you can keep in control of the business. Have fun. Enjoy life.

I have consistently found that some of the most mundane businesses are the most profitable because they go unnoticed outside their clientele and don't attract much competition.

This is a very important point. As the world breaks up into minnows and converges into many cultures, we will find that there is no one way to do business. The best way is the one that suits you and your customers.

Despite the fact that he has 150 employees and two production plants, Roy can manage the business from his home and remain in control of it without excess management and systems. What Roy has done is focus his business extremely finely. He understands it so well that he can still control it and run it much like a one-man operation—without bureaucracy or even a business plan—and still have total control over his own life. He has applied Gilder's notion of the law of the microcosm in his business. Most of the management and controls can be handled by him—he's against delegation in key management duties. For him, the one-person concept, an idea that is anathema to the traditional hierarchical CEO, greatly simplifies control. Of course, he has picked a business that he could master without a lot of electronics or specialists.

Deciding What's Best for You

You might start a rapid-growth company and become a multimillionaire, but you wouldn't have as much leisure time as Roy. Eventually you will almost certainly lose control over your business as it becomes ever bigger, ever more complex, and ever more under assault from competitive forces.

You are likely to become a workaholic. You, like Steve Jobs, are very likely to displaced as the CEO of your own successful company. In fact, you are most likely to fail in the highest-growth entrepreneurial ventures.

On the other hand, you could start a small store, a home product, or a small service business. Many of these operations are simple enough for you to control and stay on top of. But many are very competitive, unlike the boring business Roy chose. Restaurants and bars are businesses with high failure rates. Tastes change. Everyone wants to open one, and therefore the competition is high.

It's all a matter of personal choice. The important point: Know yourself, your strengths and weaknesses—and do your homework. Study and model yourself after people who have been successful in what you want to do. Don't be naive!

Whatever your choice, remember that the basic direction and changes in our economy are largely predictable. The purpose of this and my previous book, *The Great Boom Ahead,* is to point out the foreseeable trends that you can harness in your favor. None of us is big enough to change the direction of the world economy and the very fundamental social and technological shifts. But all of us can better understand the changes and get on the right horses and ride in the right direction. There are millions of ways to make a living and design your life in this new customized information economy.

You *can* understand the changes ahead of us. You *can* take the initiative to guide yourself into the future of the coming new economy and work revolution. You *can* learn what you need to start your own business or to run your own team or business within your company, utilizing today's rich world of customized information and education.

For heaven's sake, whatever you do, don't allow yourself to be dragged into the future kicking and screaming.

A final consideration. We will all have to continuously learn and adapt in this new economy. We are going to need a different approach to our education and careers. We will need a whole new education and even political system. Most important: You will have to become responsible for designing your own economic future. That will be the subject of the brief Epilogue.

Designing Your Economic Future

People entering the workforce today will have something like seven careers throughout their life instead of the one or two careers that most people in the Bob Hope generation could expect.

The Ever-Whirling Wheel of Change

Lifetime employment with a single company is only a memory. Gone is the age of corporate responsibility for your life and career.

There is a new employment contract emerging. We are shifting from an industrial, standardized economy to an informational, customized economy. We are also shifting from a society structured around stable families, farms, and factories to a more mobile, multi-career, fast-changing society in which the basic unit is the individual.

This does not discount the importance of family. It's just a recognition that the family structure is changing along with everything else, becoming a network of individuals rather than a hierarchy. Families must and will become increasingly flexible and adaptable in keeping up with our rapidly changing world. Multiple careers, rapid personal growth, and nonstop learning greatly increase the chances of revolutionizing every phase of our lives. Today's social, technological, and workplace changes are combining to create one of those great leaps in human progress, like the shift from a nomadic hunting and foraging society to an agricultural one in an earlier age.

It's no wonder people are confused, even angry. It's no wonder that one sector of our society is experimenting, leading us into this new era, while a larger part of society is defending the old ways, fighting to preserve them harder than ever. The only insight I can give you from studying cycles in human history is this:

Sweeping revolution is inevitable when the changes are fundamental, like those we're seeing in today's work revolution. We will never fully return to the social values and structures of the past, no matter how many politicians run on a platform of traditional family values.

Seeing the big picture

You've seen those three-dimensional abstract patterns that turn into images only when you stare at them in the right way, haven't you? I think there's a great analogy in that nifty little process. You can't make that picture materialize out of the pattern by looking at it the way you see a photograph. You have to focus past the plane, let your eyes glaze over, allow a kind of second sight or special vision to take over. Then, *voilà!* The picture appears right away. In the same way, you can't expect the future to materialize right in front of your eyes if you stay forever wedded to looking backward with nostalgia at the old structures and systems of work and organizations.

What each of us needs to do is to understand the fundamental changes in society and to build new cultures, institutions, communities, families, and jobs by leveraging the opportunities inherent in these changes. We are going to see a strengthening in the family as a unit in the coming decade after decades of tearing it apart, but at the same time we'll see more changes in family relationships and structure. The key to success in a new world is not to focus on the problems of old institutions and their downsizing and natural decay. It is to focus on the successful new approaches that are emerging.

The examples for success are not merely the daydreams of futurists like me. We can find windows to the future by looking into some of our most successful, leading-edge companies, institutions, and entrepreneurs.

Remember Roy from the last chapter? He has found a way to run a highly profitable business with a great lifestyle and with no formal business education, let alone a Harvard M.B.A. Small business owners need to learn from Roy, study what he does differently, and transfer what is useful to their business. A much larger company, Nucor Steel, is growing and thriving and providing high-paying jobs in an industry that is constantly downsizing and losing market share to overseas competitors. Ben & Jerry's ice cream is growing and providing fun jobs with lots of responsibility and learning.

I see no reason why most of our other companies can't adopt new structures and attitudes to allow them to become corporations of the future. Large old-line companies from AT&T to General Electric to 3M to Johnson & Johnson to Hallmark to Hewlett-Packard are making great strides in reengineering into more self-managing structures and toward large schools of minnows, although they have a long way to go. We even see many striking examples of reinventing government agencies, hospitals, and school systems. A great many of the workforce changes that will bring unprecedented productivity gains are being pioneered by our new high-tech companies, just as the greatest innovations of the assembly-line revolution came in automobiles. I have met many couples who have extraordinary marriages and families in this time of great change in family structures and high divorce rates. I have seen people like John Bradshaw teaching people how to be effective parents, something never formally taught in the past. I have met many older people who are enjoying their lives more than most young people, with stamina and health that many young people would envy. We need to learn from these individuals, companies, and institutions that are blazing the trail in this great cultural and workforce revolution.

Quit trying to streamline old business systems, old
political systems, old school systems, old family
structures. Look for people who have successfully
reinvented new approaches. Learn from those people
and chart a new life for yourself or your family or your
company or your community. Simply defending the
past is digging your own grave.

If the changes in the world seem to violate your personal, social, or
business values, look around for someone who has values similar to yours,
but has found a way to make peace with change in order to carve a place
in the new world.

Two things you can do to make a difference

The first thing we have to do to help our society make changes is to
become a part of the solution, not a part of the problem. Stop resisting
change and start doing something to turn it your way. I have lectured to
school superintendents, and they often seem to understand many of these
changes. They say it is parents and voters who are blocking their efforts
to change, trying to get them to go backward to the old basics they grew
up with instead of helping them to move forward.

Education surveys prove that the great majority of students are highly
motivated and learn very rapidly if you put them in a system that challenges their right-brain, more creative skills. But you must take the time
to understand how individuals learn differently. You must cater to their
strengths instead of beat them up for their weaknesses and force them into
a standardized approach. Kids *do* learn when they're challenged. I heard
an expert state that children lose 90 percent of their creative faculties
between ages five and seven—from entering our bureaucratic, standardized school systems. Do we really want to defend these outmoded systems
in a time when computer automation will put an absolute premium on
creativity? Let's stop complaining and learn enough to help make constructive change.

The second and most critical item is this. You can't always affect an
entire system, but you *can* affect your community by participating in it,
your company by contributing to it, your department by leading it or fol-

lowing constructively. And even if you can't have enormous effects on those institutions, you can take charge of your own life and design your own career and make your own family life work the way that bests suits you.

You can design your own future— when you take responsibility

You are likely to experience at least two and maybe as many as seven to ten careers over your life. I have already experienced four and can see at least two more coming. This is because we can learn and experience so much more in today's information-loaded, communications-rich world. We can see the great events happening around the world on television. Who really needs a Ph.D. or a formal degree anymore? Anyone who wants to learn can go directly to specialty magazines, books, seminars, home study courses, videotapes and audiotapes, CD-ROM computer libraries, and even school courses. This is the new education system. It's already here. It is about continuous learning in more interactive formats. The emphasis is on learning based on individual needs. The only trouble with it is that the education establishment hasn't adopted it yet!

Something like fifty thousand books are published every year in this country, and there are over fourteen thousand specialty magazines and a ton of newsletters and courses and so on. Education on demand is where it's at. Yes, there are basic business skills. But many of our best entrepreneurs from Bill Gates to Roy Jacobson have no business degrees. There is no one way to run a business, to proceed in a given career path, or to get education and skills.

Focus on the number one individual: yourself

We are going to have to put responsibilities for lives, careers, income, and benefits back into the hands of individuals. Start with you. Our businesses and institutions are going to have to start trusting you, allowing you a greater degree of freedom in how to get things done, letting you work where you want to—as long as you perform and deliver results to your customers.

We are going to have to be more flexible in evaluating education and job history. Have the people we're evaluating demonstrated the ability to get results? Have they learned from their experiences? Do they have the type of personality and behavioral profile to succeed in our business? Do

291

they thrive on change? Do they have personality? Are they creative in the face of change or adversity? You can't just look for a cookie-cutter employee anymore or for a stable job description.

Educational degrees will still be important in many jobs but will certainly become less important in many more. The same with functional skills. People with the right mind-set and behavioral patterns can learn fast enough to master any new skills they need. I can't help but believe that more people will wonder why we should stay in school for so many years after high school when most knowledge will be obsolete in something like five years or less and many people will go through multiple careers anyway. Isn't it far better to maintain an emphasis on continuing education throughout your life rather than going through one concentrated tunnel of schooling that stops forever at age twenty-four?

You have to start taking responsibility for your own career and learning. Don't try to change companies that don't want to change. Vote with your feet. Find companies in growing industries that are following principles like the ones in this book and work for them. If you are a middle manager, a professional, or a technical, clerical, or factory worker who gets laid off by a larger company in a mature industry, your first option is simply to seek employment with a progressive company in the same industry or with a growing company in an emerging industry. You may have to take a cut in pay at first and learn some new skills, but the long-term growth and the greater responsibilities you are likely to get should result in higher earnings capacities later. What's more, if you're creative, you can carve out your own career by starting a business within or outside your company and become your own boss. Find opportunities and advocate them in a businesslike way and then be accountable for the results and expect to be rewarded according to your results.

The simple patterns of our lives—S-curves

We all need to see our lives as a series of S-curves or careers, instead of one, as in Epilogue Figure 1. Here's how it works. We focus in an area and go through an intensive learning period in the first range of curves (0.1 percent to 10 percent). Then we go through an expansion period during which we harvest the power and financial rewards that go with that career direction (10 percent to 90 percent). We start to get bored and stop growing and yearn for the next challenge (90 percent to 99.9 percent). It is in these maturing phases that we need to invest in the next career. Set aside some

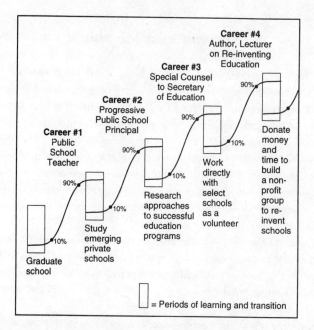

Epilogue Figure 1. A lifetime of multiple careers as a series of overlapping S-curves.

of your income and time from the old maturing path and find a new path, something that interests you more. Each new path builds on the skills, experiences, and contacts of your old path.

We will always need to save for and provide for sabbaticals or times of learning and reinspection between careers and S-curves.

Never look at a period of boredom or slowing in a path as a sign of failure. It is more a sign of success on that path, an indication of the need to learn, to change, and to start growing again.

Such learning and transition periods will always be difficult. But resistance and clinging to the old ways always make it more difficult. Allow yourself the space to get through those periods, and take advantage of counseling or objective feedback from friends.

You can beat job shock

See each new career path as a way to build broader skills and to achieve broader roles that give you a greater sense of achievement or personal freedom and control over your life. Don't let yourself get backed into a corner, resisting change, until life forces you to change on its terms. That's what's happening to most people facing job shock today. They don't feel in control. They don't understand the changes, and they are hoping for outside intervention to ride in like the cavalry to save them. Instead they are getting forced to change in the worst of ways. Many other people have been more entrepreneurial, finding ways to escape the collapsing bureaucracies and paving their own ways.

To paraphrase Shakespeare, always remain true to yourself. Constantly be identifying and reconsidering what is really important to you and what motivates you the most. Be willing to experiment enough to facilitate this creative process, but don't lose your focus and get sidetracked into trivial or superficial pursuits.

See your life as the best training ground for acquiring the skills you will need at work. If you are going to be working in self-managing teams or in more entrepreneurial business environments where you have to take charge and make decisions, then start by doing this at home. Run your personal life like a business. Have a vision of what you want to achieve. Have clear goals. Have systematic budgets and savings plans. Know your fixed and variable costs, and carefully manage your strategic investments in education and skills or promoting yourself into new careers. Learn to communicate better within your family and operate more as a team or a network of individuals at home, all participating in important family decisions.

Bottom line: This is the greatest opportunity we as individuals have had in all of history to design our own lives, our work, and our personal living environments to meet our own needs and dreams. Only the people who understand the logic of our new economy will achieve self-designed lives.

Epilogue

I hope you have enjoyed some of the new challenges and opportunities presented in this book. Don't feel you have to agree with everything I forecast or all of my opinions about the social and business changes occurring today. This book should challenge you to think differently and evaluate how you see the world changing and how you can fit in and prosper materially and spiritually in this unprecedented time of change and opportunity.

Best of luck to you!

Services Available from the
H. S. Dent Company

Keynote Speeches and Seminars for Companies, Associations, and the Public: Mr. Dent brings the complex changes in our organizations, technologies, and economy into a simple, human context that allows people at all levels to better understand how they can make changes to benefit from the unprecedented opportunities of this time in history.

Topics include:
> Job Shock: Career and Entrepreneurial Strategies for the '90s
> Four Principles for Successfully Transforming Organizations
> The Great Boom Ahead
> Growth Markets of the '90s
> Business Strategies for the '90s
> Investment Strategies for the '90s
> Boom Towns: The Next Great Population Migration

Mr. Dent can customize the talks to include any and/or all of the topics above and to incorporate information and trends from your industry or market.

Consulting Services for Businesses in Strategy and Organizational Change: Mr. Dent helps executives at highest levels of organizations bring clarity to their strategies for growth and organizational change. He has a unique capacity for communicating such strategies and simple tools for change throughout the organization to insure the effective cooperation and participation of people at all levels.

Books, Audiotapes, and CD-Roms: Attractive discounts are offered for quantity orders.

H. S. Dent Forecast: An economic newsletter. Please call for a free sample.

Call now for more information:
> Phone (415) 572-2879
> Fax (415) 312-9516

Or write:
> H. S. Dent Company
> P.O. Box 914
> Moss Beach, CA 94038